AMERICAN THOUGHT
AND RELIGIOUS TYPOLOGY

A Note to the American Edition

The English translation of this book is presented as a faithful version of the original German one which appeared in 1963. Valuable contributions to the authors and problems discussed have appeared since that time; however, to include them in the text would have meant extensive rewriting and would have altered the basic structure of the book. I trust that the critical argument of the book remains valid and can thus be regarded as a contribution to the problem of symbolism in American literature.

June, 1969   —U.B.

FOREWORD

The phenomenon of typology and its connection to literary symbolism began to interest me when a Commonwealth Fund Scholarship enabled me to study at Harvard University from 1953 to 1955. Along with other problems it was further pursued in the winter of 1957–58 during a visit for research which the Rockefeller Foundation made possible. I am grateful to both of these organizations for their generous support, as well as to the Free University of Berlin, which granted me a semester's leave for research in the winter of 1957–58. I would further like to express my thanks to the Deutsche Forschungsgemeinschaft, which generously helped defray the printing costs.

As the following work reveals in many places, the studies by Professor Perry Miller have been the stimulus for my own investigations. I am also grateful to Professor Miller for discussions and advice. I am grateful that I was able to discuss problems connected with my project with Professors John O. McCormick and Charles H. Nichols. After a careful examination of the manuscript Dr. Klaus Poenicke made valuable criticisms. Mr. Heinz Ickstadt gave me kind help in compiling the index, as did Mr. Dietmar Haack and Mr. Jürgen Peper in reading the proofs.

—URSULA BRUMM

CONTENTS

PART I

Presuppositions

1   THE PROBLEM

In *Axel's Castle. A Study in the Imaginative Literature of 1870–1930* Edmund Wilson points out that the romantic writers of America were precursors of modern symbolism. Even at that early age they had developed ways characteristic of symbolism to convey their meaning. Having investigated the development leading from Valery, Rimbaud, Laforgue, and Corbière to Yeats, Joyce, Gertrude Stein, Pound, and T. S. Eliot, Wilson observes: "It was generally true that by the middle of the century, the romantic writers in the United States—Poe, Melville, Whitman, and even Emerson, were, for reasons it would be interesting to determine, developing in the direction of symbolism." [1] Wilson himself does not inquire after these reasons because he is not investigating the origin of this American symbolism. His interest is in its influence on French literature and in the impulses which French literature in turn gave back to modern English and American literature.

Thus the prehistory of this early American symbolism also comprises certain conditions important for modern European and American literature. To reconstruct these conditions is a fascinating task for any scholar who investigates the origin and development of literary and intellectual traditions. This investigation is especially important for the Americans because the early symbolism in their literature proclaims something resembling intellectual independence, or at least a partial independence from Europe. This is what they had desired so fervently ever since achieving their political independence, although they could not really bring themselves to believe in their intellectual independence until well into the nineteenth century. If an original version of symbolism did appear in America at this early age, then the reasons for it are surely hidden away in some special American tradition, and it is this we must investigate.

The main figures of this early American symbolic movement, Herman Melville and Nathaniel Hawthorne in particular, have been analyzed in many learned books in the last thirty years. The most important and stimulating of these was F. O. Matthiessen's *American Renaissance*.[2] If in the course of the present work I have occasion to disagree with certain of Matthiessen's results, I do so fully aware of the large debt of gratitude that every student of American literature owes to his pioneer study. In his foreword, "Method and Scope," Matthiessen speaks of the books that he has *not* written. One of these would have traced the intellectual history of that creative outburst in the midnineteenth century, the esthetic principles of which he has investigated. "One way of understanding the important abundance of our midnineteenth century would be through its intellectual history, particularly through a study of the breakdown of Puritan orthodoxy into Unitarianism . . ." (p. viii). In the present study I will attempt one part of this task. I would like to demonstrate how the theory and practice of symbolism in the American classics developed out of Puritan forms of thought and belief. The problem is to identify just those forms which subsequently influenced literature and to follow their transformation from theology to literature.

This is not to deny that the ideas and techniques of European romanticism (particularly from the German literature, philosophy, and theology of the early nineteenth century) exerted a liberating and creatively stimulating influence at the very birth of American literature. Rather than being in the main direct, this influence was exerted more via the mediation of Coleridge and Carlyle. The influence on Emerson and other Transcendentalists has been investigated, and the discovery of a wealth of impulses has given rise to the questionable view that the "American Renaissance" itself was largely a product of foreign influences. This view is only partially true. One must bear in mind that if such impulses are to be absorbed, and to exert influence, they must not only respond to a need for liberation. They must also fit meaningfully into the tradition which absorbs them. Without this living affinity they provide no help at all. It is only when they respond to a spiritual need that foreign ideas can be absorbed and assimilated.

What has been accepted into the canon of American literature under the label "Transcendentalism"—a few poems, diarys, and essays—is really only part of the creative work of the Transcendentalists. These are only the by-products of a movement mainly concerned with religious problems.[3] Transcendentalists were vitally concerned with problems of Christ's divine or human nature, the significance and role of miracles, and the Eternal as opposed to the Transient in Christian faith. Emerson too dealt with these problems in his "Address." His severance from the Unitarian Church was caused by his reading the Bible in the radically literal manner of the Puritans and rejecting, just as they did, everything in the ecclesiastical rites not expressly commanded by Jesus. Emerson rejected the Holy Communion because, as he understood the Bible, Jesus only recommended it to his disciples as a "memorial dinner," and by no means intended it to be a permanent institution. The Transcendentalists were rebelling against their forefathers. Yet it was only because this heritage had such a strong grip upon them that they struggled against it so intensely.

In the twentieth century the Americans have held their spiritual ancestors, the much-abused Puritans, responsible for almost everything they find reprehensible in their country. In the seventeenth century the Puritans established a theological culture in America that endured for more than a hundred years before it hardened into a mere collection of strict moral notions and rules. In view of this inglorious fate it is well to recall that the early American Puritans were courageous and alert thinkers, passionately concerned with man's role on earth and his relation to God. True enough, they did bring the dogmas and axioms of their faith with them from Europe. But in America these rules became a part of daily life: as guides to thought and action they were continously applied and adjusted. Thus they became "streamlined"—these convictions and articles of faith for which the Puritans stood with the emphasis proper to the "elect" and "illumimated." Out of these articles of faith they developed ways of observing and interpreting the world and their own experience. These forms of interpretation shaped in turn the world view of succeeding generations and found expression in their literary works.

2 DEFINITIONS

To approach literature from the standpoint of intellectual history usually means to investigate and classify it according to its wealth or poverty of ideas, or according to the philosophy it embodies. However, our purpose in pursuing the origin and growth of symbolism is to study the formal elements of literature—to understand historically the instruments which express meaning in literature. Even though the formal elements of literature which interest us—the metaphor, the symbol, and allegory—have fixed definitions, they undergo changes as they are used over periods of time. Seen from the perspective of intellectual history, they exist neither in empty space nor as absolute values; rather, they are the offspring of intellectual traditions which can lend them quite different meanings and functions. Thus we are seeking the notions which gave rise to them and determined that they would be used in certain ways. Our inquiry concerns the categories and techniques of the intellect which the writer absorbs (largely unconsciously) from his own cultural tradition in order to depict the world and his experience as a work of art. But let us give an example. If we were to regard *Moby Dick* in this manner we would not first seek to grasp the significance of the great white whale. We would instead ask why Melville has sought to express certain insights in just this manner—in the form of an animal, an animal with a biblical ancestry, an animal whose white skin sets Melville off on metaphysical speculations. To answer this question would also be to illuminate and make precise the meaning of this symbol.

Regarded from this standpoint, literature is interpretation: it transforms world and reality in the way it assigns significance. These changing forms of interpretation are the objects of our present investigation. To simplify somewhat, we might say that the interpretation itself is a mental process which comprises two elements: the world and the mind. It also comprises two phases: the first phase is the apprehension of the world—the raw material. The second is its transformation into literature, whereby the direction of the interpretation is already prefigured in the way the world is apprehended. In this sense interpretation is significance, the world as imagination, literature.

This type of interpretation has long made use of symbol and allegory as tools. They are aids employed by man as he stands between world and significance, and their character is determined by their position between world and interpretation. Thus the symbol is characterized as belonging primarily to the world that is apprehended, the allegory to the interpretation that is intended, and they interpret in quite different directions. The symbol is a part of the world which has been singled out and ascribed a meaning. Because this part seeks to maintain its autonomy as part of the world, a creative tension can develop between it and the meaning ascribed to it. In the case of allegory we first have the idea, which we then seek to embody in figures, acts, and images with fixed and recognizable meanings. In the case of the symbol the interpretation begins with reality and aims at a certain meaning. Of course, a symbol which has already been acquired in this manner and whose meaning is recognized by all can be used in as many contexts as one pleases.[1] The decisive thing in the case of allegory is the meaning which the author has already abstracted from the world, which he then disguises in a second, artificial reality. Thus allegory is a preconceived idea which needs a fictitious reality in order to be revealed; it progresses from the idea to (artificial) reality. Because allegory has to construct its own reality, it must be a fairly complex whole, consisting of numerous parts; a symbol, on the other hand, may be no more than a simple unit.

While we are (in this simplified manner) distinguishing the symbol from allegory, we must not neglect to add that these two literary devices for reproducing the world frequently occur in mixed versions. The writer may find the symbol in reality and then interpret it, but he may also manipulate it to some extent in the service of some preconceived idea. And in filling out an allegory one may use entire passages of actual experience that has been evaluated. It is possible for allegory to grow out of the subsequent interpretation of myth and poetry that were not originally intended to be allegorical, and this may well have been the origin of allegory. Eras which have an affinity for allegory tend to interpret such works, *e.g.* Homer's epics, allegorically.[2] By regarding Homer's gods, heroes, and their deeds as personified characteristics, virtues, and activities, they created the model for later works which were purposely written as allegories.

Symbolism and allegory do not stand in equally high regard at present. In certain circles, especially in America, symbolism is greatly admired, whereas allegory is regarded as one of the inferior forms of literature.[3] I would say the reason for this does not lie exclusively in their evaluation as literary techniques:[4] rather, it is connected with the development of symbolism and allegory from the realm of religion. Both derive originally (though in different ways) from the commitment to a creed and this still has a certain effect on them. In the case of symbolism the effect is only a distant and weak one. But allegory, as the embodiment of ideas, is still anchored in a definite and consistent view of the world. The idea or message must be there before it can be allegorized, and this is why a personal faith claiming universal validity is required, or a world view with principles capable of being exemplified. For example, Spenser possessed this in his national humanistic community, and Bunyan in his Puritan one.[5]

Today we have few convictions that are dynamic, universally binding, and capable of making proselytes. Thus modern allegories cannot avoid the taint of the esoteric or eccentric. Moreover, the modern reader and critic little appreciates the allegories of earlier ages, based as they are on creeds he does not believe in.[6]

Symbolism developed in the opposite direction, but for basically the same reasons. While allegory was sinking into neglect, symbolism advanced unexpectedly into a position of general esteem. At present symbolism is regarded by many American critics as the very essence of literature. Susanne Langer, whose work is based on Ernst Cassirer's *Philosophie der Symbolischen Formen*[7] and upon the insights of modern anthropology, psychology, and semantics, has proclaimed a "philosophy in a new key." Man is, according to Cassirer, a being that lives in a symbolic universe.[8] "The symbol-making function," says Susanne Langer, "is one of man's primary activities, like eating, looking, or moving about." [9] The impulse and the ability to symbolize are regarded as distinguishing characteristics of man: they distinguish him from the animal. "Symbolization is the essential act of mind; and mind takes in more than what is commonly called thought" (p. 33). Language is the medium of the symbolic apprehension of the world, and is thus itself symbolic through and through.

Charles Feidelson's *Symbolism and American Literature* is also based on a "philosophy of symbolism." This philosophy of symbolism is regarded as the means to bridge the dualism of external world and human mind which has been dominant since Descartes. "The symbolist . . . redefines the whole process of knowing and the status of reality in the light of poetic method. He tries to take both poles of perception into account at once, to view the subjective and objective worlds as functions of each other by regarding both as functions of the forms of speech in which they are rendered." The symbolism of modern literature is said to be "a deliberate experiment with alogical structures of multiple meaning." [10] In defining the symbol in this manner Feidelson lends a quasi-philosophical status to the protean character of the modern symbol. The claims advanced by William Y. Tindall in his *The Literary Symbol* for the symbol are equally far-reaching, though they have less of a philosophical foundation. Tindall, who also refers to Cassirer and Langer, defines the symbolist novel in this way: "As tight and reflexive as poems, symbolist novels insinuate their meanings by a concert of elements. Images, allusions, hints, changes of rhythm, and tone—in short, all the devices of suggestion—support and sometimes carry the principal burden." [11] This type of symbol seems to have a sort of creative ambiguity, whereby the modern novelist establishes contact with a realm of noumena. For these critics symbolism is more than a literary technique, it is a *Weltanschauung*. At its core the symbol is part of the world and retains a reference to the reality of sense perception. But the meaning it assumes has a wide range of variability, depending upon its context. This quality has facilitated the use of the symbol in recent literature. It requires no common creed; it can be isolated and manipulated; and its possibilities of interpretation are almost unlimited. Then too, it is very well adapted to the search for fragments of meaning so characteristic of the modern artist, who has lost all religious belief and seeks significance in the world's individual phenomena.

The ambiguity and multilevel significance of the modern symbol are regarded favorably. We can discern the symbol's affinity to mythology in the distance, yet it retains the freedom of a variety of interpretations.[12] The most ancient bonds between image and meaning (which are now being called to mind again) originate in the earliest traditions and beliefs of man. There we find that certain elemental meanings were established, such as the symbols for light and for darkness, for growth and for death. With the help of folklorists, psychologists, and anthropologists, the key to many a symbol has been found in mythology. The symbols have turned out to represent the most elemental patterns of human life, connected with the most ancient vestiges of religion known to us, fertility and initiation rites. Thus modern literary symbolism regards itself as establishing contact with an ancient mythical drama. What it attempts to express is a new feeling for the mystery of human life, which, since it can no longer be bound up with a fixed creed, must be given over to the artist's individual insight. In view of the basic instability of any one man's interpretation, it is important that we remind ourselves of the symbol's reference to some mythical creed. This serves to anchor the fluctuating possibilities of the symbol's interpretation.

Whereas mythology seems to have something to offer to modern sensibility, eras that tend toward rationalism regard it less favorably. The Enlightenment was antisymbolistic as much as it was antireligious, and even Goethe, devoted as he was to enlightening the world, had to be converted to symbolism by Schiller. He finally became convinced of the usefulness of the symbol by regarding it in a largely representative manner: "A symbol is frequently representative." [13] The mystical dimensions—so important for modern philosophers of symbolism—lay beyond Goethe's notion of symbolism. Nonetheless, he regarded a symbol as the manifestation of a supernatural will. Here we encounter a vestige of faith: "Wherever the particular represents the universal as a vivid, momentary revelation of the inscrutable rather than as a dream, a shadow—there we have a true symbolism." [14] This standpoint is typical of the school of "representative" symbolism to which we may also reckon the European novel of the nineteenth century. Here the scenes and occurrences exist largely on the plane of ordinary reality—they function symbolically in the sense that they also reveal a deeper plane or universal significance. The symbol serves as a sort of shorthand, whereby the scene or character also indicates a larger, more complex whole, of which it is a part. What is represented may be a character type or group of people, the conditions of a social class or a country.[15]

In his last great work Goethe employed an allegorical-symbolical style. In *Faust* Part Two he conjures up characters and events to serve as eternally valid models of the human situation.[16] These characters and events are in part allegory and in part representative symbols, because they represent complex forces of human life in a figurative manner.[17] The purely allegorical characters are easily recognized by their names: Worry, Guilt, Hope, Hold-Fast and Have-Soon (the last two names are after Bunyan's manner). The symbolic characters are mostly of mythico-religious descent: Philemon and Baucis, Dr. Marianus, Helen of Troy. But rather than originating in the mythico-magical sphere of ritual they come from the more complex world of antique myth. These mythological characters and animals have entered into the arsenal of Western literature and thought. Goethe uses them to embody the enduring ideas and forces of the human drama. Thus Helen of Troy embodies beauty, whereby she functions allegorically. Yet at the same time she is a mythically real, even historical person, with a multilevel but definable significance which she proclaims in her own words.

We also find mythico-religious figures employed in American literature. An antique faun plays an important role in Hawthorne's *Marble Faun,* and in Melville's *Moby Dick* we encounter an Ishmael and an Ahab. But here we have no attempt to reawaken these antique or biblical figures in their historical surroundings. What we do have is a special literary technique which although it is derived from the sphere of religion is derived in a different way. We have here "shadows" which Goethe rejected in his theory of symbolism, but which were of significance for the grandchildren of the Puritans.

It is not a new insight that Hawthorne, Melville, and their New England contemporaries are the intellectual heirs of the Puritans, albeit rebellious heirs. Their inclination towards allegory and symbolism has also been traced to the same heritage by such literary historians and critics as Yvor Winters,[18] F. O. Matthiessen, and Charles Feidelson. How symbolism was nourished by Puritanism is described by F. O. Matthiessen in the following manner:

> The tendency of American idealism to see a spiritual significance in every natural fact was far more broadly diffused than transcendentalism. Loosely Platonic, it came specifically from the common background that lay behind Emerson and Hawthorne, from the Christian habit of mind that saw the hand of God in all manifestations of life, and which, in the intensity of the New England seventeenth century, had gone to the extreme of finding "remarkable providences" even in the smallest phenomena, tokens of divine displeasure in every capsized dory or runaway cow.[19]

Yet in tracing American Symbolism back to Puritanism one stumbles upon an intriguing paradox, a paradox which all of these scholars have overlooked. The paradox is that this same Puritanism out of which a literary symbolism developed was an intellectual movement decidedly hostile to images and symbols. Symbols were cause of extreme discomfort and even anger to true Puritans, and this holds not only for the symbols of the Catholic church, including the cross, but for any symbolic representations of religious doctrine whatever. Even those parts of the Old Testament where symbols were extensively used made them uneasy. Because they saw the hand of God in the events of the world they refused to create symbols themselves or to invent symbolic actions in fiction. They discerned *signs* in the world's events, which could be recognized and interpreted, but not created. In their minds only God could create symbols; not man, as the modern philosophers of symbolism have it.

In his *Symbolism and American Literature*, Chapter III, "An American Tradition," which is otherwise most valuable and stimulating, Charles Feidelson overlooks this discrepancy between modern symbolism and the Puritan conviction of the significance of natural events. He simply brands the Puritans *symbolistes manqués*. They speak of "providence" without realizing that they have to do with symbolic experiences: "The wearisome reiteration of 'providences' in the Puritan writing is actually a record of symbolic experience that never attained formal literary structure"; "The 'reading' of events was the inadequate form taken by a basically symbolic vision." [20] This estimate from the vantage point of modern symbolism is a logical consequence of Feidelson's basic position. If all literature is regarded as symbolic, the only remaining distinction is between the unsuccessful and the successful symbolism. This is an a-historical standpoint that sweeps away fundamental distinctions between different ideas and between forms of thought.[21] Significant differences in categories and two hundred years of rapid European-American intellectual development separate the concept of divine providence, which was taken with uncompromising seriousness by the Puritans, from the symbolism of recent literature. The gulf that divides them divides the religious from the esthetic outlook on life. Both these concepts are links in a single chain of development, but they do not have the same meaning. Here we are going to investigate the literary symbolism of the American classics in its various stages of development as it arises out of the Puritan interpretation of the world.

Part of the difficulty involved in tracing the intellectual background of the symbolism practiced by Hawthorne and Melville lies in the terminology. Perhaps one should say in the lack of terminology, because, when words changed their meanings, nobody bothered to clarify the new meanings and distinguish them from the old. The contemporaries of Hawthorne and Melville not only kept on using the same word after its meaning had changed, they also used the concepts "symbol" and "allegory" rather arbitrarily, without attempting to define them. They often refer to as allegory what we would surely call symbolism. One astonishing example is provided by Melville when he calls the world an allegory: "Why, ever since Adam, who has got the meaning of this great allegory—the world? Then we pygmies must be content to have our paper allegories but ill comprehended." [22] It was natural for the descendants of the Puritans to view things the other way around, *i.e.*, from God's standpoint. God's will was the primary thing, the world was its illustration. Melville regards the world allegorically in the same way as the Bible was regarded allegorically. They are both allegorical if one regards their characters and events as personifications and manifestations of God's volition. On the other hand, a nontheological interpretation (*i.e.*, one not oriented on God) of the world, nature, and human life would deserve to be called symbolic if these phenomena were simply accepted in their existence and concreteness, a deeper meaning being sought only for certain individual phenomena.

This quotation from Melville shows how difficult it is to understand his ideas and intentions. For seventy years Melville was not read because nobody understood his symbolic language. But then, when he was rediscovered, he was read with eyes that had been trained to decipher symbolist texts in the boldly speculative school of the French Symbolists. Do we see Melville's world in the same way he saw it? Do we understand his symbols the way he intended us to? Melville seldom uses the word *symbol* in his works, but we often encounter *emblem* and *emblematical*. In addition to *symbol*, Hawthorne employs *emblem* and *type*, and the latter word also occurs in Melville. Both writers further employ *sign* and *signify*.

Type, sign, and *emblem* are taken from the nomenclature of New England Puritanism. This shows that in interpreting the world both writers used concepts and methods that had developed out of Purtanism, even though they were skeptical toward the dogmas of orthodox Calvinism.[23] Both writers grew up in an atmosphere of Calvinism. Certain Calvinistic ways of thought shaped their minds and the way they viewed and interpreted the world. The substance of the Puritan faith had grown outmoded but some of its categories and methods of thought found a new use. Categories of thought derived from Calvinism or even older religious movements were being applied unconsciously to new secular situations. People ceased to believe in regeneration or depravity in the strict Calvinist sense, yet they continued to regard natural phenomena as expressions of a supernatural volition. More specifically, they regarded such phenomena as *types*, or repeat performances of previously given models.

The aspect of Calvinism that is usable from the standpoint of symbolism is the general belief that God uses natural events to give *signs* or *signals* to man. Such a sign does have a definite meaning, even though it may well be imperfectly understood. This means that of natural events one must inquire after their *significances*—a very important word to the American Puritans. By such writers as Emerson, Hawthorne, Melville, and even Poe[24] on occasion, the word *type* is used in a special sense no longer encountered today. This leads us to another kind of symbolism used by the American Calvinists, their so-called *typology*.

What is a *type* in this specific sense? Melville gives us a hint. In *Israel Potter*, while describing the naval contest between John Paul Jones's ship, the *Bon Homme Richard*, and the English *Serapis*, he says: There is "something singularly indicatory in this engagement: it may involve at once a type, a parallel, and a prophecy." By way of explanation he states that America is the "John Paul Jones of nations." Here we have a veritable definition of this Calvinistic form of the symbol. It comprises the meanings of model, parallel, and prophecy.

3 TYPOLOGY AND ITS
SIGNIFICANCE

The German language derived from the Greek the forms *Typ*, *Typus* (via the Latin form), and *Type*, whereas English uses "type" for all three forms. *Type* = "type," in the special sense of printer's type, does not interest us here. What does interest us is *Typ* = *Typus* = "type," which, in both German and English, means "kind," "basic form," "model," and "thing characteristic of a group."

Grimm's *Wörterbuch* distinguishes two fundamental meanings of *Typus* or *Typ*: "1. 'a basic form the characteristic features of which are present to a greater or lesser degree in all members of the group to which it belongs'"; and "2. 'the most characteristic specimen of any given kind, *cf.* prototype.'" The first meaning is most frequently used in the natural sciences, the second in the liberal arts. Under "*type* (L. *typus* a figure, image, form, type, character, fr. Gr. typos the mark of a blow, impression, form of character, model)" *Webster's International* [1] lists seventeen different nuances. Of these the last eleven nuances are used in various sciences. They are derived from meanings 3–5, the meanings in general use today: "3. The general character, form, or structure common to a number of individuals; 4. A particular kind, class, or order; 5. That which or one who possesses characteristic qualities; a model, standard, exemplar." These meanings, along with their use in the sciences, developed in the eighteenth and nineteenth centuries, in English as well as in German and French. Their use in French seems to have provided the model for German.[2]

Yet anyone who reads texts from the seventeenth century, or even Melville, as we have seen, encounters *type* used in a way the modern meanings do not account for. In order to understand it one must be familiar with the special theological use of this concept, which was widespread in medieval culture and persisted into the eighteenth century in certain sects. It has the meaning which *The Oxford English Dictionary*[3] gives as the first of nine: "That by which something is symbolized or figured; anything having a symbolical signification; a symbol, emblem; *spec.* in *Theol.* a person, object or event of Old Testament history, prefiguring some person or thing revealed in the new dispensation; corr. to *antitype. In (the) type*, in symbolic representation." The sources for this use extend from Henryson (*c.* 1470), Spenser, Jeremy Taylor and Fletcher up to the nineteenth century.

In English, German, and French we have "type," *Typ*, and *type* respectively, all with the same meaning. All derive from the Greek τυπος, which designates "a blow" and "that effected by a blow," *viz.* "impress," "trace," "mark," "stamp," "sculpture," "form," "figure," "image." [4] Plato uses *Typos* in the sense of model for his "Ideas." *Typos* also occurs in the New Testament with the meanings "blow," "image," "form," and "model." In addition it occurs in the Pauline Epistles with a new, derivative meaning, "anticipatory, prophetic model," which cannot be found in any earlier source.[5] Paul was the first to conceive of it as a model in the temporal sense of its being a prefiguration of subsequent persons and events.[6] At 1 Cor. 10:6 and 11 we find certain events of the Old Testament, the exodus of the Jews and their religious practices, regarded as models in the sense of prefiguration and anticipation. At Rom. 5:14 Paul speaks of Adam as "the figure of him that was to come." In other places Paul mentions other anticipatory models, and the Gospels also yield examples of this notion, which is not necessarily bound to the word *Typos*. Math. 12:40 has "For as Jonas was three days and three nights in the whale's belly; so shall the Son of man be three days and three nights in the heart of the earth," which (even though it is now regarded as an interpolation) identifies Jonas as a type of Christ. The words of Jesus at John 3:14, "And as Moses lifted up the serpent in the wilderness, even so must the Son of man be lifted up," do the same for the brazen serpent. The raised brazen serpent, at the sight of which the children of Israel are healed from the sting of the desert serpent, is a type of Christ's crucifixion. Christ is "raised" in being nailed to the Cross, and by means of his being raised he saves sinful mankind from death, just as the brazen serpent saved the Israelites. The American Puritans meditated often about this "type" of the brazen serpent and interpreted it in many different ways.

In its Latin form, *figura*, the type (in the sense of "parallel and prophecy" employed by Melville) was a concept that for hundreds of years shaped occidental ideas of human fate and world history. It also influenced literature and historiography, as we can see in the epics and mystery plays of the Middle Ages, and it dominated Christian iconography. According to this conception, the characters and events of the Old Testament are prefigurations and prophecies of future events, mainly of Christ and His works. These in turn are the fulfillment of the Old Testament types, and thus also the abolishment of its laws and rites. "A type in the biblical sense is a person, thing, action, or institution which in addition to its significance in its own historical context also prefigures a future person, thing, action, or institution (*antitypus*), the God who predetermines history having lent it this power." [7]

To establish the connection between the Old Testament and Christ was to regard history as the story of redemption. Typology is a pattern for construing the world's events as leading toward redemption. According to Hebr. 10:1 and Col. 2:17, the Old Testament is the "shadow" (*umbra*) of future redemption (*veritas*).[8] Yet the qualitative difference between *umbra* and *veritas*, Old Testament type and New Testament antitype, is sometimes so considerable that the two may almost seem to be opposites. The connection of Adam, who failed the covenant of works and cast mankind into sin, with Christ, who saved mankind from sin, manifests such an opposition. Adam is nonetheless designated by Paul himself as the most important type of Christ, although the inquiring eyes of the Fathers and medieval theologians succeeded in turning up many other types.

From the start typology was in danger of vanishing into an allegoric-symbolic interpretation of the Bible, and so its advocates were concerned to keep it separate from allegory. The type is not a symbol of Christ. It is a definite historical person or event of the Old Testament that prefigures Christ, yet exists with its own independent meaning and justification.

Nonetheless the notion of a type like that of a symbol

includes an analogy of concrete image and transcendent meaning. You could regard the type as a special sort of symbol, a prophetic symbol, where the "image" is historically given in the Old Testament and the meaning must be inferred as the "fulfillment" of the image in a certain direction. The type differs in being fixed at both of its poles of reference where the symbol is free to move in any direction of interpretation. Also peculiar to the type is the serious religious intent in regarding the processes of prefiguration and fulfillment as predetermined by God.

The view of the Old Testament as prophetic is an integral part of medieval hermeneutics,[9] where to the literal meaning of the Bible (*sensus verbalis, literalis, immediatus, historicus*) its "allegorical" or "typical" meaning is opposed (*sensus typicus, symbolicus, allegoricus, mysticus, realis*).[10] It was thought that beyond the literal meaning of the Bible, as beyond human and natural events, there lay a real, transcendent, mystical meaning, which was amenable to different ways of interpretation. The systematic development of this standpoint led to the doctrine of the threefold or, if the literal is included, the fourfold meaning of the biblical text. Historical, allegorical, tropological, and anagogical meanings were distinguished. The allegorical meaning concerns religion in general; the tropological, the moral precepts of Christianity; and the anagogical, notions of eschatology. Whenever an Old Testament passage is taken as referring to one in the New Testament, we have to do with a "typical" meaning. There is a strict school of hermeneutics which even distinguishes three kinds of types on the basis of these three ways of interpretation. The "allegorical" or "prophetic" types are the ones that refer to Christ. It is important to bear in mind that for theology "allegory" has these special meanings which differ from its meaning for literature. Whereas literary allegory is free to choose the vehicle for its meaning, biblical allegory is a form of exegesis which reveals a transcendent meaning in a given text. In a strict sense, not the event narrated in the Bible, only its revealed meaning is comparable to literary allegory, or rather, to the meaning of literary allegory. In contrast to biblical allegory, the meaning of literary allegory is clearly presented in personifications designed especially for that purpose.

Typological thought developed above all in the Latin tradition. In addition to the words *typus* and *allegoria* we often encounter there the word *figura* in the same sense of prophesying real events. In the Latin version of the New Testament *figura* is used to translate *typos*.[11] In his essay "Figura" [12] Erich Auerbach has pursued the history of this concept from the beginning to its use by Dante, clarifying its meaning and its function in the history of ideas. Auerbach, a specialist in Romance philology and one of Meinicke's former students, is to my knowledge the only literary historian who has specialized in the study of typology. His article (which should be supplemented by the substantial chapters in Heinz G. Jantsch, *Das Symbolische in der frühmittelhochdeutschen Literatur*) provides the foundation for any study of the influence of typology on literature.[13]

Auerbach begins by investigating the history of the word *figura*, which originally meant "shaped form," from its first occurrence in the first century B.C. down to the Fathers. It was Tertullian who first employed the concept *figura* or *typus* to signify prophecy. He makes Joshua into a type of Jesus, partly because of their similarity of name, and partly because Joshua rather than Moses led the children of Israel to the promised land. In a similar manner it is the grace of Jesus rather than Mosaic law that leads the second children of Israel, the Christians, to the promised land.[14] Sometimes a vague similarity is sufficient to provide a "figure." Thus Tertullian interprets the two sacrificial goats at Lev. 16:7 as figures of the first and second advents of Christ, or Adam as *figura Christi* and Eve as *figura ecclesiae*. We must stress that Tertullian by no means wanted these parallels to be regarded as allegories. The prophetic figure is a historically real fact for him, as is its fulfillment in the antitype. Their only spiritual aspect is the insight into how they are related.

From the fourth century on the word *figura* and the corresponding method of interpreting the Bible occur in almost all the writers of the Roman Church. Augustine adopts the typological interpretation and recommends it especially for sermons and missions. He enriches it with numerous new parallels, such as Noah's ark as a *praefiguratio ecclesiae*. Moses is interpreted in several ways as a figure of Christ; Hagar, the slave, is a figure of the Old Testament; Sarah, one of the new. Augustine rejects the sort of allegorical interpretation of the Old Testament practiced chiefly by Philo of Alexandria,[15] and strongly advocates the notion of the type as prophetic, which Auerbach explains in the following manner:

> Figural interpretation establishes a connection between two events or persons, the first of which signifies not only itself but also the second, while the second encompasses or fulfills the first. The two poles of the figure are separate in time, but both, being real events or figures, are within time, within the stream of historical life. . . . Since in figural interpretation one thing stands for another, since one thing represents and signifies the other, figural interpretation is "allegorical" in the widest sense. But it differs from most of the allegorical forms known to us by the historicity both of the sign and what it signifies.[16]

According to this, typology is a form of prophecy which sets two successive historical events into a reciprocal relation of anticipation and fulfillment. Yet though both events are embedded in the course of history, the theological notion of figural prophecy links them up with the more encompassing vista of divine providence. In their historical reality both poles of the figure remain anticipatory and incomplete. They reach out beyond historical events toward eternal fulfillment in the kingdom of God:

> Thus history, with all its concrete force, remains forever a figure, cloaked and needful of interpretation. In this light the history of no epoch ever has the practical self-sufficiency which, from the standpoint both of primitive man and of modern science, resides in the accomplished fact; all history, rather, remains open and questionable, points to something still concealed, and the tentativeness of events in the figural interpretation is fundamentally different from the tentativeness of events in the modern view of historical development. In the modern view, the provisional event is treated as a step in an unbroken horizontal process; in the figural system the interpretation is always sought from above; events are considered not in their unbroken relation to one another, but torn apart, individually, each in relation to something other that is promised and not yet present.[17]

Let us now go one step beyond Auerbach for a look at how the American Puritans put this typology to use. It was the preliminary, incomplete nature of the type—its promise of something yet to come—which led them to regard present and anticipated future events in the light of the biblical types. In fact, the type caused attention to be concentrated on the future, which promised its fulfillment. Jonathan Edwards regarded the "Great Awakening" as the beginning of the predicted millennium.[18]

It is not by chance that typology developed just in the first few centuries of Christianity. It performed an important service in the spread of Christianity by making it more attractive to European communities. For the Gentiles to whom Christianity was spreading, the Old Testament was not a canon of sacred legal and historical documents. But typology linked it up through the concept of prefiguration to the New Testament and the message of Christ. Auerbach points out that the passages in the Pauline Epistles that contain the doctrine of typology were written during the struggle of St. Paul's mission to the Gentiles:

> . . . nearly all are intended to strip the Old Testament of its normative character and show that it is merely a shadow of things to come. His whole figural interpretation was subordinated to the basic Pauline theme of grace versus law, faith versus works: the old law is annulled; it is shadow and *typos*; observance of it has become useless and even harmful since Christ made his sacrifice; . . . In this way his [St. Paul's] thinking, which eminently combined practical politics with creative poetic faith, transformed the Jewish conception of Moses risen again in the Messiah into a system of figural prophecy, in which the risen one both fulfills and annuls the work of his precursor. What the Old Testament thereby lost as a book of national history, it gained in concrete dramatic actuality.[19]

In his account of typology Auerbach reaches Dante but goes no further.[20] But the above quotation suggests the line of development leading from St. Paul to the Reformation, the leaders of which recurred especially to St. Paul. Thus Luther regarded typology favorably, whereas he rejected the doctrine of the fourfold meaning as frivolous.[21] Calvin was a moderate practitioner of typology, for the reason given by Auerbach, and typology itself was revived and further developed by certain Calvinist sects in the seventeenth century.[22]

Like Augustine, Calvin regarded typology as a relation between two historically real phenomena. He generally confined himself to finding models of Christ, for instance, in the tree of life (which had been used by Augustine), in the ladder to Heaven, in Joseph, in the kingdom of David, and in Melchizedek.[23] His theology provided the basis for a school of federal theology in Holland that concentrated on the idea of a covenant and was dominated by the notion of typology. This school culminates in the work of the Bremen Calvinist, Johannes Cocceius, a former student of William Ames, who in turn was a moderate typologist. One might say that Ames was a connecting link between Puritanism and Dutch Calvinism.[24] He was born in 1576 in Ipswich, Suffolk, and he belonged through his mother's family to the group from which the Plymouth Colony settlers were recruited. After studying at Cambridge, Ames went to Holland in 1610. Later on he taught in Leyden, then in 1622 he went to Franeker, where Cocceius became his student. In 1632 Ames went to Rotterdam to emigrate to New England, but death cut short his plans. However, his library did reach America. A work he had written for his lectures, the *Medulla Theologiae*, translated into English as *The Marrow of Sacred Divinity*, became the textbook of American Calvinism until well into the eighteenth century.[25] In it he employs typology primarily in his account of the covenant of grace.[26]

At the Dutch Calvinist University of Franeker, in the midseventeenth century after Ames had left, his disciple Cocceius expounded a theological system in which typology occupied a central position. Johannes Koch, alias Cocceius, was born in 1603 into a distinguished Bremen family of jurists and senators. His legal training probably influenced him to concentrate on federal theology and the problem of the validity of the Old Testament, where he derived support from the federal theology of Bullinger and Calvin.[27] In twelve folio volumes Cocceius developed a closely intertwined typological system that aroused a new interest for typology in many Protestant congregations in Europe, especially Calvinist ones. His work was carried on in Franeker by his disciple Vitringa, and from there his influence spread to certain Pietist communities in Holland and Germany.[28] Lasting into the nineteenth century, this influence was also felt by Protestant theologians. In his pioneer work on symbolism, *Symbolik des Mosaischen Cultus*, the Protestant theologian Karl Christian Bähr describes "the Cocceian form and methods of typology" as outmoded.[29] Yet typology as a means of connecting the Old and New Testaments is very much a part of Bähr's own thought:

> According to the usage generally accepted in theology, a type is like a symbol except that a reference to the future is essential to it. Its complement, which is indicated by its external features, is not something already existing here and now; it is something that will happen or appear in the future. Thus the type is a prophetic symbol. One cannot deny that the Mosaic Cult is symbolic in nature since it has already been shown to deal with imagery. Whether it is typical or not is another question, and that is, whether it prefigures persons and events of the New Testament. Many scholars doubt this, and even more deny it outright. But if you decide this question on the basis of the New Testament itself you must decide in the affirmative. There is nothing more certain than that the authors of the New Testament ascribed a typical nature to the Mosaic Cult.[30]

I have found no evidence that Cocceius had a direct influence on the American Puritans.[31] But there is no doubt

that he exerted a great influence on the Dutch Reformed
Church in America and counted many of its ministers
among his followers. The Labadist Jasper Danckaerts
traveled through the American colonies in 1679/80. In
his diary he mentions a young minister, Tessemaker, a
Voetian, who was having considerable difficulty because
all of the other Dutch ministers in America were Cocceians.[32]

Some of these Calvinist sects were probably attracted to
typology because the covenant theology, upon which the
American Calvinists based their doctrine, had a natural
affinity to it. Just like typology, the federal theology links
up the old covenant with the new, and links up Christ
with his most important type, Adam. The covenant of
works which God contracted with Adam (in which Adam
failed) had its parallel and fulfillment in God's covenant
of grace, for which Christ was the testator. The Puritans
regarded the dominating parallelism between the covenant of works and the covenant of grace as the link connecting up the Old and New Testaments.[33] Since they were
attracted to the Old Testament more than other Protestant
sects, they sought reasons to justify their preference and
ways to establish a closer relationship between the Old
Testament and Christ. This is exactly what typology provided them with.[34]

Thus we find typology referred to expressly in the Faith
of the New England Churches. Chapter VIII, "Of Christ
the Mediator," states:

> VI. Although the *Work* of *Redemption* was not actually
> wrought by Christ, till after his incarnation, yet the vir-
> tue, efficacy and benefits thereof, were communicated
> unto the elect in all ages successively from the begin-
> ning of the world, in and by those promises, types and
> sacrifices, wherein he was revealed and signified to be

the seed of the Woman, which should bruise the Serpent's head, and the Lamb slain from the beginning of the world, being yesterday and to day the same, and for ever.[35]

Here we see that the typical prefigurations of Christ belong to his image and extend the power of his act of redemption back into the time before his appearance. Yet there is a second use of typology in which it serves more to separate than to connect. In Ch. XIX, "Of the Law of God," the definition of faith distinguishes moral (the Ten Commandments), judicial, and ceremonial law, and says of the last:

III. Besides this law commonly called moral, God was pleased to give to the people of Israel, as a church under age, ceremonial laws, containing several typical ordinances, partly of worship, prefiguring Christ, his graces, actions, sufferings and benefits, and partly holding forth diverse institutions of moral duties: All which ceremonial laws being appointed only to the time of reformation, are by Jesus the True *Messiah*, and only law-giver, who was furnished with power from the Father for that end, abrogated and taken away.

What the Puritans found especially useful in this notion of fulfillment was that it entailed the abolition of practices hitherto justified. This permitted them to explain why they had done away with all of the ceremonies God prescribed for His people in the Old Testament. Both this cult of purifying, (which in the absence of typological justification might easily have conflicted with God's instructions in the Old Testament) and the covenant make typology an integral part of the religious thought of the American Calvinists.

It could be said that the covenant theology is basically a

typological idea. The Puritans took up the Adam-Christ parallel again and again until they had developed it into a drama of redemption in which Adam and Christ have parallel yet opposed roles.[36] Another use to which the American Puritans put typology was in relating their own destiny typologically to the Old Testament, which was then regarded as concrete, dramatic, universal history of providential significance. A compact such as that of the Mayflower exhibits a typological element,[37] and the emigration to the American wilderness was an exodus of the children of Israel to a "second Jerusalem."

PART II

The American Puritans:

Their Form of Thought

and Their Way

of Interpreting the World

4 SAMUEL AND COTTON MATHER

Perry Miller, who is probably the finest expert on the literary and intellectual history of the American Puritans, has pointed out that a revival of interest in typology took place in New England in the course of the seventeenth century, which thus ran parallel to the development in European Protestant groups.[1] Miller ascribes the revival mainly to the extensive work of Salomon Glassius, *Philologia Sacra*, which appeared in Jena in 1623–1636. Benjamin Keach prepared an English version of the *Philologia Sacra* under the title: *Tropologia: A Key to Open Scripture Metaphors . . . together with Types of the Old Testament*. This work was published in London in 1681 and was much read in New England.

But recent scholarship has neglected an American who also contributed to this renewed interest in typology:[2]

Samuel Mather, a member of the powerful family that wielded the most intellectual influence over New England. He was a son of Richard Mather and an uncle of Cotton Mather (who devoted a chapter of the *Magnalia* to him),[3] who had emigrated back to England. Samuel Mather studied at Harvard College and became its first fellow. He was the first minister of the second church in North Boston, which the Mathers made famous, and he was followed in its pulpit by his brother Increase and his nephew Cotton Mather. In 1650 he went to England where he became an active Nonconformist, and he was much in demand as a preacher there, as well as in Scotland and Ireland.

Characteristically enough, it was Mather's Puritan enmity towards symbols that led him to typology. He went to Ireland with Cromwell, and when the Episcopalians reintroduced the Anglican church organization after the restoration, he preached two sermons against the symbols and ceremonies of the Church of England. He was against any symbolic embellishment of the rites, the Holy Communion, such false festivals as Christmas—"especially the December festival, an imitation of an heathenish original"—and the symbol of the cross:

> He argued against *the sign of the cross in baptism, that* whatever was to be said against *oyl, cream, salt, spittle,* therein is to be said against the *cross*, which indeed never had been used, in the worship of God, as *oyl* had been of old. *That* there is as much cause to worship the *spear* that pierced our Lord, as the *cross* which hanged him, or that it were as reasonable, to scratch a child's forehead with a *thorn*, to shew that it must suffer for him, who wore a *crown of thorns: that* the *cross* thus employed is a breach of the *second commandment* in the very letter of it, being an *image* in the service of God of *man's devising*, and fetch'd, as Mr. *Parker* says, *from the brothel-house of God's greatest enemy.*[4]

Mather's words give an impression of the rabid enmity of the Puritans toward the human tendency to express a deeper meaning, and above all, a supernatural religious meaning, by means of symbols. However, the practices that could be supported by God's express instructions to Moses caused him special difficulty. A good example is the vestments the Puritans hated so much, which are derived from Aaron's garments in Moses' ceremonial law. Here Mather received help from the notion of the type and its fulfillment in Christ: "*That the Aaronical garments* being *typical* of the graces attending the Lord Jesus Christ, they are by his coming *antiquated*" (p. 39).

The notion that a church is a holy place meets the same fate: "Against *holiness of places*, he argued, *that* they were the standing *symbols* of God's presence, which made stated *holy places* under the law, and those *places* were *holy* because of their *typical relation* to the Lord Jesus Christ" (p. 40). The Puritan churches were meeting places and not holy places. Instrumental church music was not tolerated in them, because "*instrumental music* under the law was intended for *a shadow of good things to come,* which being now come, it was abolished" (p. 40 f.).[5]

As Cotton Mather reports, these two sermons brought charges of seditious preaching against the contentious Samuel Mather. He returned to England and was dismissed in 1662, along with two thousand other nonconforming ministers. He then returned to Dublin, where he was urged by friends and followers to continue his work on typology:

> Our Mr. *Mather* . . . was earnestly desired by the *nonconformist* ministers, in the city of *Dublin,* to preach upon the *types* of *evangelical mysteries,* in the dispensations of the *Old Testament*; in compliance with which

he had not proceeded very far, before he saw cause to write unto one of his brothers, *the types and shadows of the Old Testament, if but a little understood, how full are they of gospel-light and glory! having gone through diverse of them, I must acknowledge, with thankfulness to the praise of the freeness of the grace of the Lord Jesus Christ, that I have seen more of Him, than I saw before.*[6]

Samuel Mather took great pains to clarify the types, of which Cotton Mather spoke with such rich metaphor (p. 46): "Here, the *waxen combs* of the ancient and typical *cells*, being melted down is (as one expresses it) *rolled up into shining tapers, to illuminate* the students of those mysteries, *in finding out the honey, that couches in the carcase of the slain lion of the tribe of Judah*." And Samuel Mather's work bore fruit in New England, because we can surely assume that his book was read there as well as his nephew's report of his views on typology.

In sermons held in Dublin from March 1666 to February 1668, Samuel Mather presented a systematic treatment of typological theology. After his death, his younger brother, Nathanael, whom he had called over from America, published these sermons in London in 1673 under the title: *The Figures or Types of the Old Testament, by which Christ and the Heavenly Things of the Gospel were Preached and Shadowed to the People of God of Old, Explained and Improv'd in Sundry Sermons, by Samuel Mather.*[7] This work obviously aroused considerable interest, because a second edition appeared in 1702, and a new and rewritten version appeared in 1834.[8]

If Auerbach explains why the Fathers of the Church were interested in typology, Samuel Mather reveals indirectly why the Puritans came almost inevitably to typology to solve problems that arose from their mental-

ity and their theology. Puritanism was founded on redemption by grace and thus upon Christ, yet it had a great
affinity for the Old Testament. A theological movement
that prized logical consistency as much as Puritanism did
would of course seek to make up for the obvious lack of it
here. Thus the Puritans were led to those passages in the
Pauline Epistles that established a typological connection
between the Old Testament and the New. This strength-
ened the ties between the covenant of works and the covenant of grace, the fall and redemption, and Christ and his
most important type, Adam, which had already been established by the covenant theology. From this point on,
the ties were regarded as definitely typological. Samuel
Mather connects other types with Christ, *e.g.* Abraham,
Isaac, and circumcision, by means of the covenant tie.
Thus in one way typology lent the Old Testament more
significance: as a manifold anticipation (in code, yet unequivocal) of redemption by Christ. In another it reduced
its significance: as a model for cult and dogma. In this
manner it cleared away the remaining prescriptions and
rules adopted by Christianity from the Old Testament,
which were so troublesome to Puritans pressing for a removal of religion from the institutional to the personal
sphere.

Samuel Mather based his typological theology on Hebr.
4:2: "For unto us was the Gospel Preached, as well as
unto them." Typological anticipation was one of God's
ways of announcing the gospel of Christ in the Old Testament. Mather defines the type in the following manner:
"A Type is some outward or sensible thing ordained of God
under the Old Testament, to represent and hold forth
something of Christ in the New." [9] A type is always a definite kind of sign: "it is a Sign holding forth Christ"; and
"There is in a Type some *outward* or *sensible* thing, that
represents an higher spiritual thing, which may be called

a *Sign* or an Resemblance, a *Pattern* or *Figure*, or the like." [10]

Mather divides types into two main classes: personal types and real types. Some examples of individual personal types are: Adam, "the Head of the first Covenant," Enoch, Noah, Melchizedek, Abraham, Isaac, Jacob, and Joseph. Either they have been expressly confirmed by St. Paul as types, or they have been established as such by the interpretation of special circumstances concerning their birth or death, or their special deeds, statements, or sermons. Some of the Old Testament figures regarded by other interpreters as individual types are connected up by Samuel Mather as 'constellations' or 'conjunctions': Moses and Joshua; Samson, David, and Solomon; and Eliza and Jonas. In addition there are the collective types; the basic one is the people and the nation of Israel ("they were a *peculiar People to the Lord*, chosen and singled out by him from all the world");[11] His first-born; the Nazarenes; priests; prophets; and His kings from the House of David. Mather concludes this first part of his book, "The Gospel of the Personal Types," with an admonition to his readers and a challenge for them to join this select group:

> *See our own Dignity and Duty*; for all the Members of Christ do in their Measure partake of the Glory of him their Head: Therefore walk as becomes the *Israel* of God, as his *First-born*.[12]

Samuel Mather distinguishes two main groups of real types: occasional types and perpetual types. The occasional types are further subdivided into those consisting of things and those consisting of actions. The first comprises *e.g.* Noah's ark, Jacob's ladder, the burning bush, the brazen serpent, and manna, which is connected up with the

"bread of life" of John 6. The exodus of the children of
Israel from Egypt, the crossing of the Red Sea, the march
through the wilderness, the crossing of the Jordan, the
entry into Canaan, and the liberation from Babylonian
captivity are all occasional typical actions. Finally Mather
counts the ceremonial law of Moses among the perpetual
types: circumcision, sacrifices for purification, the ritual
areas of the temple and the tabernacle, the priesthood,
and the festivals, which he interprets in detail.

Like most of the typologists, Mather is aware of the special danger of real types becoming allegories because they
lack a historically fixed foundation. Thus he warns of this
danger:

> But for Men to set their Fancies a[t] Work to extract
> Allegories out of every Scripture-history, as the Popish
> Interpreters use to do, is not safe nor becoming a ju-
> dicious Interpreter.[13]

And he stresses the true nature of the real type:

> They [the real types] are not bare *Allegories*, or paraboli-
> cal Poems, such as is the Song of *Solomon*, or *Jotham's*
> Parable, *Judg.* 9:7, or *Nathan's* Parable to *David*, 2
> *Sam*: 12, but they are a true Narration of Things really
> existent and acted in the World, and are literally and
> historically to be understood.[14]

Samuel Mather's *Figures or Types* was not the only
collection of typological interpretations in New England,
and it may not even have been the most widely used one.
Yet it is a valuable aid for the understanding of subsequent American typologists. Both his account of the individual parallels and his ideas on typology in general serve
to illustrate the problems typology raised for the Puritans

and for their use of this theory. They help to clear up certain passages in Edward Taylor, Jonathan Edwards, and even in Melville.

In the third generation of New England colonists arose the man who was to chronicle their bold undertaking, in the greatness of its religious aspirations, and with the difficulties—both practical and theological—of its execution. Cotton Mather was a grandson of the renowned immigrants, John Cotton and Richard Mather, and a son of the political and spiritual leader, Increase Mather. His work, the *Magnalia Christi Americana or, The Ecclesiastical History of New England* (1702), which comprises seven books, begins with the following words:

> I write the *Wonders* of the Christian Religion, flying from the depravations of *Europe*, to the *American Strand*: and, assisted by the Holy Author of that *Religion*, I do, with all conscience of *Truth*, required therein by Him, who is the *Truth* itself, report the *wonderful displays* of His infinite Power, Wisdom, Goodness, and Faithfulness, wherewith His Divine Providence hath *irradiated* an *Indian Wilderness*.[15]

History is here above all religious history—the main motive of the Puritan emigration was a religious one—and the most important temporal events belong at the same time to the history of redemption. Thus it is no surprise that Mather employs the notion of a type in its historical aspect, the bipolar conception immanent in history as it is defined by Auerbach.[16] In the introduction to the *Magnalia* Mather outlines a historiographical program that is under the influence of the history of redemption:

> Certainly, it will not be ungrateful unto good men, to have innumerable *Antiquities, Jewish, Chaldee, Arabian, Grecian* and *Roman*, brought home unto us, with a

sweet light reflected from them on the *word*, which is our *light*; or, to have all the *typical* men and things in our *Book of Mysteries*, accommodated with their *Antitypes*: or, to have many hundreds of references to our dearest *Lord Messiah*, discovered in the writings which *testifie of Him*, oftner than the most of mankind have hitherto imagined: or, to have the *histories* of all *ages*, coming in with punctual and surprising *fulfillments* of the divine *Prophecies*, as far as they have been hitherto fulfilled; and not meer *conjectures*, but even mathematical and incontestible *demonstrations*, given of *expositions* offered upon the *Prophecies*, that yet remain to be accomplished.[17]

Even though this quotation is only a brief section of Mather's verbose introduction, it contains the pillars of his historical edifice: parallels to the ancient world; types and antitypes in general; typical prefigurations of Christ; and divine prophecies that have been fulfilled, as well as those yet to be fulfilled. He applies these principles in a manner that is disorderly, not to say confused. Mather embellishes his account with numerous quotations of every possible provenance—classical, biblical, and Reformation, and he justifies them as illustrations of the Holy Scriptures: "I considered, that all sort of *learning* might be made gloriously subservient unto the *illustration* of the *sacred Scripture*; and that no *professed commentaries* had hitherto given a thousandth part of so much *illustration* unto it, as might be given." [18] He extends the notion of typical prefiguration from the New Testament to secular history and thereby undercuts its theological significance. The result is a closely spun but arbitrary system of parallels and analogies, in which ancient history is used to illustrate the Scriptures, and vice versa, and in which both prefigure and illuminate the history of the Puritans. For Mather, New England history is an important era of human events in the plan of divine redemption, perhaps even a decisive era.

In Mather's eyes, world history—and above all, the history of the American Puritans under divine protection—is not developing toward something completely new; rather, it is developing toward the fulfillment of prophecies and the repetition of exemplary models. In order to prove this he fits his descriptions of events and people into a framework of correspondences taken from ancient, biblical, or Reformation history. Thus his frequent and extended comparisons, quotations, and enumerations are not merely (as has often been held) a vain parade of erudition or a Baroque excess of images—although these were not foreign to Mather's nature; they are based instead on the Puritan view of the world. He extends the range of the models and analogies he uses to illuminate and interpret American destiny until it encompasses the whole of world history. And he does this with astounding erudition—one should not belittle this hard-won triumph over the colonial narrowness of his surroundings. We encounter exemplary figures from secular history serving side by side with biblical figures as types and parallels for certain New England persons, and this is intended to show the dignity and significance of events in New England.

Although Mather did enlarge the notion of typology by including models from secular history, he nonetheless regarded the redemptive aspects of Puritan history as fulfillments of Old Testament prefigurations. The ever-present type for the New England Puritans' view of their own destiny was the exodus of the children of Israel from Egypt into the wilderness and then to the promised land. This conception—only a category of thought—became a factor in universal history, because it lent the Puritans the strength and endurance necessary for their trials on the stony soil of New England in the face of the dangers of

the wilderness. This basic idea is found in many variations in all the New England writers, and it also domi-
nates Cotton Mather's *Magnalia.* The analogy to the type
of the exodus of the children of Israel is encountered in
countless variations: sometimes there is only an allusion;
more often it is treated fully; and on one occasion the author is so carried away that he attempts to outdo his
model: "The most *crooked way,* that ever was gone, even
that of *Israel's* peregrination *through* the *wilderness,* may
be called *a right way,* such was the *way* of this little *Israel,* now going *into a wilderness.*" [19]

This type determines not only the history of New England but its physical features as well. The desert or wilderness where Moses and the people of Israel had to endure
serpents and hardships, and the wilderness as the place
where Christ was tempted by the devil, is the prefiguration
of the American wilderness. This type explains the temptations of the young colony as well as the character of the
Indians. According to the metaphor frequently used for
them, they are the serpents of the wilderness, under the
influence of the devil who rules there. In the seventh Book
of the *Magnalia,* which treats the "Afflictive Disturbances
which the churches of New England have suffered from
various Adversaries," Mather gives the following reason
for the temptations (Ch. 1, ¶ 1):

> It is written concerning our Lord Jesus Christ, *that he
> was led into the wilderness to be tempted of the devil*;
> and the people of the Lord Jesus Christ, *led into the
> wilderness of New-England,* have not only met with a
> continual *temptation* of the *devil* there; the *wilderness*
> having always had *serpents* in it; but also they have had
> in almost every new *lustre* of years, a new assault of
> extraordinary *temptation* upon them; a more than com-
> mon *hour and power of darkness.*[20]

In the wake of this typological influence the heathen Indians could scarcely be anything but devilish. Among the other dangers and temptations to which this figurative character of the wilderness gave birth may be counted the dissenting sects that caused trouble for the Puritans, such as the Familists, Separatists, Quakers, and Antinomians.

The declaration that New England is a New Canaan or a Second Jerusalem is not the only result of the Puritan claim to be the antitype of the people of Israel. The typological characterization of the New England leaders also has the same source. Cotton Mather provides us with numerous examples, because the main part of the *Magnalia* (the historical part) consists of biographies of the religious and secular leaders of the young colony. This is in itself a result of the typological way of thinking. Mather can only write history as the history of people who fulfill personal types.

This is not to say, however, that the dominant position of biography in Puritan historiography is due solely to typological influence. The biography of outstanding religious persons is a product of the Reformation, and its precedent is the medieval *vita* of the saint. This kind of biography was very popular in seventeenth-century England.[21] The main factors behind this were Protestant religious individualism and the concern with conscience, matters which also occupied the Puritans, as their diaries and reports of conversion reveal. Yet this tendency of the American Puritans to individualize their religious experience remains in most instances a personal estimate of chances of redemption which goes no farther than the diary, if it goes that far. Those lives of saints that are presented to the public as exemplary are viewed in the manner of types.

Kenneth Murdock has pointed out that the Puritan isolation in the wilderness is also important in this connection.[22] The Puritan emigrants and colonists did their writing amidst feelings of isolation and insecurity. In order to prove to themselves and to those who remained at home that their exodus and colonization were both justified and important, they related them to the history of Christianity and also enhanced their leaders with historical and biblical parallels. Murdock finds in this a psychological explanation for the Puritan interest in typology. It allowed them to overcome their feeling of isolation in the "howling wilderness" and to participate in the great Christian tradition of Europe, despite the great distance and the ocean that separated them geographically from it.

Puritan biographies, especially those sketched under typological influence by Cotton Mather, are characterized less by Protestant individualism than by an authoritative, stereotyped character.[23] The desire to enhance is the main cause of this. Mather's lives of saints are not intended to present individual religious experiences but to provide *exempla* of model behavior. They are a sort of Puritan hagiography with their own special pattern. This consists of an introduction, family history, theological training, regeneration, being ordained, pastoral care, sermons, virtues, and death. The conclusion is not infrequently a verse epitaph. The introduction usually mentions one or more types that determine the life and character of the person treated. In accordance with the analogy to the exodus from Egypt, the leaders of the emigration are regarded as modern fulfillments of the type of Moses. William Bradford, the leader of the Plymouth group, is described thus:

> The *leader* of a people in a *wilderness* had need be a *Moses*; and if a *Moses* had not led the people of *Ply-*

> *mouth Colony*, when this worthy person was their governour, the people had never with so much unanimity and importunity still called *him* to lead them.[24]

John Winthrop, the leader of the group that arrived in 1630, whose service as an organizer and founder of a nation earned him the epithet "Nehemias Americanus," was also a new Moses:

> Accordingly when the *noble design* of carrying a colony of *chosen people* into an *American* wilderness, was by *some* eminent persons undertaken, *this* eminent person was, by the consent of all, *chosen* for the *Moses*, who must be the leader of so great an undertaking: and indeed nothing but a *Mosaic spirit* could have carried him through the *temptations*, to which either his *farewel* to his *own land*, or his *travel* in a *strange land*, must needs expose a gentleman of his *education*.[25]

This last attribute of Winthrop, a "gentleman of his *education*" (he was of higher descent than most of the immigrants), is a prime example of the naivety with which Mather compared his New England figures to biblical patriarchs. At the same time it shows that such comparisons were taken as a matter of course.

One of the leading ministers and theologians, John Cotton, acquires a parallel to Melanchthon as well as the usual one to Moses.[26] The assistants of this new Moses are "ministers to their Moses" or they are at least credited with "Mosaic spirit." [27] Of course, this surplus of Moseses tends to reduce them from types in the strict sense to parallels that help to define character. Joshua is a favorite parallel for the outstanding figures of the second generation of Puritans, who bring New England closer to New Canaan. As we have seen above, Samuel Mather paired Moses and Joshua as a team. Thus if John Cotton is a Moses, his successor John Norton is a Joshua. This is stated in the final part of Cotton's epitaph:

> Though *Moses* be, yet *Joshua* is not dead:
> I mean Renowned *Norton*; worthy he,
> Successor to our *Moses*, is to be.
> O happy *Israel* in *America*,
> In such a *Moses*, such a *Joshua*.[28]

Various different types are prescribed for the other "Famous Divines." "Johns" and "Samuels" are often associated with their biblical namesakes, and a rather routine analogy is created through types selected more or less as a matter of courtesy toward fellow ministers. Thus Theophilus Eaton is given a parallel to the biblical Theophilus. In addition to the choice of a basic type we find in many cases an attempt to illuminate situations, acts, or individual traits of character in a typological manner. The biography of John Cotton contains in addition to the Moses and Melanchthon parallels the following: "this *Cotton* was indeed the *Cato* of his age, for his gravity; but had a glory with it which *Cato* had not," [29] because Cato was a pagan who could not share in Christian glory.

Entire segments of colonial history are supplied with biblical prefigurations and sometimes even embellished with them, as is the case with the unfortunate expedition against Canada under Sir William Phips:

> There was a time when the *Philistines* had made some inroads and assaults from the *northward*, upon the skirts of *Goshen*, where the *Israelites* had a residence, before their coming out of *Egypt*. The *Israelites*, and especially that active colony of the *Ephraimites*, were willing to revenge these injuries upon their wicked neighbours; . . . and they formed a brisk *expedition*, but came off unhappy losers in it. . . .[30]

For the relatively few cases of New England statesmen who were not at the same time religious leaders, secular categories of models had to be found. This is the case in the extravagantly laudatory sketch of Sir William Phips, one of Mather's supporters. There we find in addition to typology an express statement of the influence of prefiguration in the broader sense of parallel:

> So *obscure* was the *original* of that memorable person, whose *actions* I am going to relate, that I must, in a way of writing, like that of *Plutarch*, prepare my reader for the intended relation, by first searching the *archives* of antiquity for a *parallel*.[31]

Mather accomplishes this by examining a series of possible comparisons to people of low descent who, like Phips, had achieved fame and esteem, and then rejecting them as not really appropriate. In this manner he is able to treat some unusual features of Phips's rise to success before finally comparing him to Pizarro, doubtlessly because of Phips's service in having raised a sunken treasure.

The fact is that Mather has so intertwined the original notion of a type with Plutarch's notion of a parallel that it is in most cases impossible to ascertain what stems from the one and what from the other. We find, for instance, the following statement about John Cotton: "He had a more than common excellency in that *cool spirit*, which the oracles of wisdom describe, as *the excellent spirit in the man of understanding*; and therefore Mr. *Norton* would parallel him with *Moses* among the *patriarchs*, with *Melacthon* [sic] among the *reformers*." [32] Here we find the biblical type placed on a level with the comparison to historical religious personages, and the concept of a parallel developed from those of "type" and "similarity."

For use in his history Cotton Mather evolved a mixture of such categories of comparison as model, prefiguration, and similarity, which he adapted and applied as the need arose. This meant that on one occasion he might emphasize one of the components, on another, he might mix in at least two of them.

These theories show that Mather stands between two eras. The *Magnalia*, which appeared in 1702, is an attempt to write history from the religious standpoint. However, Mather does not really know how to apply its principles to contemporary temporal affairs.[33] Since the strict principle of the type can only be applied to the most exalted aspects of contemporary events, he recurs to the less binding principle of the parallel which is provided by ancient historiography. This is not the result of a tendency to leave behind the strict theological interpretation of the seventeenth century for a more humanistic, progressive, or secularized one; it is instead due to Mather's inability to modify theological principles in the light of a better grasp of history. He simply enlarges the theological notion of prefiguration into a vague anticipatory analogy, in back of which one can still make out God, who as the sole cause of historical events predetermines everything.

This conception of man and history is derived directly from theology and thus presents an exalted view of man. Yet it is also a matter of practical convenience: the parallels cited relieve the author from the obligation of describing his figures, and they provide the judgments already passed by history. They also relieve him of the necessity of considering that a certain development might be unique and of seeking reasons for the uniqueness. The important thing from this standpoint is that which can be compared with the past rather than that which is new and different. The giant, recently discovered continent of America, most of which was yet to be explored, was nothing but a variety

of the biblical desert, "An American Desert." This notion
of history lacks a theory of development in the sense of
something that evolves continually through time toward
an unknown goal by means of causally conditioned
changes. Rather than being conceived according to the
principle of development, it is conceived in the three
stages: prophetic prefiguration; fulfillment; and final fulfillment in the millenium. Development is only present as
the changeability of that which once existed in the past,
but it is not taken into account in this connection because
it is unimportant. People and events of contemporary history appear as slightly altered versions of previous models
or as hybrids of such models. The only forces with causal
efficacy in history are God, who reveals His will in "provi-
dencies," and the devil, who incites enemies against God's
people.[34]

In this interpretation of history, man as the sole clearly
outlined figure holds a central position. If he has the true
faith and acts accordingly he is a participant in the great
drama of divine redemption, and he derives his dignity
and significance from this very participation. All the heroes that Mather regards favorably are such participants.
They are characterized by deeds and qualities resembling
those of their great exemplary types, because this makes
them a part of the scheme of redemption. If personal and
comparatively individual qualities are mentioned at all,
they are only mentioned in a negative sense. Parallels
have been sought for them, but then rejected as not being
entirely appropriate. This view of mankind is predominantly a "typical" one, in the modern meaning of the word
too. Qualities that are common to the models are singled
out to compose types, whereas the more individual qualities receive no attention.

In addition to this influence from the history of ideas,
there are also certain psychological factors in Puritanism

itself that contributed to Cotton Mather's interpretation and presentation of New England history. We can only be astonished at the extravagant manner in which Puritan society compensated itself for its self-imposed abnegations. This society denied itself all forms of outer adornment, whether religious or of life in general, such as pomp, color, art, music, symbols, official titles, and insignia. Its dignitaries went about their duties in simple garments with no sign of hierarchical distinction. Obviously the society had a secret longing for other forms of distinction. Cotton Mather fulfilled this desire by linking up the leading men of this society in extravagant, flowery language with the heroes of the Bible, of antiquity, and of the Reformation.

The two main characteristics of Mather's interpretation are linked together: the principle of subordinating the individual to the exemplary, and the neglect of development, which is unhistorical from a modern standpoint. If someone overlooks the constant change in history and its ever-changing conditions in favor of that which never changes, he lacks the most important prerequisite of sensing differences and nuances in human character and human aspirations. This lack of interest in development and in human individuality is what distinguishes the American tradition from the intellectual movement that was winning adherents in Europe during the eighteenth century. I refer to historicism, which was initiated by Shaftsbury and Leibnitz, both of whom were contemporaries of Cotton Mather.[35] For historicism, world history is a process of development with manifold conditions, whose stages cannot be repeated, and in which individual, changing units also participate. For Mather, history is that which God has predetermined from the beginning of time, and which manifests itself by repeating eternal models.

5   EDWARD TAYLOR'S

MEDITATIONS ON THE

LORD'S SUPPER

The 1960 edition of *The Poems of Edward Taylor*[1] marks the first appearance of the complete "Preparatory Meditations, Second Series." They comprise nearly 170 poems, 128 of which have not been published before. To judge from their aim and scope these Meditations upon which Taylor labored for more than thirty of his mature years must be regarded as his main work.[2]

Taylor's Meditations, First and Second Series, are a unique document of poetical theology, a verse dialogue of a Puritan theologian with his God. Of course one can single out specific poems, some of the especially successful ones of the First Series in particular, and judge them from a purely esthetic standpoint, as has been done in American literary criticism. This approach has yielded some valuable comments on the individuality of Taylor's poetry and his relation to the metaphysical poets.[3] These are attempts to read Taylor's poetry in the light of purely literary developments, which is not, however, what the poet himself intended. If we judge these Meditations without even taking into account the Bible quotation prefixed to them and without seeking to understand it in Taylor's sense, we are ignoring his own intentions. But this is what is commonly done.[4]

Our aim is to study the Meditations more from the standpoint of theology and to inquire into their significance for intellectual history. We feel justified in doing this because their discussion of theology makes them a document of Puritan intellectual history. We shall discover that their treatment of theology has certain consequences for esthetics. Puritan dogma and Bible interpretation lead Taylor to the threshold of a symbolic interpretation of the world that he did not intend and that ran counter to his convictions.

Taylor did not want his poetry published, not even after his death. This is not only (as is thought today) because the imagery would have struck his sober New England contemporaries as dangerously sensual and thus popish, or because Taylor's own ideas were similar to the liberal Cambridge Platonism of which the New Englanders were so suspicious.[5] It seems to me to be mainly because his poetry ultimately led him to a sort of allegorical interpretation of the Scriptures, which Puritanism rejected as Catholic and medieval. Yet Taylor was by no means a secret apostate and rebel. He was a Puritan by conviction and his reflections on theology were anchored in Puritan dogma, with its Calvinist features and its theories of the covenant.

In critical evaluations of Taylor the question of his orthodoxy has been raised again and again. Kenneth Murdock believes that the poet in Taylor snatched the theologian away from the path of orthodoxy: "hot poetic emotion cannot always be kept within the limits of reasoned doctrine";[6] S. E. Lind, although he does not have a high opinion of Taylor's ability as a poet, finds his style too sensual for an orthodox Puritan.[7] Thomas H. Johnson, the discoverer and first editor of Taylor, takes him for an orthodox Puritan, yet for more of a covenant theologian than a Calvinist.[8] On the other hand, Donald E. Stanford, the editor of the 1960 *The Poems of Edward Taylor*, declares that the poet is an orthodox Puritan and Calvinist. In his dissertation, *An Edition of the Complete Poetical Works of Edward Taylor* (Stanford, 1953), he cites Calvin's *Institutiones* and the Westminister Confession in order to establish Taylor's basic harmony with their doctrines.

But Stanford's conception of orthodoxy is a bit too neat. He has little sense of the subtleties and pitfalls of this theological system, which is continually faced with the problem of bringing the whole of the Bible as well as every single sentence of it into harmony with its own doctrines. Orthodox Puritanism is not a church with a tight structure of institutions and dogmas like the Catholic church. It is rather a living, ever-renewed venture to discover the meaning of the divine word with the help of a few principles acknowledged to be correct, such as those of Calvin and other reformers.[9] The Puritans had agreed on most of these principles in their Cambridge Platform, with reference to the Westminister Confession, and one had to acknowledge them in order to be orthodox in New England. Even though they were binding on Taylor too, anyone who sought truth as passionately as he did could readily encounter conflicts, even irresolvable ones, between dogma and the word of the Bible. This holds especially for the feature of the Bible that was at once the most important and the most difficult for the Puritans: the sacrament of the Lord's Supper. In other words, it is not for disregarding Puritan dogma that Taylor is unorthodox. This very dogma, with its dialectic of "real" and "spiritual," leads Taylor's poetry to an unavoidable dilemma.

Of all the revolutionary upheavals of Protestantism, the most important for esthetics was the rejection of sacred symbols in the rites and customs of the church. The Puritans were especially radical in this respect. They regarded the sacraments (except for baptism and the Lord's Supper), all the ceremonies and holy festivals—even the Christmas festival, relics, all symbols and consecrations not established by Jesus, and even the cross, as deceitful products of papist power politics, delusions of heathen magic, and products of blasphemous superstition or of blasphemous human presumption. One and all were classed as idolatry. The Puritans condemned everything that man had added to the practice of religion without an express divine command, and they restricted the notion of consecration to the few remaining ordinances such as the sabbath and the two sacraments. They suspected a heathen core in every human embellishment of religion. This accounts for their suspicion of symbols altogether, at least when the symbols were thought to have a meaning in reference to God's will and order, which was the case with nearly all of them.

The Lord's Supper caused an enormous amount of mental exertion for Protestant theologians of all denominations. Even though it had the indisputable sanction of Jesus, in its countless performances it had come to include an element of magic, the miraculous transformation of bread and wine into the flesh and blood of Christ. Luther and Zwingli wrestled bitterly with this problem. Calvin settled on a standpoint different from both but closer to Luther. Taylor's Meditations on the Lord's Supper correspond in every way to the doctrines worked out in the Westminister Confession and repeated for the Cambridge Synods, but he found no easy solutions for the problems this sacrament held for the Puritans. The debate over whether the symbolic and transcendent nature of the miracle of the Lord's Supper was real or spiritual was an important catalyst of Protestant thought. The theory of the function of the symbol and its relation to a transcendent as well as to an immediate reality received important distinctions and was otherwise furthered by this debate. Taylor is a good example of this development.

Since the Puritans could not take the Catholic path of making religion mystical, they followed involuntarily the path of making the real world symbolical, whereby all phenomena were regarded as expressions of the divine volition. It is ironical that all this skepticism and debate about symbolism increased the use of symbolism as a way of thought. What little remained of Puritan art, including music, was purified of sensual and symbolic elements, and the consecration of symbols was rejected. But in their place the Puritans introduced the potential symbolization of all natural phenomena as signs or signals. They are ascribed in a transcendent though not a magic manner to the personal intervention of a God. This Puritan symbolism of the signs was in fact as little supported by the express word of God as was Catholic symbolism. What sanctioned it in the eyes of the Puritans was the ingenious parallels uncovered between the signs and the manifestations and events of the Bible. This general development is illustrated by Edward Taylor and the progression toward an all-encompassing symbolism within his Meditations.

Edward Taylor entitled his poetic theological Meditations thus: "Preparatory Meditations before my Approach to the Lords Supper. Chiefly upon the Doctrine preached upon the Day of administration." He began the Meditations of the First Series in July 1682 at about the age of forty. At the beginning we find several Meditations that are not prefixed with a Bible quotation, and these are interspersed with Meditations on verses from the Song of Solomon. There follow Meditations on verses from various books of the Old and New Testaments, and toward the end quotations from the Pauline Epistles and John predominate. These quotations all center on a small group of themes: the glory of God and Christ, the effects of their infinite grace, and the hope of redemption through grace, to which confessions of human unworthiness are contrasted. Taylor has already begun to ponder whether man is able to find images worthy of God's greatness, a theme of later Meditations:

> When thy Bright Beams, my Lord, do strike mine Eye,
>   Methinkes I then could truely Chide out right
> My Hide bound Soule that stands so niggardly
>   That scarce a thought gets glorified by't.
>   My Quaintest Metaphors are ragged Stuff,
>   Making the Sun seem like a Mullipuff.[10]

Edward Taylor occupied himself with the Preparatory Meditations, Second Series from 1693 to October 1725. He was about fifty-one years old when he started on them, and about eighty-three when he finished. Their thematic history ranges from elucidations of the Bible and the world by typological parallels to a metaphorical interpretation of God and the world based on the images of the Song of Solomon. Three phases may be clearly distinguished in the Meditations of the Second Series:

1) Meditations 1–61, which extend from 1693 to 1704, are dominated by the typological interpretation of the Bible;

2) Meditations 62–114 (1704 to 1713) are concerned

with various Bible passages, most of them from the New Testament and especially from the Pauline Epistles and John. They develop more and more in the direction of the "spiritual" interpretation. The Lord's Supper and transubstantiation are treated several times;

3) Meditations 115–165 (1713 to 1725) are, with the exception of 154, 155, 158, and 159, wholly concerned with words of the Song of Solomon. The word of the Bible has now become entirely symbolical, and topics specifically connected with the Lord's Supper have disappeared.

It is obvious that Taylor's thought in the years 1693 to 1699 was strongly influenced by typology. We do not know what occasioned this. Possibly one of the extensive typological works of this decade reached his hands.[11] Each Meditation 1 to 30 of the Second Series is occasioned by a typological Bible passage, or one that is regarded typologically, and among them are many of the passages which provide the main support for typology itself. Meditation 1 is occasioned by Col. 2:17: "Which are Shaddows of things to come and the body is Christs"; Meditation 3 by Rom. 5:14:" Who is the Figure of Him that was to come"; Meditation 4 by Gal. 4:24: "Which things are an Allegorie" (here = type), etc. Taylor's intense interest in typology lasted until 1704. Meditation 61 is an interpretation of John 3:14: "As Moses lift up the Serpent in the wilderness so must the Son of man be lift up," in which Jesus acknowledges the principle of typology. We find interpretations of types and parallels in Meditations 31 to 60 also. But after 1704 typology largely serves a single purpose, though a quite important one: it helps solve the difficult problem of the Lord's Supper.[12]

Taylor must have regarded the adoption of typological

theology for his poetry as marking a new chapter or a wholly new epoch in his own thought. Otherwise he would probably not have made it the beginning of a second series of Meditations. There is no lapse of time between the First and Second Series.[13] He treats typology extensively in Meditation 1 of the Second Series on Col. 2:17, "Which are Shaddows of things to come and the body is Christs":

> The glory of the world slickt up in types
>   In all Choise things chosen to typify,
> His glory upon whom the worke doth light,
>   To thine's a Shaddow, or a butterfly.
>   How glorious then, my Lord, art thou to mee
>   Seing to cleanse me, 's worke alone for thee.
>
> The glory of all Types doth meet in thee,
>   Thy glory doth their glory quite excell:
> More than the Sun excells in its bright glee
>   A nat, an Earewig, Weevill, Snaile, or Shell.
>   Wonders in Crowds start up; your eyes may strut
>   Viewing his Excellence, and's bleeding cut.[14]

It is characteristic that the notion of the type is here extended from the Old Testament to the world: all the glorious things of the world are types pointing to Christ. Later, connections between particular types are discussed. In Meditation 4, on Gal. 4:24, "Which things are an Allegorie," the parallel is Isaac–Christ (in reality Isaac–New Testament), which the notion of the covenant (Gen. 17:19) made so important for the Puritans. Here Taylor relates the type to his own destiny and implores God not to take the unfortunate Hagar and her son Ishmael as the model for the Puritans in the wilderness, or for himself. In the second stanza this idea turns into a pun on the word "figure":

> Then, my Blesst Lord, let not the Bondmaids type
>   Take place in mee. But thy blesst Promisd Seed.
> Distill thy Spirit through thy royall Pipe
>   Into my Soule, and so my Spirits feed,
>   Then them, and me still into praises right
>   Into thy Cup where I to swim delight.
>
> Though I desire so much, I can't o're doe.
>   All that my Can contains, to nothing comes
> When summed up, it onely Cyphers grows
>   Unless thou set thy Figures to my Sums.
>   Lord set thy Figure 'fore them, greate, or small.
>   To make them something, and I'l give thee all.

The words used in Gal. 4:24 to characterize this typical connection (Gal. 4:22 and 23: "For it is written, that Abraham had two sons, the one by a bondmaid, the other by a freewoman. But he *who was* of the bondwoman was born after the flesh; but he of the freewoman *was* by promise") are rendered in the King James Bible with: "Which are an allegory" (Luther says: "Die Worte bedeuten etwas"). Thus Taylor employs "allegory" here, in the theological sense of the word, for type:

> Nay, Abrams Shine to thee's an Allegory,
> Or fleeting Sparke in th' Smoke, to typify
> Thee, and thy Glorious Selfe in mystery.

However, this is an isolated instance of the use of "allegory," and, so far as I know, Taylor does not use the word again in his Meditations. One could almost believe that he is observing the distinction between type and allegory made by the typologists as well as Samuel Mather.[15]

Taylor goes through the most important types, one after the other, with systematic thoroughness. In Meditation 1 he gives us a general exposition of typology; this is followed by the first-born in 2, Adam in 3, Isaac in 4, Isaac and the ram in 5, Jacob in 6, Joseph in 7, Moses in 9, Joshua in 10, Samson in 11, David in 12, and Solomon in 13. This corresponds to their order in the Bible, which was also followed by Samuel Mather. Taylor's division also corresponds to Mather's in that personal types are treated before real types. There are even resemblances between Taylor's groupings and those of Mather, but the resemblances are not pronounced enough to support the hypothesis that Taylor followed Mather's work. It is likely that he was acquainted with Mather's work but as a conscientious theologian he could not have relied on Mather alone. He must have consulted other works too and developed his own ideas into an independent interpretation of the Bible on the basis of their contributions. Yet Taylor does follow Mather for longer stretches because he treats sacerdotal, prophetic and kingly types in Meditation 14, the Nazarites in 15, the kings of the House of David in 16, and the various aspects of ceremonial law in Meditations 17 to 28: sacrifices, altar, table, tabernacle, holy days, and Passover. In Meditation 29—where Taylor follows the Bible's order rather than Mather's—he treats the construction of the ark, and in 30, Jonas.

The elucidation of these prefigurations is a unique exercise in bold comparisons. Meditation 11 states the following about Samson:

> An Angell tells his mother of his birth.
> An Angell telleth thine of thine. Ye two
> Both Males that ope the Womb in Wedlock Kerfe
> Both Nazarited from the Womb up grew.
> He after pitchy night a Sunshine grows
> And thou the Sun of Righteousness up rose.
>
> His Love did Court a Gentile spouse, and thine
> Espous'd a Gentile to bebride thyselfe.

His Gentile Bride apostatizd betime.
    Apostasy in thine grew full of Wealth.
    He sindgd the Authours of't with Foxes tails.
    And foxy men by thee on thine prevaile.

The Fret now rose. Thousands upon him poure.
    An asses Jaw his javling is, whereby
He slew a Thousand, heap by heap that hour.
    Thou by weake means makest many thousands fly.
    Thou ribbon like wast platted in his Locks
    And hence he thus his Enemies did box.

He's by his Friend betray'd, for money sold,
    Took, bound, blindfolded, made a May game Flout
Dies freely with great sinners, when they hold
    A Sacred Feast. With arms stretcht greatly out,
    Slew more by death, than in his Life he slew.
    And all such things, my Lord, in thee are true.

The modern critic finds these comparisons forced and bizarre. But after several readings he discovers that the imagination that produced them has been trained in a wholly different school. Whereas modern man grasps things according to their historical development by recognizing their differences, Taylor does the same by seeking and discovering identities. To be more precise, he finds an identical deeper meaning in things that are quite heterogeneous, and which can only be compared under a more encompassing principle. This positing of identities that Taylor and those of a similar cast of mind exercised with such devotion is based on a dogmatic foundation. As Puritanism waned this foundation became weaker and finally disappeared altogether. But the intellectual practice of daring explanatory comparisons and identifications became transformed into a literary symbolism.[16] This development began in America at Taylor's time. As another ex-

ample one can take the wealth of bold comparisons on
Solomon as a type of Christ in Meditation 13. Here Taylor
has nearly left the strict confines of the parallelism of
types, especially by virtue of his bold embellishments of
the antitype, Christ:

> Did He Gods Temple Build, in glory shown?
>   Thou buildst Gods House, more gloriously bright.
> Did he sit on a golden ivery Throne
>   With Lions fenc'd? Thy Throne is far more White
> And glorious: garded with Angells strong.
> A Streame of fire doth with the Verdict come.
>
> Did he his Spouse, a glorious Palace build?
>   The Heavens are thy Palace for thy Spouse.
> Gods house was by his pray're with Glory filld.
>   God will for thine his Church in Glory house.
>   Did Sheba's Queen faint viewing of his glory?
>   Bright Angells stand amazed at thy Story.

It is difficult to decide how much of this is still a precise
typological connection and how much veers toward symbolic speculation.

The border is even easier to cross in the case of nonper-
sonal types, where some object or phenomenon represents
one of Christ's qualities. Meditations 20 to 30 are concerned with such types of Old Testament rites and objects
of worship. Meditation 20 treats Hebr. 9:11, "By a Greater,
and more Perfect Tabernacle"; Meditation 21, Col. 2:16
and 17, "In respect of an Holy Day, of a New Moon, or a
Sabbath. Which are figures"; Meditation 22, 1 Cor. 5:7,
"Christ our Passover is sacrificed for us"; Meditation 23, 1
John 2:2, treats Aaron's garments and his sacrifices as a
type of Christ; Meditations 24 to 29 treat similar themes;
and Meditation 30 treats Math. 12:40, "As Jonah was
three Days, and three nights in the Whales belly. So must,

etc." Typological parallels are turned unintentionally into symbolic constructions, for instance when the tabernacle as a type of Christ becomes "Christ my Tabernacle":

> Thou art my Tabernacle, Temple right,
>   My Cleansing, Holiness, Atonement, Food,
> My Righteousness, My Guide of Temple Light
> In to the Holy Holies, (as is shewd)
> My Oracle, Arke, Mercy Seat: the place
> Of Cherubims amazde at such rich grace.[17]

Christ is not only a tabernacle but cleansing, holiness, atonement, food. Countless relations and identifications can be established by this sort of threefold connection between a sacred object, Christ, and a supernatural meaning. But in the process the clearly defined function of the type can easily lose its precision and its fixed form, because this sort of type has the exterior form of a symbol or even the explanatory character of an emblem.[18] Taylor occasionally refers to one and the same thing as "emblem" and "type." Meditations 26 and 27 are both about Hebr. 9:13 and 14, "How much more shall the blood of Christ, etc.," the part of the Epistle to the Hebrews which explains that the meaning and effect of the Feast of Tabernacles and its sacrifices are fulfilled and annulled for Christians by the expiatory death of Christ. In other words, it designates the Old Testament feast as a type of Christ the savior. Meditation 26 states:

> The Dooves assign'd
> Burnt, and Sin Offerings neer do the feate
> But as they *Emblemize* the Fountain Spring
> Thy Blood, my Lord, set ope to wash off Sin.

On the other hand Meditation 27 states, with a mingling of type and fulfillment so bold as to remind us of myth:

The slain Dove's buri'de: In whose Blood (in water)
    The Living Turtle, Cedar, Scarlet twine,
And Hysop dipted are (as an allator)
    Sprinkling the Leper with it Seven times
    That *typify* Christs Blood by Grace applide
    To sinners vile, and then they're purifide.[19]

Even more so than the personal type, this real type of thing entices the poet on to daring identifications of highly disparate things and thus paves the way to an extravagant uncovering of symbolic connections. The stanzas in Meditation 29 on 1 Pet. 3:20, "While the Ark was Building," serve to illustrate this:

Oh! For an Ark: an Ark of Gopher Wood.
    This Flood's too stately to be rode upon
By other boats, which are base swilling tubs.
    It gulps them up as gudgeons. And they're gone.
    But thou, my Lord, dost Antitype this Arke,
    And rod'st upon these Waves that toss and barke.

Thy Humane Nature, (oh Choice Timber Rich)
    Bituminated ore within, and out
With Dressing of the Holy Spirits pitch
    Propitiatory Grace parg'd round about.
    This Ark will ride upon the Flood, and live
    Nor passage to a drop through Chink holes give.

This Ark will swim upon the fiery flood:
    All Showrs of fire the heavens rain on't will
Slide off: though Hells and Heavens Spouts out stood
    And meet upon't to crush't to Shivers, still
    It neither sinks, breaks, Fires, nor Leaky prooves,
    But lives upon them all and upward mooves.

All that would not be drownded must be in't
    Be Arkd in Christ, or else the Cursed rout

>   Of Crimson Sins their Cargoe will them sinke
>   And suffocate in Hell, because without.
>   Then Ark me, Lord, thus in thyself that I
>   May dance upon these drownding Waves with joye.

The ark as a type is developed here with the technique of the metaphysical conceit. This highly incongruent image of the ark for Christ yields such comparisons as "Thy Humane Nature" with "Choice Timber Rich" and "Bituminated ore," which are in fact unrelated and can only be connected meaningfully by way of the type. By itself, the metaphor "Choice Timber Rich" states only that Christ's human nature is "choice," "precious." However, the governing identification of the ark with Christ opens further possibilities of interpretation: Christ's human nature is of the choice material best able to bear us over the "fiery flood" of raging sin.[20] The ark itself turns into a metaphor for this service of Christ. Taylor has made the biblical type of the ark yield metaphorical imagery of symbolic intensity.

After Taylor finished his systematic treatment of types, he turned again to the words of Jesus from John 6:51, which he had already treated twice before, in Meditations 8 and 9 of the First Series: "I am the Living Bread, that came down from Heaven." Four years later, in Meditations 80, 81, and 82, he takes up John 6:53: "Unless yee eate the Flesh of the Son of Man, and drinke his blood, you have no life in you." [21] But it is not until Meditations 102 to 109, thirty years after he started these "Preparatory Meditations before my Approach to the Lords Supper," that Taylor takes up the Lord's Supper verses proper, the words of Jesus in the three synoptic gospels that prescribe in a similar manner the observance of the Lord's Supper. Taylor employs above all Matt. 26:26 and 27 and once Luke 22:19 and 20):

> And as they were eating, Jesus took bread,
> and blessed it, and brake it, and gave it to
> the disciples, and said, Take, eat; this is
> my body.
> And he took the cup, and gave thanks, and
> gave it to them, saying, Drink ye all of it.

It is amazing that Taylor did not approach the central theme of the Lord's Supper, the transubstantiation of bread and wine, until so late a date, and even then in such a hesitant, indirect manner. He did take John 6:51, "I am the Living Bread that came down from Heaven," as the basis for Meditations 8 and 9 of the First Series and 60 (A) of the Second, but this passage is concerned with the feeding of the Five Thousand rather than the Lord's Supper. It could be maintained that the image "living bread" in Meditation 60 is developed according to the technique of the metaphysical conceit, but it was already given in the biblical text rather than created by the poet. But it is more important to note that this designation of Christ as the bread of life has no direct connection with the Lord's Supper and the mystery of transubstantiation. "I am the Living Bread" is a brief parable based on the manna type rather than a magic transformation. Jesus discusses this with the grumbling people in John 6. The Jews demand in a realistically typological manner that Christ should pass out manna to them,[22] whereas Christ replies:

"Your fathers did eat manna in the wilderness, and are dead. This is the bread which cometh down from heaven, that a man may eat thereof, and not die. I am the living bread which came down from heaven." The evangelist either rejects this type or interprets it in another way (the teachings of Christ are manna), and stress is laid on the distinction that Christ and not manna is what really saves mankind from death.[23]

Taylor takes the manna–Christ parallel as the basis for Meditation 60 (A). It obviously affords him a better explanation of why we should eat the "Living Bread," Christ, than he finds in the Lord's Supper verses proper:

> I'm sick; my sickness is mortality
>> And Sin both Complicate (the worst of all).
> No cure is found under the Chrystall Sky
>> Save Manna, that from heaven down doth fall.
>> My Queasy Stomach this alone doth Crave.
>> Nought but a bit of manna can mee save.

There is a second stage of approach to the interpretation of the Lord's Supper in poems 80, 81, and 82 of the Second Series, on John 6:53: "Unless ye eat the Flesh of the Son of man, and drink his blood, you have no life in you." In Meditation 80 Taylor takes up first the last part of the quotation, "Life." But then in Meditation 81 he attacks the real problem:

> What feed on Humane Flesh and Blood? Strange mess!
>> Nature exclaims. What Barbarousness is here?
> And Lines Divine this sort of Food repress.
>> Christs Flesh and Blood how can they bee good Cheer?
>> If shread to atoms, would too few be known,
>> For ev'ry mouth to have a single one?

The solution he proposes is a "metaphorical" interpretation of the Scriptures:

> This Sense of this blest Phrase is nonsense thus.
>> Some other Sense makes this a metaphor.
> This feeding signifies, that Faith in us
>> Feeds on this fare, Disht in this Pottinger.
>> Faith feeds upon this Heavenly Manna rare
>> And drinkes this Blood, Sweet junkets: Angells Fare.

"Some other Sense makes this a metaphor" suggests that
Taylor was familiar with the practice of the threefold or
fourfold allegorical interpretation of the Bible, which the
reformers Luther and Calvin rejected because of its tendency toward excessive allegorization. The remaining
stanzas of the poem expand this metaphorical interpretation: Christ's "flesh and blood"—"Christs works, as Divine
Cookery, knead in/ The Pasty Past (his Flesh and Blood)
most fine/ Into Rich Fare"—are taken up by the soul as
Spirituall Food.

> Thy Flesh, and Blood and Office Fruites shall bee
>   My Souls Plumb Cake it eates, as naturally,
> In Spirituall wise mixt with my soul, as wee
>   Finde food doth with the body properly.

Meditations 102 to 109, which treat the proper Lord's
Supper passages of Matthew and Luke, differ from the
above Meditations on passages from John in that they reveal in many places a serious struggle to find the correct
interpretation. They are in part polemical and not always
easy to understand. The central problem of Calvinism is
clearly manifested in these Meditations: the conflict of
faith and reason, which is most acute in the problem of
the Lord's Supper. The faith of the Puritans was based on
the word of the Bible. Thus it was jeopardized when the
New Testament commanded the Puritans to believe something which their rational convictions forced them to rele-
gate to the sphere of magical and heathen idolatry: the
transformation of bread and wine into the flesh and blood
of Christ. The Puritans exercised reason and common
sense even on the cardinal questions of their faith. Thus
one reads in their profession of faith the following comment on the transformation of bread and wine:

> The doctrine which maintains a change of the substance
> of bread and wine into the substance of Christ's body
> and blood (commonly called *transubstantiation*) by con-
> secration of a priest, or by any other way, is repugnant
> not to the scripture alone, but even to common sense
> and reason, overthroweth the nature of a sacrament,
> and hath been and is the cause of manifold supersti-
> tions, yea of gross idolatries.[24]

Whereas other sacraments could be regarded as products of the Catholic Church, Jesus himself had said:
"Take, eat; this is my body." The solution the Puritans
proposed for this intellectual dilemma is a masterpiece of
dogma. At the same time it is an interesting document in
the history of ideas, because it points toward symbolism
and by virtue of its ambiguity even anticipates it to some
extent. The solution is a dialectical conception of reality
in which one and the same thing or act can be both real
and spiritual. The chief principle of the Calvinist definition of the Lord's Supper is the following:

> Worthy receivers outwardly partaking of the visible ele-
> ments in this sacrament, do, then, also, inwardly by
> faith, really and indeed, yet not carnally and corporally,
> but spiritually receive and feed upon Christ crucified,
> and all benefits of his death; the body and blood of
> Christ being then not corporally or carnally in, with, or
> under the bread and wine, yet as really, but spiritually
> present to the faith of believers in that ordinance, as the
> elements themselves are to their outward senses.[25]

As we have seen, Taylor made "the Flesh of the Son of
Man, and . . . his blood" into "spiritual food," which
raises the question whether he did not go so far with his
metaphorical interpretation that he left the "really and indeed" behind. He makes a fresh attempt in Meditations

102 to 109 to master the "mystery" (the word he uses himself) of the Lord's Supper. He classifies it under the all-encompassing institution of the "New Covenant," the "covenant of Grace." It is the seal of the covenant of grace, its visible and legitimate accomplishment, as he repeats in almost every one of these eight poems: [26]

> Unto the Articles of this Contract
>   Our Lord did institute even at the Grave
> Of the Last Passover, when off its packt.
>   This Seale for our attendance oft to have.
>   This Seal made of New Cov'nant wax, red di'de,
>   In Cov'nant blood, by faith to be appli'de.[27]

The notion adumbrated here, that this seal of the covenant of grace reveals, fulfills, and annuls the types of the old covenant, is developed fully in Meditation 103. This is another important role taken by typology for the Puritans, who were drawn so powerfully to the Old Testament. It helps explain why the numerous religious practices prescribed by God in the Old Testament are no longer valid. They are types prefiguring Christ that are fulfilled and annulled by his advent. Taylor regards the various elements of the Lord's Supper—the "seal of the covenant of grace" —also as the fulfillment and annullment of such types. With their help he is able to account for Christ's flesh and blood being bread and wine by establishing a typological connection of them with manna and the Paschal lamb.

> New Covenant worship Wisdom first proclaims
>   Deckt up in Types and Ceremonies gay.
> Rich Metaphors the first Edition gains.
>   A Divine key unlocks these trunks to lay
>   All spirituall treasures in them open Cleare.
>   The Ark and Mannah, in't, Christ and Good Cheere.

> This first Edition did the Cov'nant tend
>   With Typick Seales and Rites and Ceremonie
> That till the Typick Dispensations end
>   Should ratify it as Gods Testimony.
>   'Mong which the Passover (whose Kirnell's Christ)
>   Tooke place with all its Rites, graciously spic't.
>
> But when the Pay day came their kirnells Pickt.
>   The Shell is cast out hence. Cloudes flew away.
> Now Types good night, with Ceremonies strict,
>   The Glorious Sun is risen, its broad day.
>   Now Passover farewell, and leave thy Place.
>   Lords Supper seales the Covenant of Grace.
>
> But though the Passover is passt away.
>   And Ceremonies that belong'd to it,
> Yet doth its kirnell and their Kirnell stay
>   Attending on the Seale succeeding it.
>   The Ceremony parting leaves behinde
>   Its Spirit to attend this Seale designd.[28]

In the incompletely rendered passages from Matt. 26:26 and 27 (or Luke 22:19) affixed to the titles of these eight Meditations, the words "This is my body" are conspicuously absent. If this saying of Jesus' is taken literally, it does not fit in with the Calvinist conception of the Lord's Supper at all. In Meditation 108 Taylor takes up the problem of the Lord's Supper just as it is mirrored in the Cambridge profession:

> Can Bread and Wine by words be Carnifide?
> And manifestly Bread and Wine abide?

The answer is a rejection of the Catholic and Lutheran views. Rather than being transformed bodily, they are *sign* and *signal*:

What monsterous thing doth Transubstantiation
And Consubstantiation also make
Christs Body, having a Ubique-Station,
  When thousands Sacraments men Celebrate
  Upon a day, if th'Bread and wine should e're
  Be Con-, or Trans-Substantiated there?

If in Christs Doctrine taught us in this Feast,
  There lies No ly. (And Christ can never ly)
The Christian Faith cannot abide at least
  To dash out reasons brains, or blinde its eye.
  Faith never blindeth reasons Eye but cleares
  Its Sight to see things quite above its Sphere.
. . . .
The Sign, bread, made of th'kidnies of Wheate
  That grew in Zions field: and th'juyce we sup
Presst from the grape of Zions Vine sweet, great
  Doth make the Signall Wine within the Cup.
  Those Signals Bread and Wine are food that bear
  Christ in them Crucified, as spirituall fare.

When reason is applied to the sacrament of the Lord's
Supper, it makes bread = flesh and wine = blood into
signs and signals that indicate the sealing of the covenant.
Although these two concepts were not specifically Calvinist (the sacrament is a "sign" for Catholics too), they received added importance for the Calvinists due to their
tendency to remove mystery from the sacraments. The
Calvinist no longer regards the essence of the sacrament
as lying in its magic transformation, but rather in its spiritually transforming effect. It establishes a relation they
regarded as sacred between the divine sign and the eluci-
datory meaning. In Ch. XXVIII, "Of the Sacraments," of
the New England profession of faith it is stated thus:
"There is in every sacrament a spiritual relation, or sacramental union between the sign and the thing signified;

whence it comes to pass that the names and effects of the one are attributed to the other." In this manner the sacrament is defined as a symbolic connection. It is a sacred symbol that unites the sign and the thing signified by means of a spiritual relation or sacramental union. When "sign" and "signal" are used for elements of the Lord's Supper and for functions of the sacrament in general, they acquire the rank of theological concepts. They indicate the reference of some terrestrial object to the transcendent kingdom of God, and Taylor employs them along with "signification" and "to signify" in this sense. Not only are the sacraments signs of God: any terrestrial event, even the most commonplace one, is potentially a similar sign. Thus "sign" and "signal" are special words in Puritan literature, because they always announce the possibility of a transcendental reference. Along with "emblem" and "metaphor" they belong to the vocabulary employed by the Puritans to express the transcendency of the world, and we must carefully observe the special importance with which these words are used by the nineteenth-century heirs of the Puritans.

Taylor was aware that the human vocabulary was inadequate to describe God:

> I fain would praise thee, but want words to do't:
>   And searching ore the realm of thoughts finde none
> Significant enough and therefore vote
>   For a new set of Words and thoughts hereon
>   And leap beyond the line such words to gain
>   In other Realms, to praise thee: but in vain.[29]

Whenever Taylor chooses metaphors for God's glory he speaks of them with humility as insufficient. He twice speaks of "quaint metaphors" in the "Meditations, First Series":

> My Quaintest Metaphors are ragged Stuff,
> Making the Sun seem like a Mullipuff.[30]

The same occurs in Meditation 82:

> My tatter'd Fancy; and my Ragged Rymes
> Teeme leaden Metaphors: which yet might serve
>   To hum a little touching terrene Shines.
> But Spirituall Life doth better fare deserve.[31]

On the other hand, the biblical metaphors for Christ or God are "silver" or "sparkling metaphors":

> Thou gildest ore with sparkling Metaphors
>   The Object thy Eternall Love fell on
> Which makes her glory shine 'bove brightest stars
>   Carbuncling of the Skies Pavillion
>   That pave that Crystal Roofe the Earth's Canopy
>   With golden streaks, border'd with Pomell high.[32]

What does Taylor mean with this concept "metaphor," which occurs in two so distinct usages? In these Meditations a metaphor is an image with a spiritual meaning, *i.e.*, a meaning related to God:

> And hence these Metaphors we spirituallized
>   Speake out the Spouses spirituall Beauty cleare:
> And morallizd do speake out Enemies
>   And hence declare the Spouses Lovely deare
>   To be the best and Enemies hath though they
>   Assaulting her shall perish in th'assay.[33]

The imagery of the Bible and God's own creations are His metaphors, but man must try to depict God's greatness with inadequate images. This notion of the metaphor and its concomitant tendency toward spiritualization in general were not without dangers, dangers which the Puritans took seriously. Taylor was aware of them too, or at least he was aware of the first, the danger that the distinction between divine metaphor and human metaphor (used by men to depict God's greatness) would be lost. The second great danger was that the Bible's basis in concrete reality would vanish in a metaphorical or some new form of allegorical interpretation, in which every scene would receive a parallel spiritual meaning. Taylor's inclinations urged him along this path. The stanza cited above shows him on the way to the manifold interpretation of the Scriptures practiced in the Middle Ages; he explicitly applies the allegorical and tropological interpretation. In the "Meditations, Second Series" one can see exactly how his fantasy develops more and more toward allegory. From historically fixed types he turns to a typological, metaphorical interpretation of the Lord's Supper (Christ's flesh = manna or "spiritual Bread"), and from there he advances to a purely metaphorical, allegorical interpretation of the Song of Solomon, where all the images are "spiritualized."

In his final fifty Meditations Taylor chose almost exclusively phrases from the Song of Solomon as the basis of his reflections on the Lord's Supper. This late period of his thought is dedicated to representing God by allegory and symbol. Obviously he cannot interpret the Song of Solomon in a real sense, but only in a figurative or (theologically) allegorical one. This is exactly what Taylor does. He makes religious meanings perceptible and intelligible by using metaphors as tools. But his metaphors are more than just tools for him. The myrrh, the cedars of Lebanon, the nard and turquoise all have a special reality in the

sphere of God's transcendent glory. These late Meditations
are a unique and glowing song of God's glory.

In the First Series of Meditations Taylor chose from the
Song of Solomon only the very popular verses Cant. 2:1, "I
am the Rose of Sharon" (Meditation 4) and "The Lilly of
the Vallies" (Meditation 5, and again in Meditation 69,
Second Series). In the Second Series, Meditation 19 is on
Cant. 1:2, "While the King sitteth at his table, my Spick-
nard sendeth forth the smell thereof," and this verse is
taken up again eight years later in Meditation 62. Meditation 63 takes up Cant. 6:11, "I went down into the Garden
of Nuts, to see the fruits," etc., which is continued in Meditations 64 and 65: "To see—if the Vine Flowrisht, and
the Pomegranate bud"; "To see the Fruits of the Vally."
Meditation 79 is on Cant. 2:16, "My Beloved is mine and I
am his," and Meditations 83 to 86 are on Cant. 5:1: "I
come into my Garden," etc.; "I have gathered my Myrrh
with my Spice"; "I have eate my Hony Come with my
Hony. I have drunk my Wine with my Milk"; "Eat Oh!
Friends. Drink, yea drink abundantly Oh! Beloved." Meditations 96 to 98 are on Cant. 1:2, "Let him kiss me with
the Kisse of his mouth" and "Thy Love is better than
Wine." [34]

In the final phase of his preoccupation with the Song of
Solomon, which began in 1713, Taylor took far bolder
verses as his theme. Now it is spices, perfumes, and precious stones that predominate in his poems. Meditation
121, "His Lips are like Lillies dropping sweet smelling
Myrrh" (Cant. 5:13) is bolder than similar verses chosen
earlier, but tame in comparison to Meditation 123 (A) on
Cant. 5:14, "His Belly [i.e. bowells]: is as bright Ivory
overlaid with Saphires," or Meditation 148 on Cant. 7:1,
"How beautiful are thy feet with Shooes, oh Prince's
daughter; the Joynts of thy Thighs are as jewells," etc.,
and other comparable ones.

Here Taylor's fantasy bursts the confines of Puritan sobriety and succumbs to the charm of biblico-Oriental word pictures. "Jasper," "Beryll," "Carbuncles," "Crystall," "Pomegranates," "Almonds," "Myrrh," "Cedars of Lebanon," "Olives," "Ivory," "Olivant," "Silk," and "Satin" are all precious objects, upon whose foreign, unseen beauty Taylor intoxicates himself. The rural, domestic, and homely imagery—taken from weaving, baking, or bowling—used so effectively in the early poems diminishes in importance in the later. Instead Taylor yields to an imagery of precious objects that is intended to render God's glory visible. The most daring images become "spiritualized." On Cant. 7:1, "How beautiful are thy feet with Shooes, oh Prince's daughter: the Joynts of thy Thighs are as jewells," etc., Taylor says:

> Her Spirituall Shooes ore laid with Spirituall Lace
>   Studed with spirituall pearls and precious Stones,
> Fitted to stick in glory's Crown where Grace
>   Shines in't as brightest Carbuncles ever shown
>   Which makes her path she walks in ware a shine
>   As she walks to Christ, glazd with rayes divine.[35]

And then he says to Cant. 7:2 (Meditation 149), "Thy Navill is a round Goblet . . . thy belly is a heap of Wheate set about with Lillies":

> Thy Spirituall Navill like the Altars Bowle
>   Filld full of Spirituall Liquor to refresh
> The Spirits babes conceived in thy Soule
>   The Altars Bason that its blood to dress
>   The Altar sprinkled with it and t'atone
>   Herself and hers and ease her of her Grone.

This tempts one to recall the mature periods of other great poets where a similar tendency to allegorize the world is manifested. Taylor hesitates as little as medieval interpreters did to "spiritualize" shoes, lace, pearls, precious stones, or even the navel. Any thing in this world has for him a potential transcendent meaning. If this meaning is obvious to all true believers, then the thing is an "emblem." [36] Meditation 149 says on "Thy belly is a heap of Wheate set about with Lillies":

> Here's Spirits of the Spirits Chymistrie
> And Bisket of the Spirits Backhouse best
> Emblems of Sanctifying Grace most high
> Water and Bread of spirituall life up dresst.

This absolute spiritualization of all images far surpasses what the Puritans considered theologically permissible. But this is not solely the tendency of old age to allegorize, it also stems from tendencies and problems inherent in Puritan theology. If Taylor proceeded in his old age to a complete allegorization of the world, one reason for this was that his imagination was more vital and sensual than those of his colleagues. But another was his religion. It had trained his imagination to discover connections between the terrestrial and divine worlds, and to discover types and prefigurations. His allegorization of the Song of Solomon is at bottom very similar to typology. That the Song of Solomon had its significance in anticipations of Christ was generally admitted, and it is in this general manner, but with an exuberance of the imagination, that Taylor interprets all of its images.

It is a strange anomaly in the American literary tradition that certain of its finest and most interesting works have not become known until long after their composition. One such case is Melville's *Moby Dick*, which was not really "discovered" until seventy years after it was published; another, though not so crass, is the long-neglected work of Henry James. Emerson had to develop his ideas without knowing of Taylor's "Meditations" or Jonathan Edward's *Images or Shadows of Divine Things*.[37] But Edward Taylor's meditations and poems, which lay buried away for more than two hundred years, were the greatest loss to the development of American literature. No one dreamed what a luxurious garden of flowers and spices had grown up in the turnip patch of the Puritan fantasy. No one profited from its beauty and riches.

Although it is an undertaking of dubious value, it is nevertheless intriguing to speculate on the effect Taylor might have had on the young American literature. First of all he would surely have aroused the ire of his fellow theologians, who would have condemned his rich, sensual imagery and his radical spiritualization as the latest form of idolatry. It is difficult to say whether a tradition of religious or intellectual poetry might have grown from his example. At that time poetic talent was rare in the tiny, sparsely populated country, and it is doubtful whether the Meditations would have aroused any latent ability.

It is entirely possible and even likely that if the Meditations had been printed, they would have set off a controversy extending inevitably to the theological and literary terms used by Taylor, a controversy perhaps not wholly sterile. When Taylor uses "type," "emblem," "sign," or "metaphor," he is using literary terms in a theological sense. They are the links which he uses to connect up the world of real events—including that of the Bible—with the transcendent, divine realm. For Taylor, these terms show the different ways in which the terrestrial world is an expression of God's grandeur and His will. Of course the eighteenth century would have modified this conviction and shifted the emphasis from the transcendent to the here and now, and from divinity to nature. The discerning and subtle Jonathan Edwards would possibly have disagreed with Taylor but would certainly not have failed to profit from him. Possibly America would by a better use of its own heritage have reached the point sooner where someone could have said as Emerson did in 1836: "Every natural fact is a symbol of some spiritual fact," or "Words are signs of natural facts. The use of natural history is to give us aid in supernatural history; the use of the outer creation, to give us language for the beings and changes of the inward creation." [38]

6 JONATHAN EDWARDS AND RALPH WALDO EMERSON

> For surely the Scriptures have taught us, that the type should give way to the antitype, and that the shadow should give way to the substance.[1]

Jonathan Edwards, the "last" and most important of the American Puritans, has enjoyed a remarkable renaissance in recent years. He has been acknowledged as a forerunner of Transcendentalism and as a force that helped shape American literature.[2] He is even being read, for instance, in the volume of selections carefully edited by Clarence H. Faust and Thomas H. Johnson, who have gathered the pieces of most interest to the modern reader.[3] These selections reveal Edwards as a theoretician in natural science, as a psychologist, as a philosopher, and in the case of the famous sermon "Sinners in the Hands of an Angry God," also as a theologian. What they do not reveal is the extent to which Edwards was a typologist and that his theory of the coherence and the processes of the world was derived from typology. His typologically dominated works have most likely been left aside on purpose as being too abstruse and tedious for the modern reader. Among them we may count many if not almost all of his sermons, his exegesis ("Passages of Scripture"), and the historical work *Thoughts on the Revival of Religion in New England.*

God Glorified in the Work of Redemption is world history seen theologically from the fall of Adam to the end of the world.[4] But the *Revival of Religion in New England* is contemporary history. It deals with the events that entered history as the "Great Awakening," in which Edwards was a direct participant. This revival movement, which did produce some rather dubious and hysterical outbreaks, lay open to attack from the clergy itself, against whom Edwards defended it with a passion born of conviction. The only portion of his defense that is read today is his letter to a colleague, Benjamin Colman, the "Narrative of Surprising Conversions," [5] and not the more fundamental and comprehensive work *Thoughts on the Revival of Religion in New England.*[6] Only in this treatise do we discover why Edwards took part heart and soul in the events of the Great Awakening. He regarded this movement with overwhelming expectations in the belief that it marked the beginning of the millennium.

Edwards' attitude toward the revival is connected with his view of religious affections. To these he devoted several sermons some years later, which he subsequently worked up into a treatise. Affections are powers of the human soul bound up with the will and located primarily in the heart. Though some uses of the affections are false and deceptive, and others are connected up with man's animal nature, these affections are nonetheless the vital force of religion. This allows Edwards to account for the abuses of the revival movement as regrettable but under-standable (and scarcely avoidable) by-products of an enormous activation of the religious powers in man. He does not doubt for a moment that the revival is God's work (p. 310):

> There are many things in the word of God, that show that when God remarkably appears in any great work for his church, and against his enemies, it is a most dangerous thing, and highly provoking to God, to be slow and backward to acknowledge and honor God in the work, and to lie still and not to put to a helping hand.

For the clergy it is almost criminal negligence to stand by idly, because whatever lies behind the numerous conver-sions and the overall revival of religious life must be something special. Edwards thinks that it is the prepara-tion for the millennium: "It is not unlikely that this work of God's Spirit, that is so extraordinary and wonderful, is the dawning, or at least, a prelude of that glorious work of God, so often foretold in Scripture, which in the progress and issue of it shall renew the world of mankind" (p. 313).

There is something remarkable in the discovery of an acute eighteenth-century mind believing that the world-wide revival proclaimed by God has already begun.[7] It is equally remarkable in the context of American intellec-tual history to find this belief—already anachronistic at that time—bound up with a future-oriented belief in the American nation as the chosen land. Edwards sets out to show why God wants this project begun in America. It is not only "in some measure to balance things," since Europe and Asia have already had their share of great religious events, but also because America is especially deserving of it.

> The other continent hath slain Christ, and has from age to age shed the blood of the saints and martyrs of Jesus, and has often been as it were deluged with the church's blood: God has therefore probably reserved the honor of building the glorious temple to the daughter, that has not shed so much blood, when those times of the peace, and prosperity, and glory of the church shall commence, that were typified by the reign of Solomon.[8]

Long before the separation from Europe, we encounter here a purely religious rather than a political version of the view that Europe is corrupt and guilty of shedding blood, whereas America is peace-loving, happy, and innocent.

Edwards finds the proof of this incipient revival of mankind in typical prefigurations.

> Most of the great temporal deliverances that were wrought for Israel of old, as divines and expositors observe, were typical of the great spiritual works of God for the salvation of men's souls, and the deliverance and prosperity of his church, in the days of the gospel; and especially did they represent that greatest of all deliverances of God's church, and chief of God's works, of actual salvation, that shall be in the latter days; which as has been observed is above all others, the appointed time, and proper season of actual redemption of men's souls.[9]

Edwards finds types for this "actual salvation, that shall be in the latter days" in Solomon's kingdom, in Isaiah, in the Feast of Tabernacles, and in many other Old Testament signs. Then he attempts to prove that these types were coined for America, or more specifically, for New England. Isaiah's prophesies indicate that God will perform his final and greatest work for mankind in the wilderness, because "When God is about to turn the earth into a Paradise, he does not begin his work where there is some good growth already, but in a wilderness." [10] The rescue of Hezekiah and his city from the Assyrians and the turning back of the sun, which Isaiah tells of at II Kings 20:9 to 11 are types for the resurrection of Christ and for "the Sun of Righteousness." From this Edwards infers that:

> The Sun of Righteousness has long been going down from east to west; and probably when the time comes of the church's deliverance from her enemies, so often typified by the Assyrians, the light will rise in the west, until it shines through the world, like the sun in its meridian brightness . . . And if we may suppose that this glorious work of God shall begin in any part of America, I think if we consider the circumstances of the settlement of New England, it must needs appear the most likely of all American colonies, to be the place whence this work may principally take its rise. And if these things are so, it gives more abundant reason to hope that what is now seen in America, and especially in New England, may prove the dawn of that glorious day: and the very uncommon and wonderful circumstances and events of this work, seem to me strongly to argue that God intends it as the beginning or forerunner of something vastly great.[11]

The argument is buttressed and clenched with the type of Babylonian captivity, followed by those of Joshua, the wilderness, and Canaan, which the Puritans had referred to themselves all along:

> When God redeemed his people from their Babylonish captivity, and they rebuilt Jerusalem, it was, as is universally owned, a remarkable type of the spiritual redemption of God's church; and particularly, was an eminent type of the great deliverance of the Christian church from spiritual Babylon, and their rebuilding the spiritual Jerusalem, in the latter days; and therefore they are often spoken of under one by the prophets: and this probably was the main reason that it was so ordered in Providence, and particularly noted in Scripture, that the children of Israel, on that occasion, kept the greatest *feast of tabernacles*, that ever had been kept in Israel, since the days of Joshua, when the people were first settled in Canaan (Neh. VIII. 16, 17); because at that time happened that restoration of Israel, that had the greatest resemblance of that great restoration of the church of God, of which the *feast of tabernacles* was the type, of any that had been since Joshua first brought the people out of the wilderness and settled them in the good land.[12]

Auerbach has explained how the principle of the type contains an expansion into future time.[13] Edwards took this possibility seriously. He jumped to the bold conclusion that the prefigured millennium was beginning here and now. But we must avoid the mistake of regarding this view of history as a mere curiosity or outmoded way of thought. It is the early theological version of that nineteenth-century American view of history which looked rather to the future than to the past. After independence and the founding of the nation this kind of history was written in the conviction that all human events were developing toward the fulfillment of man's aspirations in America. This hope is found at the core of the world views of writers such as Emerson, Whitman, and Mark Twain. It can also be discerned in the ideas of such historians as Bancroft and Motley.

It has to be admitted that this tendency of the late eighteenth- and nineteenth-century American mind to look toward the future was also derived from the optimistic theories of civilization and progress of the French Enlightenment. Condorcet is especially important in this connection. He followed the progress of civilization through the ages to an America that had just achieved independence, which in his view represented the final and highest stage of civilization. However, the theologically-based faith in the future is a preparatory form that preceded rationalist influence. It had nationalistic aspects, and we can trace exactly how it was transmitted to nineteenth-century thinkers.

Thus the characteristic bent of the American mind toward the future is not solely due to the European influence that arrived with the eighteenth-century Enlightenment and was then continuously reinforced by European immigrants fleeing the burdens of history. The nineteenth-century immigrants welcomed the lack of history in their new land, where they wanted to put their economic and political ideals into practice. In the case of the Puritans these practical aspirations were bound up with others stemming from biblical prophecies and the conception of the type.

And so the future-directed ideas of the American colonists received their first literary expression in the typological form of thought. In this tradition we encounter for the first time an ideal, future America, namely, in a work by Timothy Dwight, a grandson of Jonathan Edwards. This late Puritan, who for many years distinguished himself as

president of Yale University, was a patriot from the group
of Connecticut Wits. In 1785 he composed a lengthy verse
epic, *The Conquest of Canaan*. This work is an exhaustive
and verbose account of the conquest of Canaan after the
Book of Joshua, a topic that seems way off the track for an
American patriot at the time of the Revolution. It is in fact
nothing other than a typological version of the American
battle for independence. For the Calvinist Dwight, the biblical event is a prefiguration and analogy of the liberation
of America,[14] and in Bk. X he extols the new Canaan,
America, in glowing colors:

> Far o'er yon azure main thy view extend,
> Where seas, and skies, in blue confusion blend,
> Lo, there a mighty realm, by heaven design'd
> The last retreat for poor, oppress'd mankind!
> . . . .
> Far from all realms this world imperial lies;
> Seas roll between, and threatening storms arise;
> Alike unmov'd beyond Ambition's pale,
> And the bold pinions of the venturous sail:
> Till circling years the destin'd period bring,
> And a new Moses lifts the daring wing,
> Through trackless seas, an unknown flight explores,
> And hails a new Canaan's promis'd shores.[15]

In our context, which is in the final instance a literary
one, Edwards' typological arguments are interesting for
another reason. There is a conspicious feature about the
types chosen by Edwards. He almost never relates them to
concrete antitypes, and very seldom to Christ as a person.
They refer almost exclusively to "spiritual" fulfillments.
The liberation from Babylonian captivity is "a remarkable
type of the spiritual deliverance of God's church"; in general "Most of the great temporal deliverances that were
wrought for the Israel of old [are] typical of the great spirit-

ual works of God for the salvation of men's souls." In the
sermon "The Folly of Looking Back in Fleeing Out of
Sodom" Edwards explains that the flight from Jerusalem
commanded by Jesus "was a type of fleeing out of a state
of sin." [16] Similarly, Lot fled in a rush without looking
back: "Because his fleeing out of Sodom was designed on
purpose to be a type of our fleeing from that state of sin
and misery in which we naturally are." [17] Edwards also relates the Feast of Tabernacles as well as many other types
to some inner state of man or of the church, an inner state
that as a rule has not yet occurred or has only occurred
partially and is instead awaited at the end of time. But
this facilitates a severance of the type from Christ at one
pole of its relation and also in a certain sense from concrete historicity at the other. The more the fulfillment
loses its concrete historical character and becomes a spiritual correspondence, the more this mode of interpretation
approaches the allegorical, and the more the type approaches the symbol. The antitype, which was once a determinate aspect of Christ's life and works, now changes
more and more into an inner meaning. It is related to the
concrete type (Feast of Tabernacles, Lot's flight, the escape from Babylon) as a symbolic meaning is related to
its symbol. Thus the successors of the Puritans began by
using the concept "type" for a sort of symbol similar to the
type, and ended up by using it as a synonym for symbol.

Edwards sometimes speaks of a symbol in the positive
sense: for instance, in regard to Christ's symbolic act of
washing feet. This act cannot be typical in the strict sense
because rather than prefiguring Christ it is carried out by
him. On this Edwards comments:

> Which action, as it was exceeding wonderful in itself,
> so it manifestly was symbolical, and represented some-
> thing else far more important and more wonderful, even

that greatest and most wonderful of all things that ever
came to pass, which was accomplished the next day in
his last sufferings. There were three symbolical representations given of that great event this evening; one
in the passover, which Christ now partook of with his
disciples; another in the Lord's supper, which he instituted at this time; another in this remarkable action
of his washing his disciples' feet. Washing the feet of
guests was the office of servants, and one of their meanest offices: and therefore was fitly chosen by our Saviour
to represent that great abasement which he was to be the
subject of in the form of a servant, in becoming obedient
unto death, even that ignominious and accursed death
of the cross, that he might cleanse the souls of his disciples from their guilt and spiritual pollution.[18]

Just as in his interpretation of the type, Edwards also
ends up in this interpretation of Christ's symbolical action
with a state of the soul, namely, regeneration. The subsequent assimilation of type to symbol can be understood on
the basis of this case.[19] In certain instances Edwards' sermons approach allegory, as do so many theological pres-
entations. In every case where an abstract theme is the
primary matter and biblical or typological correspondences are sought to illustrate it, the function of allegory is
fulfilled, at least in theory.

Cotton Mather enlarged the type into parallel and analogy. Edwards weakened the strict theological conception
of the type in another way, by making it bear a meaning
expressed in imagery. Thus not long before the end of the
Calvinist era, symbolism and allegory lay ready for future
hands to take them up.

At his early, sudden death Jonathan Edwards left behind aphorisms that Perry Miller published as *Images or
Shadows of Divine Things by Jonathan Edwards*. Some

long, some brief, these aphorisms are notes toward a comprehensive system of correspondences that was intended to bring together divine revelation (the Bible), nature, and history in an orderly, hierarchical whole. The basic correspondence postulated by Edwards is between the spiritual world and the natural world, where inferior things are derived from superior:

> 8. Again it is apparent and allowed that there is a great and remarkeable analogy in God's works. There is a wonderfull resemblance in the effects which God produces, and consentaneity in His manner of working in one thing and another throughout all nature. It is very observable in the visible world; therefore it allowed that God does purposely make and order one thing to be in agreeableness and harmony with another. And if so, why should not we suppose that He makes the inferiour in imitation of the superiour, the material of the spiritual, on purpose to have a resemblance and shadow of them? We see that even in the material world, God makes one part of it strangely to agree with another, and why is it not reasonable to suppose He makes the whole as a shadow of the spiritual world? [20]

This system of analogies spreads through all nature, so that the lower forms are imperfect imitations of the higher. Thus the animals are inferior imitations of man, the plants of animals, etc.:

> 59. If there be such an admirable analogy observed by the creatour in His works through the whole system of the natural world, so that one thing seems to be made in imitation of another, and especially the less perfect to be made in imitation of the more perfect, so that the less perfect is as it were a figure or image of the more perfect . . . Why is it not rational to suppose that the corporeal and visible world should be designedly made

and constituted in analogy to the more spiritual, noble, and real world? It is certainly agreeable to what is apparently the method of God's working.[21]

The instrument Edwards uses to establish these analogies is the concept of the type. From the original correspondence of Old Testament and Christ, which also marks a value increment from prefiguration to fulfillment, from shadow to truth, he transfers it to the enlarged correspondence of natural world and spiritual world. Image 45 gives a biblical text in support of this. But the real reasons for this extension to the cosmos lie in the respect the rising natural sciences were winning for the natural world and its laws.[22] There is an argument that reveals some of the thought behind this in Miscellany No. 362, appended to Image 58:

> Indeed, the whole outward creation, which is but the shadows of His being, is so made as to represent spiritual things. It might be demonstrated by the wonderful agreement in thousands of things, much of the same kind as between the types of the Old Testament and their antitypes; and by there being spiritual things being so often and continually compared with them in the word of God. And it is agreeable to God's wisdom that it should be so, that the inferior and shadowy parts of His works should be made to represent those things that are more real and excellent, spiritual and divine, to represent the things that immediately concern Himself and the highest parts of His work. Spiritual things are the crown and glory, the head and soul, the very end, the alpha and omega of all other works . . . Thus the inferior dispensation of the Gospel was all to shadow forth the highest and most excellent which was its end; thus almost everything that was said or done, that we have recorded in Scripture from Adam to Christ, was typical of Gospel things. Persons were typical persons; their actions were

> typical actions; the cities were typical cities; the nations
> of the Jews and other nations were typical nations; their
> land was a typical land; God's providences towards them
> were typical providences; their worship was typical wor-
> ship; their houses were typical houses; their magistrates,
> typical magistrates; their clothes, typical clothes; and
> indeed the world was a typical world. And this is God's
> manner to make inferior things shadows of the superior
> and most excellent; outward things shadows of spiritual;
> and all other things shadows of those things that are the
> end of all things, and the crown of all things. Thus God
> glorifies Himself and instructs the minds that He has
> made.[23]

Edwards' goal was as ambitious as it is obvious. Deeply
influenced by Locke's philosophy, he wanted to make the
natural world (the only one accessible to human compre-
hension) into the image of and key to the transcendent
world of religion, which could thus be understood indirectly. Edwards recognized the danger that the natural
laws discovered by Newton could achieve an authority of
their own alongside the authority of divine revelation.
Thus they had to be interpreted as types and copies of divine truths. The book of nature would have to be interpreted by means of the book of revelation:

> The book of Scripture is the interpreter of the book of
> nature two ways, viz., by declaring to us those spiritual
> mysteries that are indeed signified and typified in the
> constitution of the natural world; and secondly, in ac-
> tually making application of the signs and types in the
> book of nature as representations of those spiritual mys-
> teries in many instances.[24]

Edwards realized that the only theology that could
thrive in the modern era was one that had a place for na-

ture and cosmic forces in its scheme.[25] He regarded the law of gravity as a type of the "spiritual world" in the following manner:

> The whole material universe is preserved by gravity or attraction, or the mutual tendency of all bodies to each other. One part of the universe is hereby made beneficial to another; the beauty, harmony and order, regular progress, life, and motion, and in short all the well-being of the whole frame depends on it. This is a type of love or charity in the spiritual world.[26]

The modern discovery, the telescope, "Whereby heavenly objects are brought so much nearer and made so much plainer to sight and such wonderfull discoveries have been made in the heavens, is a type and forerunner of the great increase in the knowledge of heavenly things that shall be in the approaching glorious times of the Christian church." [27]

History recedes into the background compared with these intense efforts to connect nature with the transcendent world. Edwards had little interest in secular history, and church history was already revealed typologically. Thus he envisaged no threat to theology from the side of historiography. He only makes use of two historical events in the service of typology: "the constitution of the Roman polity" (Image 91), and (very extensively) the Roman world conquest, which is interpreted with all its triumphal marches and victory celebrations as a "remarkeable type of Christ's ascension" (Image 81).

From true types or natural "images of divine things" Edwards distinguishes those correspondences in which one natural event expresses another symbolically. In such cases he speaks of "significations":

> There are many things in the constitution of the world
> that are not properly shadows and images of divine
> things that yet are significations of them, as children's
> being born crying is a signification of their being born to
> sorrow. A man's coming into the world after the same
> manner as the beasts is a signification of the ignorance
> and brutishness of man, and his agreement in many
> things with the beasts.[28]

One may count these "significations," which Edwards obviously regards as an inferior form of relation between
earthly things, among the methods of modern symbolism.
On the other hand his types are a special sort of symbol
with a fixed transcendent meaning. Thus "Hills and
mountains [are] types of heaven" (Image 64); "Ravens,
that with delight feed on carrion, seem to be remarkeable
types of devils, who with delight prey upon the souls of the
dead" (Image 61); and "It is a sign that the beautiful variety of the colours of light was designed as a type of the
various beauties and graces of the spirit of God that divine
and spiritual beauties and excellencies are so often represented in Scripture by beautifull colours" (Image 58). On
several occasions we find the sun and the silkworm employed as types of Christ, in analogy to traditional typology. Finally, Edwards also sets an aspect of the intimate
human sphere he obviously considered important in an
exalted relation. Images 5, 9, 12, 32, and 56 treat love and
marriage as a type of the relation of Christ to the church:

> We are told that marriage is a great mystery, as repre-
> senting the relation between Christ and the church
> (Eph. 5, 32). By mystery can be meant nothing but a
> type of what is spiritual. And if God designed this for a
> type of what is spiritual, why not many other things in
> the constitution and ordinary state of human society and
> the world of mankind? [29]

These sketches of "Images or Shadows of Divine Things," which occupied Edwards his entire life,[30] are a grandiose attempt (even though we find it futile) to subordinate the entire natural world—cosmos, earth, man, and history—to the power of the divine will by clamping together in a typical relation the natural and supernatural worlds. The type thus becomes a way of regarding natural phenomena as expressions and products of an analogous transcendent world. The transformation of the entire world accessible to human experience into an indicator of a higher religious meaning does of course diminish its reality. Yet this lends it at the same time a superior reality through its harmony with the spiritual world.

The modern reader has some difficulty realizing that Edwards' reasoning is neither abstruse nor naive. Grant him his presuppositions and Edwards develops a consistent and comprehensive world picture; however, it is a typico-transcendent one rather than a mechanico-casual. If the Bible is the word of God, then it follows that its contents establish eternal models. If nature is the creation of God, then it is natural for its phenomena to mirror its origin and for God to express something in them. It is in the form of types, or in the broader sense, of shadows that God projects his rules into the world of nature. They explain the world after the principle of identity rather than that of causality. In Edwards' theory it is not so much the isolated phenomenon as it is the natural world itself that is a type in relation to the divine world. It is not an isolated act of God's volition to create a particular type; it is rather "God's *manner* to make inferior things shadows of the superior and most excellent" (my italics). But the reference to the "superior and most excellent" automatically does away with the bipolarity and historicity of the original type concept. If natural and historical phenomena represent copies rather than temporally previous models of something superior and spiritual, this means that the antitype here approximates a deeper, purely spiritual meaning instead of being a concrete historical person or event. Edwards' concept of the type approaches that of the secular symbol, from which however the methodical and parallel character of its reference as well as the law that it always contains a transcendent meaning still serve to distinguish it. As the above statement shows, however, the approach to the Platonic doctrine of eternal ideas and their shadowy terrestrial copies occurs as early as Edwards and not first with Emerson. But Edwards actually only lays bare a component that belonged to the notion of the type from the very beginning. A Platonic influence was present at the very inception of the notion of the type by the Fathers.[31]

"The use of natural history is to give us aid in supernatural history." This sentence is not from Edwards' *Images or Shadows*; it is from Emerson's manifesto of Transcendentalism, his essay "Nature." And since it reveals a shift of accent to nature as the centrally important power of revelation it could not be from Edwards. Yet it seems to be in a direct line of descent from Edwards' conception. Emerson could not have been acquainted with Edwards' *Images or Shadows of Divine Things*, but he grew up in the same theological culture as Edwards. The inner resemblance of the two statements is due to the continuous development of modes of thought of a single cultural tradition rather than to direct borrowing, since the latter would only have meaning or even be possible on the basis of an inner affinity. In his essay "From Edwards to Emerson" Perry Miller has pointed out Emerson's Calvinist origin and his intellectual affinity to Edwards.

Miller gives cautious voice to his conviction in this statement:

> . . . it may be permissible to suggest that the gulf be-
> tween Edwards and Emerson is not so deep nor so wide
> as a strictly doctrinal definition would lead us to believe.
> What is persistent, from the covenant theology (and
> from the heretics against the covenant) to Edwards and
> to Emerson is the Puritan's effort to confront, face to
> face, the image of a blinding divinity in the physical uni-
> verse, and to look upon that universe without the inter-
> mediacy of ritual, of ceremony, of the Mass and the con-
> fessional.[32]

In this essay Perry Miller shows that Emerson's "latest
form of infidelity" is only a new variety of the mystical,
pantheistic enthusiasm that arose again and again in Puritanism from the time of Anne Hutchinson. The Calvinistic dogmas of God's omnipotence to create and His power
to predetermine the destinies of all earthly creatures lead
almost inevitably to the idea that God must somehow be
inherent in nature and its creatures:

> The point might be put thus: there was in Puritanism a
> piety, a religious passion, the sense of an inward com-
> munication and of the divine symbolism of nature. One
> side of the Puritan nature hungered for these excite-
> ments; certain of its appetites desired these satisfactions
> and therefore found delight and ecstasy in the doctrines
> of regeneration and providence.[33]

This belief in the internal connection of the natural and
divine worlds provides the foundation upon which Emerson the theologian assimilated Platonism, Neoplatonism,
Swedenborg,[34] and others who held similar views on the
correspondence of the natural and supernatural worlds.[35]
Although the Transcendentalist movement was a here-
tic backsliding from Christianity in the eyes of the Calvinists, and even in those of the Unitarians, its innermost

aims were religious ones. The debates on the nature of Christ, on the nature and significance of miracles, and on the literal authenticity of the gospels are its intellectual driving force, and it received impulses toward an independent, critical approach from the writings of Herder, Schleiermacher, and Strauss's *Leben Jesu*. The literary fruits of Transcendentalism are much less numerous than the religious disputes and writings. But their acceptance into literary history makes them seem to us today the more important or even the essential part of Transcendentalism.

At the core of Transcendentalist thought we find the controversy over the person of Christ and his status between man and God, as well as over the miracles performed by Jesus according to the testimony of the gospels.[36] Emerson began his career as a Transcendentalist in 1832 in a characteristic manner: with a critical treatment of the sacrament of the Lord's Supper in a sermon entitled "The Lord's Supper," [37] which led to his separation from the Unitarian Church.

Once again we find that in this religious culture it is the Lord's Supper that serves as a catalyst. Emerson goes one step further toward removing religion from the institutionalized sphere: he claims that Jesus did not command the rite of the Lord's Supper for all people and for all time; he only intended for his disciples to repeat it in his memory. Emerson appears to arrive at this conviction by biblical criticism: he compares the texts of the three synoptic gospels and finds Jesus' words in Luke "this do in remembrance of me" (Luke 22:19) too weak for the establishment of a sacrament that is to be repeated forever. Yet this argument is not strong enough to cope with the statement of Jesus that caused Taylor such a struggle: "This is my body which is broken for you. Take it, eat. This is my blood which is shed for you. Drink it." [38] Emerson's solution is as simple as it is heretical: Jesus "always taught by parables and symbols"; the saying is symbolical.

The concept of type also has its role in Emerson's thought. He applies the old Puritan conviction that the religious customs of the Old Testament are types to the Lord's Supper. The washing of feet and the Passover are typical, yet it cannot be maintained that they are annulled by Christ's advent, because he performs them himself in the concrete sense. Foot-washing was not adopted in the rite of the Lord's Supper. Emerson gives two reasons for this: first, because it was an Oriental custom not appropriate for Western nations; second, "because it was typical, and all understood that humility is the thing signified." The transition to a symbolic connection has been established, in this instance within the sphere of religion. The type, which is in this case a ritual custom that as such contains a certain element of symbolism, has a significance, a metaphorical meaning, "humility."

Thus the disciples followed the instructions of Jesus, continues Emerson, and held religious meetings in which they broke bread and drank wine "as symbols." This was natural because they lived in the same place and were bound together in the commemoration of Christ: ". . . nothing could be more natural than . . . that they, Jews like Jesus, should adopt his expressions and his types." [39] Emerson has obviously adopted the concept of type from his own religious tradition and applied it here correctly for Old Testament and Jewish customs. However, he links it up with a "signification," a general symbolic meaning, at the same time as he omits the antitype, Christ, as the specific fulfillment. Even though he is aware of its original meaning he uses "type" in certain cases as a synonym for "symbol."

Emerson uses the concept of the type for his interpretation of nature just as Jonathan Edwards did. But he went one step further than Edwards in modifying Calvinist principles. Edwards' Image 156 states: "The book of Scripture is the interpreter of the book of nature in two ways . . ." [40] In a late work, "Poetry and Imagination," which is however based on early lectures and notes, Emerson summarizes thus: "Natural objects if individually described and out of connection, are not yet known, since they are really parts of a symmetrical universe, like words of a sentence; and if their true order is found, the poet can read their divine significance orderly as in a Bible." Then he adds the following, also parallel to Edwards' ideas: [41] "Each animal or vegetable form remembers the next inferior and predicts the next higher."

Edwards makes inferences about nature on the basis of the Bible: "The book of Scripture is the interpreter of the book of nature. . . ." Emerson on the other hand allocates prime importance to the book of nature, in which just as in the Bible "divine significances" can be read. "Whilst common sense looks at things or visible Nature as real and final facts, poetry, or the imagination which dictates it, is a second sight, looking through these, and using them as types or words for thoughts which they signify." [42] Nowhere did Emerson expressly define "type" as applied to nature, nor distinguish it from "symbol," "emblem," or "sign," all of which occur in similar contexts in his writings.

All these concepts are concerned with nature's being anchored in a superior being and with the message nature thereby holds for man, above all for the poet who can read the divine message in nature. [43] In his essay "The Poet" Emerson calls the poet the "translator of Nature into thought," and even more enthusiastically, the "liberating god." [44]

Nature offers all her creatures to him as a picture-language. Being used as a type, a second wonderful value appears in the object, far better than its old value; as the carpenter's stretched cord, if you hold your ear close enough, is musical in the breeze. "Things more excellent than every image," says Jamblichus, "are expressed through images." Things admit of being used as symbols because nature is a symbol, in the whole, and in every part.[45]

Here we have "type" and "symbol" in close proximity; an explanatory sentence adds "emblem":

Beyond this universality of the symbolic language, we are apprised of the divineness of this superior use of things, whereby the world is a temple whose walls are covered with emblems, pictures and commandments of the Deity,—in this, that there is no fact in nature which does not carry the whole sense of nature; and the distinctions which we make in events and in affairs, of low and high, honest and base, disappear when nature is used as a symbol.[46]

The notion that plain, base things could be poetically equal to exalted things was essential for the subsequent development of American literature. Emerson explains it and supports it with reference to the original biblical type of circumcision, which he regards as symbolic (theologically, it is a type for baptism, for the admittance of believers to a church covenant): "The circumcision is an example of the power of poetry to raise the low and offensive. Small and mean things serve as well as great symbols. The meaner the type by which a law is expressed, the more pungent it is, and the more lasting in the memories of men. . . ."[47]

These examples show us that "symbol" is the concept

for that which carries meaning in nature—nature in the broad sense of the NOT ME, as Emerson defines it in the introduction to "Nature." The specific features concerning the origin or use of what is meaningful are designated by "sign," "emblem," or "type." The "sign" demands attention like a consciously given sign (either God's or the poet's);[48] the "emblem" reveals metaphorically: "the world is a temple whose walls are covered with emblems"; and "type" is a piece of reality in which a law, a principle, or something superior manifests itself in an impressive form. It is a part of visible nature employed by God the creator and by the poet who recognizes it to express such a law or meaning.[49] "Throw a stone into the stream, and the circles that propagate themselves are the beautiful type of all influence," is how it is put in Part IV, "Language," of the essay "Nature." [50] An inner harmony links up God, nature, and the human mind, and this is why man can recognize and express divine principles in the images nature affords him. "Every natural fact is a symbol of some spiritual fact. Every appearance in nature corresponds to some state of the mind, and that state of the mind can only be described by presenting that natural appearance as its picture." [51]

The connection of nature to a superior law on the one side and to the human mind in which this law is also present on the other closes the ring in which symbol and type are also doubly connected. Now nature occupies the central position as source of knowledge which the Bible once held in New England. It is the medium of revelation, the means of knowledge, and the matter for poetic representation of deciphered revelation. The same nature which the first Puritans found inimical and savage received by virtue of Emerson's heresy the consecration which made it the ground of symbols and knowledge, and thus a vital element in American literature.

PART III

The Heirs of the Puritans and

Their Literary Works

7 NATHANIEL HAWTHORNE

1. The Problem of Allegory

Herman Melville takes experience as his point of departure and attempts to shape its amorphous abundance. On the other hand Hawthorne takes as the starting point for his creative work either an idea, the abstract core of a concrete experience, or one of life's more vivid and graphic problems. In the *Notebooks* Hawthorne jotted down for his stories such ideas as the following: "Cannon transformed to church-bells," or "To make one's own reflection in a mirror the subject of a story." [1] Melville has an expansive narrative style, Hawthorne a terse and precise one. Hawthorne's stories are not so much evocations of reality as abbreviations of it. In certain respects his method compares to that of modern shorthand. Radical compression and omission result in a transcription which is less a copy than a version of reality restricted to the basic difficulty, of which the central motifs[2] are represented by certain "shorthand" signs.

Hawthorne's work is full of such signs of different sorts. They often embody the meaning of the story to the extent that they provide its title also, as in "The Snow Image," "Howe's Masquerade," "The Prophetic Picture," "The Great Carbuncle," and "The Maypole of Merrymount." The elixir is a sign that occurs in several pieces. We encounter it in "A Virtuoso's Collection," "Dr. Heidegger's Experiment," and in the incomplete works, *The Dolliver Romance* and *Septimius Felton*. "The Earth's Holocaust" is a sign for mankind's destructive revolutionary acts, and "The Great Stone Face" is one for the ideal of the true American, who is awaited like a true messiah and whom it is hoped the country will one day produce.

The birthmark and the bosom serpent are also signs in the stories to which they give the titles, as is Owen Warland's butterfly in "The Artist of the Beautiful," but they are a less complex, allegorical kind of sign. The ones mentioned previously are more complicated. They comprise metaphorical, symbolic, and allegorical elements, as well as realistic and historical ones, and they are the pictorial or dramatic correlates of quite definite, multilevel meanings intended by the artist. In some cases they serve as the vessel or framework for a number of symbols or symbolic actions. "The Earth's Holocaust," "Howe's Masquerade," and "A Virtuoso's Collection" belong in this category. These signs could be taken as varieties of Eliot's objective correlative if they were not so highly contrived and essentially non-realistic. Eliot's objective correlative is, if this *contradictio in adjecto* may be permitted, a realistic allegory which is intended to engender a specific emotion.[3] One could say that Hawthorne's signs are "imaginative correlatives," intended to express real emotional problems.

Most critics regard Hawthorne essentially as an allegorist. F. O. Matthiessen regards him as one whose imagination leans mainly toward allegory: "With all the forces conditioning his art that we have noted—the scantiness of material and atmosphere, his lack of plastic experience, his steady moral preoccupation—it is no wonder that the favorites of his childhood, Spenser and Bunyan, rose again to the surface when he began to write, and helped determine his bias to allegory." [4] In *Maule's Curse, or Hawthorne and the Problem of Allegory* Yvor Winters views Hawthorne as the born allegorist: "Hawthorne is, then, essentially an allegorist; had he followed the advice of Poe . . . and had thrown his allegorizing out the window, it is certain that nothing essential to his genius would have remained." [5] "Of Hawthorne's three most important long works—*The Scarlet Letter, The House of the Seven Gables,* and *The Marble Faun*—the first is pure allegory, and the other two are impure novels, or novels with unassimilated allegorical elements" (p. 157). Richard Fogle advances the opinion in *Hawthorne's Fiction: The Light and the Dark* that "Allegory is organic to Hawthorne, an innate quality of his vision." [6] In this study Fogle accepts allegory as an artistic form and defends it: "Hawthorne still suffers from our prejudice against allegory" (p. 7). Hyatt H. Waggoner criticizes F. O. Matthiessen's interpretation of Hawthorne in his *Hawthorne, A Critical Study.* Waggoner does not think that Hawthorne can be regarded simply as an allegorist in Spenser's footsteps. He also sees that Hawthorne's tales are neither allegories in the usual sense nor symbolic in the sense of modern symbolism: "Most of Hawthorne's best tales exist, like the stories of Conrad Aiken, in a realm somewhere between symbolism and allegory, as those terms are used today." [7]

No doubt Hawthorne is close to allegory. Certain of his

tales are clearly allegorical, and others contain allegorical elements or tendencies. It can be proved that he took Spenser's *Faerie Queene* as his model in some stories.[8] "The Celestial Railroad" is oriented in all its details on Bunyan's *Pilgrim's Progress*, and one suspects that as a pure allegorist Hawthorne is mainly imitative. "The Celestial Railroad" is an allegory based on another allegory, and the second allegory supplies the key to the correspondences, which Hawthorne treats with a dash of irony for his own purposes.

However, Hawthorne is seldom a pure allegorist. At the core of his stories we find some human problem presented in a concrete situation rather than an abstraction. The problem is most often too complex to be allegorized; a combination of real elements and symbolic elements is required. An examination of Hawthorne's literary techniques reveals that he employs allegorical principles only on occasions and even then only halfway. It was from elements of his own cultural tradition that he developed his characteristic forms of style, and they touch allegory occasionally without being identical with it.

Yet the basic feature of the tale "Egotism, or The Bosom Serpent" is an allegorical one. Together with "The Christmas Banquet" it belongs to the "Allegories of the Heart" published in *Mosses from an Old Manse*. One of the entries for 1836 in the *American Notebooks* reads: "A snake taken into a man's stomach and nourished there from fifteen years to thirty-five, tormenting him most horribly. A type of envy or some other evil passion." [9] This might be based on Cotton Mather's *Magnalia Christi Americana*, which Hawthorne is known to have studied. Following a discussion of envy, the General Introduction, ¶ 6, of the *Magnalia* records the incident of a young man after whose death a serpent with several tails was found in his heart.

Accordingly, it is not the historical characters—the

man, his wife, and his friend—that are treated allegorically. Their names suggest individuality: Roderick Elliston, Rosina, George Herkimer. What is allegorized is
a quality, egotism, which comprises envy, and is represented by the serpent. As allegory in general is a system of
abbreviations from the standpoint of realism, so the serpent functions as an abbreviation. It spares the writer
from presenting Elliston's egotism and selfish faults at
length and verifying them. The serpent seems to have
been a metaphor originally. "What do people say of me?"
Roderick Elliston asks his faithful servant. "Sir! My poor
master! that you had a serpent in your bosom." [10] This
figure of speech acquires more and more the aspect of
reality—the serpent hisses and gnaws at Elliston's heart.
But then it is classed as a symbol again: "The snake in his
bosom seemed the symbol of monstrous egotism to which
everything was referred, and which he pampered, night
and day, with a continual and exclusive sacrifice of devil
worship." [11] We are not told whether it is a metaphor or a
real serpent with a symbolic meaning.

This reference to the devil betrays the serpent's origin
in the history of ideas. It comes from the Bible, of course,
from Genesis, and it is the agent of evil, of alienation from
God, and of the Fall. Roderick Elliston believes—since all
mankind is affected by the Fall—that every man must
have a similar serpent in his bosom. Thus he makes "his
own actual serpent—if a serpent there actually was in his
bosom—the type of each man's fatal error, or hoarded sin,
or unquiet conscience." [12] It is also "the true type of a mor-
bid nature." [13] Elliston rids himself of the serpent as soon
as he succeeds in forgetting about himself. His friend ap-
prises him: ". . . whether the serpent was a physical rep-
tile, or whether the morbidness of your nature suggested
that symbol to your fancy, the moral of the story is not
less true and strong. A tremendous Egotism, manifesting

itself in your case in the form of jealousy, is as fearfull a fiend as ever stole into the human heart." His wife Rosina says, "The serpent was but a dark fantasy, and what it typified was as shadowy as itself." [14] In other words, the serpent exists somewhere between reality and symbolism. It belongs either to the one or to the other, but it cannot be said for sure which. It is not mere chance that the serpent is described as a "type" in several ways. In origin it is a type, *i.e.*, a symbol fixed by God. It appears in the Old Testament account of the creation as the archetype of evil —"The type of each man's fatal error"—and has reappeared ever since that time, whether in fact or in the mind, on every occasion man has succumbed to evil. In Hawthorne the reality of thought, idea, and imagination continually interpenetrates physical reality to such an extent that ideas, thought, supersensual things, and even chimeras can exert influence just like real, palpable things. The concept of the type comprises both concrete phenomena and inherent as well as transcendent meanings, which makes it extremely useful for Hawthorne's purposes.

Thus in Hawthorne we again encounter the "type" concept in an expanded, literary form. This use of the concept represents a stage of its transition from the original theological meaning to the generalized symbolic function as the figurative (in the present case biblical too) representation of a quality. This can be noticed in the introductory tale of Hawthorne's first published work, *Twice Told Tales*, "The Gray Champion." In a characteristic way this story combines the historical with the symbolical, reality with apparition. Like so many of Hawthorne's tales, it is concerned with the invisible forces behind historical phenomena: in this case with the Puritan desire of liberty and its continued influence in American history. Hawthorne makes this mental reality concrete by fixing it historically and temporally; indeed, by fixing it quite precisely. He localizes it in a Boston street on an afternoon in April 1689. Sir Edmund Andros, the detested and tyrannical governor of New England and deputy of James II is riding through Boston with his counsellors and red-coated English soldiers. He intends to intimidate the complaining New England populace by putting on a show of military force. It is obvious, as it always is in Hawthorne, that this scene has an emblematic character: "The whole scene was a picture of the condition of New England, and its moral, the deformity of any government that does not grow out of the nature of things and the character of the people." [15]

From the crowd of hostile spectators there suddenly emerges the figure of an ancient and venerable man in old-fashioned, Puritan dress. It is obvious that he is a patriarch of the first, heroic generation of Puritans, but nobody knows just who he is. He halts the parade of bold oppressors and announces to the startled tyrant Andros that his time has run out. James II has abdicated and William III is now king—this news does not reach Boston until the next day, by ship. But who is this unknown patriarch with prophetic knowledge, who disappears after his performance without leaving a trace? He says of himself: "I am here, Sir Governor, because the cry of an oppressed people hath disturbed me in my secret place; and beseeching this favor earnestly of the Lord, it was vouchsafed me to appear once again on earth, in the good old cause of his saints." [16] (where of course Puritan saints are meant). He is said to have been seen again at the beginning of the War of Independence and at the defense of Bunker Hill. He will appear again every time tyranny threatens from within or danger from without, concludes Hawthorne, "for he is the type of New England's hereditary spirit; and his shadowy march, on the eve of danger, must ever be the pledge, that New England's sons will vindicate their ancestry." [17]

What sort of literary conception or construction is this "Gray Champion," "the type of New England's hereditary spirit"? It is a sign and an abbreviation. The desire of the New England populace for liberty, which in reality was documented on many occasions and by different persons, is concentrated in this one figure. "The Gray Champion" is thus the personification of an idea or attitude, and to this extent is related to allegory. But since the attitude is historically fixed it is embodied in a concrete historical figure. This is what distinguishes it from allegory, which has traditionally represented this idea as "libertas" or "Victoria." Although he does not come from the Old Testament —the Puritan patriarchs have a certain relation to those of the Bible in any event—this gray saint corresponds in many features to the original conception of the type. Moreover, he is expressly designated a type: he is a historically fixed figure having a prophetic meaning at the same time. He is a prefiguration, which becomes fulfilled or reappears in certain situations. In the present case it assumes a shape whenever the desire of the Americans to maintain their liberty or dignity is put to the test. In a genuine typological manner he rises from the past to point out the future: ". . . his shadowy march . . . must ever be the pledge, that New England's sons will vindicate their ancestry." [18] The gray patriarch's hybrid nature comprises historically real and abstractly ideal existences. He is a conception settled between type and allegory, having features of both.[19]

Hawthorne employs three concepts to designate an image or person that represents a certain meaning: "symbol," "emblem," and "type." Along with derivatives such as "symbolic," "symbolize," "emblematic" (no verb is formed), "typic," and "typify," the three concepts occur with almost the same frequency.[20] The three concepts are used wherever the modern writer would use "symbol," and in many instances Hawthorne makes no noticeable distinction among them. But in certain situations he is obviously concerned with special features of the relationship. When he is concerned with some special significance or specific nuance intended in the relation of image to meaning, he uses "emblem" and "type" in the narrower senses: "type" designates all the variations of the original biblical meaning of the concept; "emblem" is used for the image set up intentionally and publicly as a sign.

The three concepts all occur in "The Minister's Black Veil" with reference to the black veil Father Hooper wears over his face. The veil is above all an emblem, since Hooper after deliberating the matter put it on intentionally as a sign or almost as a mark of distinction. Thus the black veil is referred to successively as a "mysterious emblem," [21] at the funeral as an "appropriate emblem," and finally as "only a material emblem [that] had separated him from happiness." [22] But the veil is also "a type of innocent sorrow," [23] and "type" is here almost a consciously applied symbol. The veil embodies innocent sorrow as the flag flying at half-mast proclaims mourning. An allegorical element is even present in the awareness of its being an image chosen to represent an abstract idea. But it would be unthinkable for Hooper himself, the strict Puritan minister, to regard the veil as an allegory. In Calvinist eyes that would give the stern emblem a frivolous character. He calls it a "type," and this lends the symbol he contrived himself (which is nonetheless weighted with theological gravity) the air of religious authenticity.

The veil is "the symbol of a fearfull secret" between

Hooper and his congregation. When his betrothed asks him to reveal his purpose, he replies: "Know then, this veil is a type and a symbol, and I am bound to wear it ever, both in light and darkness, in solitude and before the gaze of multitudes, and as with strangers, so with my familiar friends." [24] It is obvious that neither Hooper nor Hawthorne regards "type" and "symbol" as the same thing. They are aware of the theological origin of "type." For Hooper this concept has not only the symbolical reference, it also has the much stronger power of obligation. It has a religious authority which obliges him to wear his veil until death. Here the type is a figurative representation which, through its origin or its significance, borders on the realm of the religious and the supernatural.

"The Minister's Black Veil" is called by Hawthorne "A Parable." Like "Young Goodman Brown," "The Man of Adamant," "The Gentle Boy," and "The Prophetic Pictures," this tale is a parable for certain basic features of Puritanism. "The Prophetic Pictures" is concerned with predestination; "The Man of Adamant" embodies hardened, misanthropic fanaticism; and "Young Goodman Brown" shows how a young and friendly man turns morose from the Puritan distrust of human nature. Father Hooper exemplifies the Puritan inclination to display the blackness and depravity of fallen human nature. Rather than having a firm, strong character, Hooper is weak. Hawthorne calls him "a gentlemanly person," a good but by no means energetic preacher, and a man of weaker character than his betrothed, Elizabeth.[25] Hooper is an exhibitionist—and Hawthorne presents this with his usual mild cold-bloodedness—but he is basically a timid and inhibited man. He conceals his own peculiar sin (which is not specified) behind the mask of universal human iniquity, and in the end he bitterly accuses his own people of hard-heartedness and hypocrisy:

"Why do you tremble at me alone?" cried he, turning his veiled face round the circle of pale spectators. "Tremble also at each other! Have men avoided me, and women shown no pity, and children screamed and fled, only for my black veil? What, but the mystery which it obscurely typifies, has made this piece of crape so awful? When the friend shows his inmost heart to his friend; the lover to his best beloved; when man does not vainly shrink from the eye of his Creator, loathsomely treasuring up the secret of his sin; then deem me a monster, for the symbol beneath which I have lived, and die! I look around me, and, lo! on every visage a Black Veil!" [26]

Hawthorne is correct in calling this tale a parable: what expresses the intended meaning is the plot itself; it is a simile for the deeper theme. It is far more difficult to decide what the specific elements and images, such as the black veil, are intended to represent. Hooper does not reveal this, and his betrothed, who questions him, fails to discover what it is. The black veil has something to do with secret sin, but in the final instance it is as much a symbol for Hooper's Puritan mind as an emblem for human iniquity. Here we encounter a quality that makes Hawthorne unfit for a simple, unambiguous allegory: His skepticism and the complexity of his mind prevent him from finding direct personifications and embodiments for simple abstractions. When he did attempt this technique he was apt to get so entangled in the ambiguities of his images and symbols that his readers could find no key to the allegory. This is the case in, *e.g.*, "Rappaccini's Daughter." I take the minority view that this allegorical tale is unsuccessful because it is overloaded with allegorical elements, some of which are inconsistent with others.

The symbol of the black veil has another interesting feature. Like the scarlet letter "A" that Hester Prynne had to wear, this emblematic symbol, which is worn deliberately to provoke, acquires an existence of its own. Both the black veil and the scarlet letter emerge from the passive, representative character of the symbol and become, if not active, at least contributing elements of the action. The scarlet letter on Hester's breast transforms first her and then her surroundings. It sets her off from the anonymous group of all sinners and makes her, a confessed sinner, almost venerable. The black veil, which was really only intended to signify a mystery, creates a gulf between Father Hooper and his congregation. By transforming Hooper's life into one of isolation, it makes it almost tragic.

The character of Christ as a model plays almost no role in Hawthorne's work, in contrast to Melville's.[27] Thus Christ is not the type of any of his characters, and whenever Hawthorne uses the type concept it is without reference to Christ. Usually it has no connection to the theologically recognized types of the Old Testament either. To my knowledge a genuine Old Testament type is used only in the posthumous *Dolliver Romance*. Even there it is not without a certain ambiguity which, due to the fragmentary character of that work, cannot be eliminated entirely. The old apothecary Dr. Dolliver has put up "the Scriptural Device," the brazen serpent, as a sign of his profession, and this is obviously an association of the Aesculapian serpent with the brazen serpent of the Bible. The brazen serpent that Moses at God's command raised up in the desert to heal snakebites (Num. 21:6–9) served, as we have shown,[28] as a type for Christ's crucifixion. As the serpent saved the Jews from deadly snakebites, so Jesus on the Cross saves mankind from its sins and vanquishes death. Dolliver obviously chose this "symbolic serpent," as Hawthorne calls it, as a symbol for his miraculous potion, which could vanquish death. But the potion is discredited when his son suffers reverses in his experiments. Now the other biblical serpent, the one from paradise, is shoved into the interpretation: "It was the general opinion that Satan had been personally concerned in this affliction, and that the Brazen Serpent, so long honored among them, was really the type of his subtle malevolence and perfect iniquity." [29] Christ is supplanted by the devil, religion by black magic. There is a diabolical principle at work in the miracles of medicine and experimentation— an idea that occurs several times in Hawthorne.

Hawthorne did not again use such authentic theological types as that of the brazen serpent. He sought his types in Puritanism and in New England. He does find types there, but he does not invent them. Hawthorne's types are not embodiments of abstract ideas which the human mind has come up with for literary purposes. Instead they are things, persons, and scenes, allegedly real or veritably real, and the writer discovers a deeper meaning expressed in them. For him, a grandson of the Puritans, this deeper meaning has been placed there by a superior being: types are God's allegories.[30]

The narrator of "The Vision of the Fountain" visits a poor pastor who is sitting silently with his family before a gloomy, smoldering fire in the fireplace. The narrator meditates: "Dreamy as the scene was, might it not be the type of the mode in which departed people, who had known and loved each other here, would hold communion in eternity?" [31] In "Footprints on the Sea Shore" waterfowl are "the types of pleasant fantasies." [32] In every case "type" designates a reference inherent in the things, a parallelism of the inner and outer worlds which goes back in the final instance to the connection of all created things. This calls to mind the saying of Edwards:[33] "External things are intended to be images of things spiritual, moral, and divine," and his definitions of the connections between natural phenomena and spiritual meanings.

As early as Edwards we find products of technology such as the telescope imbued with a similar meaning. We encounter more of the same in Hawthorne when the locomotive, "the steam fiend," becomes "the type of all that go ahead," [34] whereas the old apple dealer (in the story of the same name) represents those who will never take part in progress. Hawthorne comes from the same tradition Edwards helped shape, but for him God is only behind the scenes and is no longer named. For Edwards, spring is "a season of the outpouring of the spirit of God"; [35] for Hawthorne, who composes a hymn to spring in "Buds and Bird Voices," it is "with its outgushing life, the true type of movement." [36] But the only reference to a creator is a furtive "Thank Providence for spring!"

Hawthorne's notion of the type has a special reference to the heart: figures and appearances are outer manifestations of what takes place in the hidden regions of the heart. Above all it is the evil in the heart that projects itself outward. Or, seen from the other direction, the pernicious phenomena of the terrestrial world are types of the power of evil that leads an invisible existence in the human heart: "The heart, the heart—there was the little yet boundless sphere wherein existed the original wrong of which the crime and misery of the outward world were merely types." [37]

As evil presses outward, so does the consciousness of the evil deed. Hawthorne tried again and again to depict the force with which the secret sin cries out for confession and thus redemption. The inability to confess his sin is what destroys Dimmesdale. When Chillingworth tries to snatch the dark secret from Dimmesdale's heart, he does it with a "Gothic" trick, a weapon taken from the arsenal of the "Gothic" novel. He shows Dimmesdale a handful of weeds and claims he found these "ugly weeds" on the grave of some unknown person: "They grew out of his heart, and typify, it may be, some hideous secret that was buried with him, and which he had done better to confess during his lifetime." [38] Dimmesdale objects that the unfortunate person may have wanted to confess but could not. Chillingworth does not accept this argument: "Wherefore not; since all the powers of nature call so earnestly for the confession of sin, that these black weeds have sprung up out of a buried heart, to make manifest an unspoken crime?" Dimmesdale rejects this version: "That, good Sir, is but a fantasy of yours. . . . There can be, if I forebode aright, no power, short of the Divine mercy, to disclose, whether by uttered words, or by type or emblem, the secrets that may be buried with a human heart." [39] Opinion differs only over the manner of the connection. It goes without saying for both that there is a direct parallelism between God and the world, meaning and event, the moral law and nature. Chillingworth adopts the "modern," "Gothic," pseudo-scientific standpoint. Dimmesdale takes the classical Puritan one, with the difference for him, as the creature of a "romantic" writer, that the heart intrudes in the simple relation of God to type. God no longer fixes types and emblems peremptorily as manifestations of His will. He causes the inner working of the human heart to manifest themselves as types in earthly things.

"Emblem" sounds old-fashioned to us today. It is seldom used, and then only in the sense of an ornamental, heraldic, or at any rate, a rather official distinction. It originally meant an inlay, a ship's figurehead, or a man-made ornament or object provided with a motto or a message.[40] From this final meaning there grew the collections of emblemata that were so popular in the sixteenth and seventeenth centuries, which provided copies with explanations and quotations.[41]

Hawthorne often uses "emblem," as often if not more so

than "type" or "symbol." All three have, like "sign," a tinge of didacticism in his hands. They are intended to convey something, and one of his uses of "emblem" is to give special stress to this quality. The Puritans had extended the meaning of "emblem." Events and natural phenomena can be "emblems," because every earthly phenomenon is potentially a sign used by God to proclaim His will like an inlaid motto to mankind. Moreover, since the word "symbol" always recalled the detested symbols of the Catholic Church, "emblem" was widely used as a substitute. It is the meaningful image or sign, the phenomenon that contains a message from God. It is a message or a meaning that is always fixed and precise, even though it may not always be clearly recognized. But this introduces a shift of meaning the consequence of which was never fully realized. Whereas the emblem was originally an artificial, man-made image, it was now a natural image. On the other hand, the strict Puritans regarded the symbol as a man-made and thus blasphemous religious symbol, as for example the cross. But the nature of the case makes a fixed dividing-line impossible. Since God predestines man's deeds and projects, they can have the character of divine signs also. In the end every visible object becomes a potential emblem, behind which an ever paler God stands in an ever more puzzling relationship.

For Hawthorne the world is full of emblems. God, nature, and man all create emblems. He sees in "mud, an emblem of all stains of undeserved opprobrium";[42] Lady Eleanore, in "Lady Eleanore's Mantle," places her foot on the slavishly prostrated body of her admirer and thereby creates an emblem "of aristocracy and hereditary pride trampling on human sympathies and the kindred of nature";[43] and the maypole of Merry Mount is a "venerated emblem" for the community. The American Puritans were more emblematists than allegorists (as Yvor Winters and others hold).[44] They regarded an allegorical world, or any fictional world not concerned with biblical themes, as blasphemous, because man's inventive powers are thereby pitted against God's power of creation. They had no leeway for literary themes beyond the Bible and the real world, and even these could only be interpreted, not altered. Of course these rules were relaxed with the decline of Puritanism in the eighteenth century, but even down to Hawthorne's time we find basic features of the Calvinist view of the world influencing literary styles, including Hawthorne's.[45] This Calvinist conception of the emblematic structure of reality contains a strict principle of selectivity. Only a certain kind of event or phenomenon can be regarded as a true emblem and thus as significant, and more restricted yet, only characteristic features are pertinent (these may nonetheless be plain, every day features). This world view discards as insignificant and superfluous all the circumstantial and decorative features, and all features peculiar to the individual in the human situation.

In the famous "negative catalogue" of his monograph on Hawthorne, Henry James listed all the "items of high civilization" missing in Hawthorne's America, to account for the rigidity and meagerness of his fictional world. Even though it lacked an Eton, Harrow, Ascot, etc., this America was in fact chock-full of vital material; it was not, however, the material traditionally regarded as worthy of notice or literature. Hawthorne's fictional world is austere only because his field of vision is restricted to that which is exemplary and indicative of a deeper meaning. There was of course the possibility of treating the other, nonemblematic aspects of life in literature, simply for their intrinsic emotional and human interest. Hawthorne took this possibility into consideration once, in the "Custom House Preface," but never followed it up in his tales and novels. He saw the possibilities and the perspectives of a fresh standpoint, but tradition exercised a stronger influence on his mind. He sought the emblematic features of reality rather than reality itself: his world is constructed solely of emblematic elements.

2. THE CYCLICAL VIEW OF HISTORY

Hawthorne also views history from this emblematic standpoint. He was not, as were his European contemporaries, interested in ascertaining the unique character of an era, taking all factors into account with scientific objectivity. His country's past interested him in so far as it was an expression of the Puritan spirit. Hawthorne is to date the only great American novelist besides Faulkner to take his nation's past as the theme for his literature. The American genius has generally been less concerned with what was than with what is and what will be. But Hawthorne looked back. A good number of his stories have historical themes, and this includes his most important tales. Of the four novels two are historical: *The Scarlet Letter* and *The House of the Seven Gables*. And one, *The Marble Faun*, has a romantic historical theme.

But Hawthorne is not interested in the historicity of history. History only provides him with the temporal coordinates for unchanging moral categories. The past like the present is the stage upon which man succeeds or fails —more often than not, he fails. Hawthorne does not view history as an epic of things arising and perishing. He views it dramatically, as scenes and performances: it is like the technique of the tableau, where costumes and *décor* change yet everything is combined to impart a meaning. This is why the actors on his historical stage are not so much individuals who exist uniquely in their own right as they are types which embody certain principles and demonstrate specific meanings. Hawthorne does not regard time and history as being in continual change and flux. Rather, he regards them as something cyclical and recurring, where the same situations and types recur over and over again in different masks and costumes.

The House of the Seven Gables is the novel of a family, and it is also a historical novel in a symbolic way, since the Pyncheon house stands for the "house" of Puritanism. The house of the seven gables illustrates not only the fate and guilt of the Pyncheon family but that of Puritanism too.

The peculiar structure of this novel can be clearly seen when we compare it with another novel about the fate and decline of a family, *e.g.*, *Buddenbrooks*. The confrontation of one novel with another one so different from it gives us a vivid picture of two different ways of treating a similar theme. First we have the differences in the ideas of time and history. For Thomas Mann, time is something that passes, continually changing people with their fates before it discards them irretrievably. For Hawthorne time is something that is fulfilled. With certain variations it again and again brings forth similar constellations, and these recurrences are fulfillments of the original points of departure. History is not the eternal change and transformation that brings forth new possibilities and individuals in every generation. It is the cyclical recurrence of typical events and figures, whose differences are only superficial and unimportant.

In his discussion of *The House of the Seven Gables*, the Hawthorne novel he appreciated most, Henry James makes the following comment on its characters:

> They are all figures rather than characters—they are all pictures rather than persons. But if their reality is light and vague, it is sufficient, and it is in harmony with the low relief and dimness of outline of the objects that sur-

round them. They are all types, to the author's mind, of something that is bound up with the history, at large, of families and individuals, and each of them is the center of a cluster of those ingenious and meditative musings, rather melancholy, as a general thing, than joyous, which melt into the current and texture of the story and give it a kind of moral richness.[46]

There is a pattern in the action corresponding to this "figural" quality of the characters. The beginning of *The House of the Seven Gables* presents us with a case of guilt that sets the action off on its tragic course. The same for *The Scarlet Letter* and *The Marble Faun*.[47] All these "Puritan" novels of Hawthorne are basically modeled on the biblical pattern. In the beginning there is the fall, the guilt, and then comes the story of regeneration.[48] Hawthorne himself calls *The House of the Seven Gables* "This long drama of wrong and retribution." [49]

In *The House of the Seven Gables* Hawthorne depicts the Fall of Puritanism, the burden of guilt it incurs by religious fanaticism, lust for power, and greed. Colonel Pyncheon, a respected and powerful Puritan dignitary—he is called a "stalwart Puritan" and an "iron-hearted Puritan"—covets the land of the simple crafstman, Matthew Maule. His claim is a dubious one, and it is not until Maule is tried and executed at the time of the witch-hunt that Pyncheon succeeds in taking possession of the land. He demanded that Maule be condemned, and Maule cursed him from the gallows: "God will give him blood to drink." "But the puritan soldier and magistrate was not a man to be turned aside from his well-considered scheme." In place of Maule's modest cabin he builds a spacious, sturdy house intended for many generations of his descendants. As the foundation is being laid, the water in Maule's well turns brackish. On the day of the opening ceremony of the house Maule's curse is fulfilled. Pyncheon is found dead in a chair beneath his own portrait, without wounds but with blood on his collar.

This might be called the prologue of the novel, an event that occurs one hundred and fifty years before the action proper of the novel starts. It is a short story that actually contains enough material for a novel itself, and it is wholly self-contained. Hawthorne develops the novel from this short story by using it as a prefiguration—or "type" if you please—of the history of the entire Pyncheon family.[50] "Family" and "descendants" signify to Hawthorne the continuity of a definite type of person. The descendants of Maule and those of Pyncheon have the same qualities and talents, and even encounter the same circumstances of life again and again:

> In almost every generation, nevertheless, there happened to be some one descendant of the family gifted with a portion of the hard, keen sense, and practical energy, that had so remarkably distinguished the original founder. His character, indeed, might be traced all the way down, as distinctly as if the Colonel himself, a little diluted, had been gifted with a sort of intermittent immortality on earth. At two or three epochs, when the fortunes of the family were low, this representative of hereditary qualities had made his appearance, and caused the traditional gossips of the town to whisper among themselves, "Here is the old Pyncheon come again! Now the Seven Gables will be new-shingled!" From father to son, they clung to the ancestral house with singular tenacity of home attachment.[51]

As we see here, the author is less than half-convinced that these similarities can be explained by heredity. It is not only qualities that recur, but also "typical" acts and situations, with the symbols that indicate them: Maule's well, the lost deeds to the huge tract of land, "the crimson stain" of blood on the Pyncheons who died so suddenly, and the ominous portrait of the Colonel. Of the Colonel the following is said:

> Those stern immitigable features seemed to symbolize an evil influence, and so darkly to mingle the shadow of their presence with the sunshine of the passing hour, that no good thoughts or purposes could ever spring up and blossom there. To the thoughtful mind there will be no tinge of superstition in what we figuratively express, by affirming that the ghost of a dead progenitor—perhaps as a portion of his own punishment—is often doomed to become the Evil Genius of his family.[52]

Maule's curse runs through the novel like a *leit-motif* and is fulfilled several times. Three other Pyncheons die in the same manner as the Colonel. The last one is Judge Pyncheon, and we hear that another Pyncheon died the same way a hundred years earlier. Thirty years before the action of the novel another descendant of the Colonel died in the same mysterious fashion. This time it was taken for murder, and the nephew of the deceased, Clifford, spent thirty years in prison for the supposed crime. We are told that the dead man had discovered the injustice of the Pyncheon claim to the land, and that death alone prevented him from making amends to the descendants of Maule, who also survived according to the "type" of their ancestor. The main narrative of the novel begins with the release from prison of Clifford, who was innocent of any crime. It covers a period of only a few short weeks, but episodes from the previous two centuries are woven into the account.

According to Hawthorne's own definition *The House of the Seven Gables* is not a novel but a romance, because "the Marvellous" is given a place in it.[53] The reason he gives is a curious one, somewhat provincial and naive: "The point of view in which this tale comes under the Romantic definition lies in the attempt to connect a bygone time with the very present that is flitting away from us." [54] Thus it is a romance because it treats a historical theme: "It is a legend prolonging itself, from an epoch now gray in the distance, down into our own broad daylight, and bringing along with it some of its legendary mist, which the reader, according to his pleasure, may either disregard, or allow it to float almost imperceptibly about the characters and events for the sake of a picturesque effect." [55] There is a strange uncertainty and vagueness in Hawthorne's words. Instead of defending the principles of his art, he courts the reader's favor by allowing him to regard or disregard the romance style of the book as he pleases. The veil of the legendary is there "for the sake of a picturesque effect." But when we investigate the matter we find that it is a pall of gloom, and that the main agent of the "Marvellous" in this romance is a deadly curse. This is what connects the past with the present. Its origin is not difficult to trace. It comes from the inventory of the Gothic novel, the persistent influence of which on the American novel in general and on Hawthorne in particular has already been investigated. In *Nathaniel Hawthorne and the Tradition of Gothic Romance*,[56] Jane Lundblad has enumerated the "Gothic" elements and pointed them out in Hawthorne. But she does not consider why certain requisites of horror, such as the curse, so fascinated Hawthorne's imagination.

Jane Lundblad regards "Gothic" romance as an influence alongside of Puritanism.[57] But in Hawthorne's case they seem to me to be connected. There are several dispositions of the mind—mystery, the gloomy presentiment, anxiety, and the readiness to enjoy terror (think of the macabre delight in the witch trials and other misdeeds found in Puritan chronicles and diaries)—common to the Puritans and their descendants devoted to romance. They may even have been inherited from the Puritans. A closer look reveals that many of the romantic requisites of terror are components of religion that have been degraded and usurped by superstition. As such, they are especially attractive for a society like Hawthorne's that has just been released from theological constraint and still wavers between theology and science, without being able to decide for one or the other.

The curse is unmistakably related to predestination. It is predestination secularized, romanticized, and converted into superstition. In *The House of the Seven Gables* Hawthorne links up Maule's curse clearly to divine predetermination. "God will give him blood to drink," says Maule, and this curse predetermines the way the Colonel and those of his descendants who resemble him will die. When the curse is fulfilled on Judge Pyncheon, Maule's descendant Holgrave registers the event with astonishing composure:

> Even in her agitation, Phoebe could not help remarking the calmness of Holgrave's demeanor. He appeared, it is true, to feel the whole awfulness of the Judge's death, yet had received the fact into his mind without any mixture of surprise, but as an event pre-ordained, happening inevitably, and so fitting itself into past occurrences that it could almost have been prophesied.[58]

Another miraculous element connecting up the past with the present in *The House of the Seven Gables* is the rebirth many times over of the same types in the Maule and Pyncheon families, and the parallelism of the prologue with the action proper. Here too we encounter a mixture of theological and romantic elements, because

this conception comprises the notion of the type, predestination (of an entire family), the curse, and superstition. The main action of the romance, the principle
agents of which are Hepzibah and Clifford Pyncheon,
Phoebe, Holgrave, and Judge Pyncheon, stands in the
relation of parallel and fulfillment to the seventeenth-
century prologue referred to above as a prefiguration, in
which we first encounter Colonel Pyncheon and the "wizard," Matthew Maule. The characters parallel to Colonel
Pyncheon and Maule are Judge Pyncheon and Maule's
descendant Holgrave, although time has worked a certain
transforming influence on the latter. The curse is fulfilled
again, this time for the last time, and is thereby annulled.
A collateral descendant of Pyncheon, Phoebe, marries
Holgrave, who is a descendant of Maule.

Hawthorne makes the parallelism between the Puritan
ancestor and his nineteenth-century descendants almost
too obvious. At Judge Pyncheon's first appearance, step-
ping into Hepzibah's store, Phoebe imagines that the ancient Puritan is standing opposite her: "The fantasy
would not quit her, that the original puritan, of whom she
had heard so many sombre traditions,—the progenitor of
the whole race of New England Pyncheons, the founder of
the House of the Seven Gables, and who had died so
strangely in it,—had now stept into the shop." [59] Then the
parallel—Hawthorne himself says "the above drawn parallel"—is elaborated for several pages, only to be taken up
again several times later on. Judge Pyncheon threatens to
commit the unfortunate Clifford to an insane asylum if he
does not reveal where he supposedly hid the wealth of
their murdered uncle. In this decisive conflict Judge
Pyncheon affects Hepzibah as he previously had Phoebe:
"Hepzibah almost adopted the insane belief that it was her
old Puritan ancestor, and not the modern Judge, on whom
she had just been wreaking the bitterness of her heart." [60]

The curse and death overtake Judge Pyncheon in the very chair in which the Colonel died. The dead man is found by Holgrave, who—"for the hereditary reasons that connect me strongly with that man's fate"—makes a photograph of him. This daguerrotype is intended to prove that Judge Pyncheon as little died by violence as his Puritan ancestor or his supposedly murdered uncle did. He died from something resembling apoplexy brought on by Maule's curse, to which a guilty conscience and divine retribution obviously contributed also.

Now Holgrave reveals himself as a Maule:

> "My dearest Phoebe," said Holgrave, "how will it please you to assume the name of Maule? As for the secret, it is the only inheritance that has come down to me from my ancestors. You should have known sooner (only that I was afraid of frightening you away) that, in this long drama of wrong and retribution, I represent the old wizard, and am probably as much a wizard as ever he was." [61]

Holgrave actually does resemble the earlier Maule in having a plebian, revolutionary bent and mesmeric, hypnotic powers. The latter correspond to the "magnetic" powers that cost Matthew Maule his life in the seventeenth century. The correspondence of Holgrave to Maule is on the whole not so close as that of the Pyncheons, yet Holgrave's role too is determined by parallelism to his ancestor. Even in Phoebe's case there is a principle of parallelism at work, because she is prefigured, or at least partially so, by Alice Pyncheon. On one occasion she is hypnotized involuntarily by Holgrave. Alice had been hypnotized by a Matthew Maule, a grandson of the first Matthew Maule and an ancestor of Holgrave, whose hate of the Pyncheons led him to destroy her.

The guilt of the Pyncheons and their downfall illustrate and represent the fate of Puritanism. It too betrayed its mission out of lust for power, selfishness, and religious fanaticism. The Puritan ruling class declined at the same time as the Pyncheon family. The nineteenth century belongs to Maule, the "plebian," the democrat. This is the historical result of the novel. However, as we explained above, instead of being presented realistically this development is the fulfillment of a prefiguration, or the result of a basic situation that was established at the start.

Similar to the temporal aspects, there is also a principle of parallels and correspondences in regard to the spatial aspects of the novel, *i.e.*, the scenes and physical objects. The world in and around the house of the seven gables is symbolic in the sense of being emblematic. It consists only of things with emblematic qualities, which, in the form of moral correspondences or parallels, reveal something about the characters or the meaning of the action. Hawthorne does not use symbols of the indefinable and suggestive type that can hint at aspects of the human situation too vast and too deep to be grasped. Like the Puritans he employs as symbols the solid objects of everyday life, which are made into signs and emblems by their unmistakable connections with meanings. Their meanings are easy to figure out and are generally more illustrative than profound.

First of all we have the dismal house itself, once magnificent and pretentious, which symbolizes the unjust claim to power of its Puritan builder. But then the garden affords us a true arsenal of correspondences. It too consists mainly of references to the characters of the narrative. At one time it extended far and wide, but now it is hemmed in by neighbors' houses. The garden is overgrown with weeds, but it has one tall rose bush left. Though attacked by mildrew the rose bush still has blossoms, as

Phoebe immediately notices—thereby beholding her own symbol. The character and mission of Holgrave is also manifested in the garden. He is the practical man who can cope with life and who will subsequently carry on the family line. He spades, hoes, and weeds the garden, and plants something practical like beans, the blossoms of which attract industrious bees and birds. Hepzibah and Clifford, the two weak descendants of the family, have no models in the prologue of the novel. But there is at least something corresponding to them in the garden, although the correspondence is ironical. This is the rooster and the hens, which are said to be an "immemorial heirloom in the Pyncheon family." [62] Their progenitors were supposed to have been as large as turkeys, but now the poor decadent chickens are reduced to the size of pigeons, and it is only seldom that they produce one of their tiny eggs. Hawthorne alludes almost too much to their ironic parallel to the Pyncheon brother and sister:

> The distinguishing mark of the hens was a crest of lamentably scanty growth, in these latter days, but so oddly and wickedly analogous to Hepzibah's turban, that Phoebe—to the poignant distress of her conscience, but inevitably—was led to fancy a general resemblance betwixt these forlorn bipeds and her respectable relative.[63]

Maule's well is a special type of independent symbol. It occurs throughout the book and thus has the character of a *leit-motif*. I would characterize its peculiar nature by calling it a "speaking" symbol, because it is capable of saying different things in different situations. The well water is clear as long as the land is in Maule's possession. After the land has been annexed and as Colonel Pyncheon is excavating for his house, the water turns murky and unpalatable (only the degenerate Pyncheon chickens can drink it). The well has a magic attraction on Clifford. In it he sees strange faces and figures that alternately frighten and delight him:

> The truth was, however, that his fancy—reviving faster than his will and judgment, and always stronger than they—created shapes of loveliness that were symbolic of his native character, and now and then a stern and dreadful shape that typified his fate.[64]

Rather than being a usual symbol the well is an organ of divine providence, because at the end of the novel it casts up pictures of the future: "Maule's Well, all this time, though left in solitude, was throwing up a succession of kaleidoscopic pictures, in which a gifted eye might have seen foreshadowed the coming fortunes of Hepzibah and Clifford, and the descendant of the legendary wizard, and the village maiden, over whom he had thrown Love's web of sorcery." [65] Thus we have an ending that contains a new beginning: the well produces models of that which is to come.

Is *The House of the Seven Gables* a "Romance"? Surely only in a distant, transformed sense. The tale remains within the compass of the middle class, and it is characterized more by a certain homely charm and busyness rather than by a truly romantic range of emotions. If we look closely behind the veil of wonders with which Hawthorne sought to cover them, we find that the characters and actions are affixed to a strangely archaic framework.

The "romance" elements are a disguise for the original theological notions of predestination and cyclical recurrence, which are anchored by Hawthorne more in a moral principle than in divine omnipotence. Because Colonel Pyncheon does Matthew Maule a serious wrong out of base, selfish motives, Maule's curse continues to take its toll until the Pyncheon line vanishes into feebleness, and into the Maule family line. This morally founded predestination must be regarded as the serious core of Hawthorne's charming little work. One would scarcely say that the views of man and history sketched by Hawthorne are profound and significant, yet he is more earnest and strict than were most of his romance predecessors with the scheme of retribution that governs his narrative. Hawthorne's relation to romance was not a marriage of kindred souls from which his work would profit or become enriched. It was instead a marriage of convenience by which he made himself acceptable to his surroundings and his public. Certain limitations of his genius and his personality are revealed in the fact of his preferring a marriage of convenience that softens or conceals the harsh contours of his being and his dark inner convictions to letting his stern inner voice speak. Melville's inner demon bore him beyond such considerations.

The preface of *The Marble Faun* like that of *The House of the Seven Gables* is regarded as an important statement of Hawthorne's esthetic aims. It contains the famous passage intended to explain why the "Romance of Monte Beni" is set in Italy rather than in America:

> Italy, as the site of his Romance, was chiefly valuable to him [the author] as affording a sort of poetic or fairy precinct, where actualities would not be so terribly insisted upon as they are, and must needs be, in America. No author, without a trial, can conceive of the difficulty of writing a romance about a country where there is no shadow, no antiquity, no mystery, no picturesque and gloomy wrong, nor anything but a commonplace prosperity, in broad and simple daylight, as is happily the case with my dear native land. It will be very long, I trust, before romance-writers may find congenial and

easily handled themes, either in the annals of our stalwart republic, or in any characteristic and probable
events of our individual lives. Romance and poetry, ivy,
lichens, and wallflowers, need ruin to make them grow.[66]

But Hawthorne did not intend to portray Italian manners and character: "The author proposed to himself
merely to write a fanciful story, evolving a thoughtful
moral." One suspects that this preface too conceals at
least as much as it reveals. The first two pages are
addressed to the "gentle, kind, benevolent, indulgent and
most beloved and honored reader," whom Hawthorne
fears that he has lost in the seven or eight years ("so
many, at all events, that I cannot precisely remember the
epoch") since his last novel. Preambles like this were in
accord with the taste of the time. Moreover, it provided
Hawthorne the mask of the happy, amiable conversation-
alist, behind which he tried to conceal the Puritan sternness he constantly regarded as a liability.

What he announces as "merely a fanciful story" is in
truth the story of the Fall, the drama of mankind incur-
ring guilt. Again it is clad with romance embellishments,
with which Hawthorne thought he was conforming to the
taste of the times. But what he offered his readers differed
so much from their usual fare that in answer to their pro-
tests he added a "Conclusion" to the tale, in which he tried
to defend his bold hints about Donatello's faun-like ears:

> The idea of the modern Faun, for example, loses all the
> poetry and beauty which the Author fancied in it, and
> becomes nothing better than a grotesque absurdity, if
> we bring it into the actual light of day. He had hoped to
> mystify this anomalous creature between the Real and
> the Fantastic, in such a manner that the reader's sym-
> pathies might be excited to a certain pleasurable degree,

without impelling him to ask how Cuvier would have classified poor Donatello, or to insist upon being told, in so many words, whether he had furry ears or no.[67]

But the problem was not that his readers, who were accustomed to romance, insisted on seeing characters in "the actual light of day." They were disturbed because they sensed that this unreal, imaginary trait did not belong in the realm of romance. This character is again a romanticized descendant from the realm of theology.[68]

It is characteristic of Hawthorne the Puritan that the first and only novel to result from his European experience is a new and more specific treatment of the Fall: "the story of the fall of man! Is it not repeated in our romance of Monte Beni?" [69] In Europe Hawthorne came to realize that this theme was more complex than he had imagined before. America came into being with the Calvinist certainty of original sin and innate depravity, but Europe had possessed a pristine innocence and simplicity before they were destroyed by the Christian notions of the Fall and original sin. The legendary innocence of Adam before the Fall had actually occurred there. It was depicted plastically for his own eyes to see in the ancient works of art that Hawthorne met with in Italy. In uncertainty Hawthorne posed the question whether these ancient statues indicated the innocence of paradise or a naive and natural amorality. What happened to the innocent people of the ancient world, and how did they fall into universal human guilt?

These are the questions Hawthorne seeks to answer in *The Marble Faun*. It must be unusually difficult to present the fall of ancient man in a novel. How was the gap between the ancient heathen world and the modern age to be bridged? Hawthorne thought (or wanted it thought) that he used romance techniques to solve his problem. In fact, he gave the concept of the type a romantic disguise. He bridges the two millennia by giving his protagonist, Count Donatello of Monte Beni, the type of a faun of classical antiquity: "it was he whom they called Donatello," it says at his second appearance, "and whose wonderful resemblance to the Faun of Praxiteles forms the keyote of our narrative." [70] The type of the faun, which represents natural ingeniousness and innocent amorality, is at the same time connected with that of Adam before the Fall. Hawthorne identifies the still innocent Adam with pre-Christian man of classical antiquity and shows how he must become guilty in order to rise to greater maturity and humanity. [71]

Two factors create the type of the faun. The first is the astonishing resemblance of Donatello to the marble Faun of Praxiteles, which their visit to the Capitoline Museum reveals to his three friends, and which is pressed on them again and again:

> The portraiture is perfect in character, sentiment, and feature. If it were a picture, the resemblance might be half illusive and imaginery; but here, in this Pentelic marble, it is a substantial fact, and may be tested by absolute touch and measurement. Our friend Donatello is the very Faun of Praxiteles. [72]

The second is the way the type of the faun for Donatello is anchored in his family history, which makes this family history represent the history of mankind. The family of the Count of Monte Beni reaches back to the era of the Roman kings, even to the Golden Age, [73] and its progenitor was a faun:

> One story, or myth, that had mixed itself up with their mouldly genealogy interested the sculptor by its wild, and perhaps grotesque, yet not unfascinating peculiarity.

He caught at it the more eagerly, as it afforded a shadowy and whimsical semblance of explanation for the likeness which he, with Miriam and Hilda, had seen or fancied, between Donatello and the Faun of Praxiteles.

The Monte Beni family, as this legend averred, drew their origin from the Pelasgic race, who peopled Italy in times that may be called prehistoric. It was the same noble and poetic kindred who dwelt in Arcadia, and— whether they ever lived such a life or not—enriched the world with dreams, at least, and fables, lovely, if unsubstantial, of a Golden Age. In those delicious times, when deities and demigods appeared familiarly on earth, mingling with its inhabitants as friend with friend,— when nymphs, satyrs, and the whole train of classic faith or fable hardly took pains to hide themselves in the primeval woods,—at that auspicious period the lineage of Monte Beni had its rise. Its progenitor was a being not altogether human, yet partaking so largely of the gentlest human qualities, as to be neither awful nor shocking to the imagination. A sylvan creature, native among the woods, had loved a mortal maiden, and—perhaps by kindness, and the subtile courtesies which love might teach to his simplicity, or possibly by a ruder wooing—had won her to his haunts.[74]

In the course of centuries the wild blood of the faun became tamer by mingling with gentler human blood, yet it still gave the descendants a special vitality. In addition it lent them certain peculiar hereditary features such as the pointed, furry ears. But these only occurred now and then in certain specially favored descendants. Hawthorne makes much of these ears, which are the true emblem of the faun's nature. Donatello refuses to show his ears, and this itself makes one suspect they are faun-like. In the Monte Beni family history there are legends about connections to nymphs and to Bacchus. These legends are part of family history but any indication of faun's ears is rejected by them. "It might, however, be considered as typifying some such assemblage of qualities—in this case, chiefly remarkable for their simplicity and naturalness—as, when they reappear in successive generations, constitute what we call family character." [75] Shortly thereafter we are told that Donatello has all the peculiar hereditary traits of his family. He is "a genuine Monte Beni, of the original type." [76] This quotation, in which "type" also corresponds to modern usage in the sense of "the general character or form common to a number of individuals" (see above, p. 2 f.), shows the transformation from the theological to the modern usage, which is also illustrated clearly in the quotation previous to it. If the prophetic model of the progenitor is fulfilled again and again in succeeding generations, the result is a homogenous group of the same type of person.

The fusion of romance elements with typological ideas in the Monte Beni genealogy is easily recognized. How this mode of presentation differs from allegory is also obvious. It is not the personification of ideas, but the representation of hypothetically historical events in the concrete. What the notion of the type provides is the capability of bridging great intervals of time to link up a distant era with the present. Romance attempts something similar, but it uses the past for its picturesque effects rather than for its intellectual content. Where Hawthorne agrees with romance is in avoiding "actualities," since he too seeks a world "where actualities would not be so terribly insisted upon." But he does not avoid reality as romance does for escapist reasons: he avoids it because it does not provide sufficient opportunities of expressing meaning. "The idea of the modern Faun, for example," says the Conclusion, "loses all the poetry and beauty . . . , if we bring it into the actual light of day." "The actual world" is of no use for Hawthorne—though he occasionally regrets this, as in the

"Custom House Preface." The fictional world he creates could be called an emblematic one, since it is composed of images with determinate meanings, *i.e.*, persons, things, and situations indicating definite meanings. In his description of Miriam's studio Hawthorne hints at this conception of a world of types and models that radiates meaning, in opposition to the actual world: "One of those delightful spots that hardly seem to belong to the actual world, but rather to be the outward type of a poet's haunted imagination, where there are glimpses, sketches, and half-developed hints of beings and objects grander and more beautiful than we can anywhere find in reality." [77]

This statement supplements the one quoted above from "The Earth's Holocaust": "The heart, the heart,—there was the little yet boundless sphere wherein existed the original wrong of which the crime and misery of this outward world were merely types." Both touch—if only peripherally—the basic conception of Hawthorne's standpoint and his fiction, which is never stated outright. This is the belief that an analogy obtains between the outer and the inner worlds so that the things and events of the outer world can be emblems or types of those of the inner. "The outward world," or "the actual world," as Hawthorne, with a trace of annoyance, prefers to call it, fulfills this requirement very imperfectly. Only certain aspects of reality express the hidden impulses of the heart. Among these aspects we may count "crimes and miseries," and this explains their fascination for the writer. Since the actual world seldom provides what "a poet's haunted imagination" wants from it, the poet must transform it according to his own principles. This is where romance provides a welcome help: it yields a collection of conventions according to which one can disregard or transform reality with impunity. Hawthorne transforms it to correspond to his notion of the inner world of morality, so that it can be the "type" of this inner world. "External things are intended to be images of things spiritual, moral, divine," said Jonathan Edwards, and he used the types of the Bible to explain the world of nature. Hawthorne sees that this world is also a product of the human will; thus, he regards its phenomena as types and emblems of the human heart and will.

Like all Hawthorne's novels *The Marble Faun* has a quite restricted number of characters. There is one European couple: Donatello and Miriam; and one American: Hilda and Kenyon. There is also the mysterious, frightful and nearly silent character: the monk, Miriam's model. Of the five, Kenyon is the most natural and the closest to the usual novel character. Although he is not consistently a center of consciousness as James defines it, he is the representative of the narrator for long stretches of the novel. He accompanies the action and comments on it without furthering it by his own activity. In other words, he stands mostly outside the romance element of the book, to which the other four belong, each in his own way.

Donatello's partner is Miriam, who also represents an aspect of the European version of the Fall, or rather Hawthorne's American conception of it. Innocent yet stained with guilt, she embodies the fusion of the highly cultivated aristocracy with guilt. Personally she is guiltless, but there is a tinge of infamy about her. The Europe of classical antiquity manifests itself anew in Donatello; what manifests itself in Miriam is the Renaissance. She is beautiful, fascinating, and creative, yet overshadowed by unscrupulous crimes of a decadent, unnatural kind. Accordingly, she is equated by analogy with a Renaissance personality, the unfortunate, guiltless yet guilty Beatrice Cenci, who together with her brother murdered the father who had violated her. With a look that urges Donatello on to murder, Miriam partakes of the guilt in the death of her persecutor. In addition she has some mysterious connection with the Cencis or their heirs, because she has Hilda take the package given her for safe-keeping to the Cenci palace. Hawthorne uses the portrait of Beatrice by Guido Reni, who was so highly regarded in America at the middle of the nineteenth century, in order to fit Miriam-Beatrice into his "romance." Hilda, the Puritan, innocent American girl, who is Miriam's friend, is so fascinated by this portrait that she is able to make a copy of it at her home after intense gazing has impressed it on her memory. She was not permitted to copy the portrait outright. In the course of the narrative Guido Reni's portrait and Hilda's copy again and again yield interpretations of Miriam's character and fate.

Here the type—antitype or prefiguration—fulfillment relation is linked with the magic connection Hawthorne always saw between a person and his portrait. Rather than a mere likeness Hawthorne sees in a portrait a mysterious representative that can even manifest a volition or an emotion in some critical situation.[78] The Puritan, Colonel Pyncheon, lived on in the house of the seven gables in the form of his portrait that stared so gloomily. When Matthew Maule's son offers to get the lost deeds to the large tract of land for the Colonel's grandson if he got the house of the seven gables in return we learn that:

> All through the foregoing conversation between Mr. Pyncheon and the carpenter, the portrait had been frowning, clenching its fist, and giving many such proofs of excessive discomposure, but without attracting the notice of either of the two colloquists. And finally, at Matthew Maule's audacious suggestion of a transfer of the seven-gabled structure, the ghostly por-

trait is averred to have lost all patience, and to have shown itself on the point of descending bodily from its frame.[79]

Edward Randolph's portrait too is supposed to have interfered in the decisions of a later era.[80] The painter is said to have "foreshadowed" future destinies with his portrait; thus the portrait that predetermines events assumes one of the functions of the type here too.

"There were many stories about Miriam's origin and previous life, some of which had a very probable air, while others were evidently wild and romantic fables" (p. 37 f.). Both the various conjectures given us and the vague, summary treatment of Miriam's descent and earlier life show how little intrinsic importance Hawthorne ascribed to romance elements, which in the present case are closer to being Gothic elements. What Hawthorne does consider important in the Beatrice-Miriam analogy is the idea of the reincarnation of the Renaissance figure, which serves to link that era up with the present. The gloomy, Gothic details of Miriam's past with all their potential interest are treated so negligently that the reader does not even find out what the horrible event in her past actually was. We are only told that a "mysterious and terrible event" some years ago made her name known to the world. Nor are we told whether or not the evil monk who persecutes her is in fact her rejected fiancé of old: he is simply "the evil fate that had haunted her through life." [81]

Her persecutor assumes the form of the "evil monk," a cliché borrowed from the Gothic novel, where it was obviously used, especially in Protestant countries, to give vent to anti-Catholic sentiment. Several models are provided for this mysterious persecutor, all of whom represent antichristian evil. When the monk appears in the catacombs of St. Calixtus the guide takes him for the ghost of Memmius, a persecutor of Christians condemned to haunt the catacombs forever:

> This man, or demon, or man-demon, was a spy during the persecutions of the early Christians, probably under the Emperor Diocletian, and penetrated into the catacomb of St. Calixtus, with the malignant purpose of tracing out the hiding-places of the refugees. But, while he stole craftily through those dark corridors, he chanced to come upon a little chapel, where tapers were burning before an altar and a crucifix, and a priest was in the performance of his sacred office. By divine indulgence, there was a single moment's grace allowed to Memmius, during which, had he been capable of Christian faith and love, he might have knelt before the cross, and received the holy light into his soul, and so have been blest forever. But he resisted the sacred impulse. As soon, therefore, as that one moment had glided by, the light of the consecrated tapers, which represent all truth, bewildered the wretched man with everlasting error, and the blessed cross itself was stamped as a seal upon his heart, so that it should never open to receive conviction.[82]

Of course this fable of the man condemned to eternal damnation for letting his moment of grace slip by does run counter to modern sentiment, but Hawthorne seems to find no fault with the Calvinist conception of depraved man that lies behind it. In this version of the Fall Hawthorne makes him a deputy of Satan. The remarkable thing is that this character too, by virtue of its type, Memmius, is extended back in time like Donatello to ancient paganism. The tragedy of Memmius lies in his being unable to accept the grace of redemption through Christ. This makes him evil, and then his evil nature forces him to persecute Christianity. There is a further identification in the same direction. Miriam's persecutor has a striking similarity to an evil demon in a drawing attributed to Guido Reni, who is being trampled under the feet of the archangel Michael. This new parallel once more fixes the antichristian nature of the monk, because the demon is the absolute embodiment of sin and enmity toward Christianity.

The monk along with his several transformations is probably the weakest role in Hawthorne's drama of the Fall. Hawthorne had moved beyond Calvinist dogma in his conception of sin. He did conceive of sin as a grave human failing, but he also regarded it as a necessary condition of becoming mature and human. However, his conception of evil, as it is embodied in the monk, is shallower than the usual Puritan one. It is in fact the latter conception in disguise, watered down with certain legendary features and several picturesque Gothic effects. This figure embellished with Gothic features stands in no relation whatever to the idea brought forward by Miriam and Kenyon at the end of the novel, namely, that sin is "a blessing in . . . strange disguise." Yet therein lies the whole point of the story:

> Was that very sin,—into which Adam precipitated himself and all his race,—was it the destined means by which, over a long pathway of toil and sorrow, we are to attain a higher, brighter, and profounder happiness, than our lost birthright gave? Will not this idea account for the permitted existence of sin, as no other theory can? [83]

But the monk represents sin as inexplicable enmity toward God, as evil by nature and by principle, and as meaningless evil. This is the evil that pursues man to bring on his downfall just as Satan in the form of the serpent brought on the Fall of Adam and Eve. The weakness of this novel, which is interesting in many respects, lies in the discrepancy between these two conceptions of sin.

The two Americans, Kenyon and Hilda, stand apart from the European drama of sin and are really only spectators, even though they are interested in the fate of Donatello and Miriam as friends. Hilda does intervene in the action to the extent that when Miriam seeks solace for the guilt she has incurred, Hilda rejects her for fear of losing her own innocence.

Hilda embodies innocence, and she might almost be called an allegorical figure, were it not for certain other specific and characteristic features. She is a New England girl, often called "the daughter of the Puritans," and she is also a painter, or to be more precise, a copyist. She has definite historical and personal qualities in addition to the abstract ones, yet she is near allegory. She might be called an emblematic character. She is a person with qualities specified historically and geographically, yet she also stands for an idea, innocence.[84]

The author's characterization of Hilda is emblematic. For her "coat of arms" she is given the dove, the biblical image of purity and innocence. Doves inhabit her tower and the shrine with the eternal flame at the image of the Virgin Mary. The connection of the daughter of the Puritans with the Catholic Virgin Mary—whose cult the Puritans of course detested as popish, pagan, and "idolatrous" —is Hawthorne's cautious way of using irony to give the New Englanders and Puritans a piece of his mind. He does this obviously not only to emphasize Hilda's purity but also to convey that Hilda's innocence was, like Mary's, physical too, and that her life had its limitations, since its essence consisted in her being a virgin. The pale, ideal type of New England girl that had been formed by Hawthorne's time actually had more in common with Mariolatry than respectable New Englanders, who detested it as "idolatry," ever suspected. Hilda's subsequent quest for refuge in St. Peter's and her longing to confess serve to confirm this. But Hawthorne does not state this heretical view outright. He establishes an unspecified connection between Hilda and Mary without enlarging upon it.

On the other hand Hawthorne makes it almost too obvious that the doves are symbols of Hilda's character. She is not only "like a dove" but even "Hilda, the dove," and her dwelling in the tower is called a "dove cote." Once it is even said that she flies down from her dovecote. The doves are another "speaking symbol." Like Maule's well in *The House of the Seven Gables* they signal special events and changes. When Kenyon seeks Hilda in vain in her den in the tower, he finds the doves fluttering about nervously. Two of them, Hilda's favorite pair, try to get him to help by flying down to him as if to alight on his shoulder. When Hilda does not return after several days, the doves desert the tower: "only a single dove remained, and brooded drearily beneath the shrine. The flock, that had departed, were like the many hopes that had vanished from Kenyon's heart; the one that still lingered, and looked so wretched,—was it a Hope, or already a Despair?" [85]

It is not the purpose of this study to examine the total significance of Hawthorne's entire work. What we are investigating is whether and how Hawthorne's literary techniques and imagery are connected with the Puritan, Calvinist culture of New England, in the late phase of which he grew up. We have discovered that an influence was exercised on Hawthorne by the category of typical connection as modified from the type and the parallel by the erudite Cotton Mather, whom Hawthorne read so assiduously. In addition to Hawthorne's notion of the symbol the category of typical connection also influenced his view of history and man's role in it, which thus had to be taken into account in our investigation.

Though fruitful for the development of symbolism this conception was intellectually obsolescent in the nineteenth century. However, it must be taken into consideration when discussing the artistic failure of Hawthorne's final years. The reasons given for this have been declining health and the national disaster, the Civil War. Waggoner thinks that the growing discrepancy between Hawthorne's own gloomy vision and the era's optimistic and materialistic belief in progress made him feel ever more insecure.[86] But there was an even more specific discrepancy between Hawthorne's plan to critically illuminate the history of the Puritans and make it useful for the present and future, and his adherence to their outdated typological and cyclical view of history. The only change made by Hawthorne was to replace religious factors by moral ones as the moving principles of history. This limitation leads to a stagnation mirrored in the final works, upon which Hawthorne labored in vain.

The posthumous novel fragments, "The Ancestral Footstep," "Dr. Grimshawe's Secret," "Septimius Felton," and "The Dolliver Romance," are governed by two signs Hawthorne experiments with in various combinations: the elixir of life and the bloody footprint. These two signs obviously represent an important interest of his final years. Both contain what is in the modern sense an antihistorical tendency; their meanings make them bridge time and obliterate it. The elixir of life is *eo ipso* inimical to time and everything transitory. The sign of the bloody footprint impressed on the threshold of the English ancestral manor was the theme that had intrigued Hawthorne ever since his stay in England. It was the theme of America and England, depicted in the fate of an American seeking his

lost English inheritance, which his ancestor had been un-
justly forced to flee.

Whereas the miraculous, rejuvenating drink, the elixir
of life, had already appeared in "Dr. Heidegger's Experiment" and "A Virtuoso's Collection," Hawthorne first became acquainted with the petrified bloody footprint in
England in 1855. A Mrs. Ainsworth told him the legend
that came with the manor, Smithell's Hall, she had recently purchased, whereupon Hawthorne noted in his
diary:

> The tradition is that a certain martyr, in Bloody Mary's
> time, being examined before the then occupant of the
> Hall, and committed to prison, stamped his foot in ear-
> nest protest against the injustice with which he was
> treated. Blood issued from his foot, which slid along the
> stone pavement of the hall, leaving a long footmark
> printed in blood; and there it has remained ever since, in
> spite of the scrubbings of all after generations.[87]

Thus Hawthorne found this sign rather than invented it,
and it impressed him so much that he wanted to make it
into the governing symbol of a novel. In his mind the
martyr from the time of Bloody Mary was changed into an
American.

Hawthorne began the fragment "The Ancestral Footstep" in Rome in 1858 and worked on it until the Faun of
Praxiteles, which he saw in the Villa Borghese, diverted
his interest to another project, *The Marble Faun*.[88] Two
years later, after *The Marble Faun* had been published, he
again started to work on the theme that resulted in the
posthumous "Dr. Grimshawe's Secret." It is clear from
these elaborations of the original sketch that the footprint
was only a form or vehicle, without a specific content.
Hawthorne was obviously fascinated by this image of

something as perishable as a footprint immortalized in stone. He made it into an emblem that was intended to express Europe's injustice to its American sons. But Hawthorne was unable to decide exactly what injustice had been perpetrated on the emigrant. Here his artist's imagination failed him or, if you please, his historical acumen. In the fragment called "G" he suggested several possibilities, but none of them satisfied him.[89] The ancestral footstep remains a hollow impression that perpetuates the trace of an injustice without being able to indicate what injustice it was.

The ancestral-footstep theme is that of an American in quest of his origin. It is a historical theme that reaches back beyond the New England past, a past that yielded subject matter for many of Hawthorne's best narratives. But we recall that in them he treats the past as stationary or, from an esthetic standpoint, in a tableau technique. He can also treat it as a cycle, for instance in *The House of the Seven Gables*, where "typical" characters and constellations recur. In *The Marble Faun* he bridged a two thousand-year gap in time with the concept of the timeless type, which contained its ration of eternity. But confronted with the problem of development, which the English-American theme required in one form or another, Hawthorne capitulated. Even an emblem as suitable for romance treatment as the petrified footprint could not help him here.[90] He always regarded history in a modified religious sense as a moral institution; never in the modern way as a play of forces, ideas, and powers. In the end he was left with the bloody impress of a mysterious wrong, the meaning of which he could not grasp. The failure of his final years shows that Hawthorne never really belonged to his own era intellectually. His greatness lay in rising above passing time; his tragedy, in having worked with a worn out system of thought that no longer fit in with nineteenth century ideas.

The conviction that the world functions according to a moral principle manifesting itself in signs and emblems was the unassailable foundation of his thought. Yet he had the vaguest and most dubious notions of how the principle became established and exerted its power. Thus it ultimately rested on Puritan convictions that had ceased to convince him. Here it becomes evident that the ultimate basis of faith was no longer compatible with reason. Thus, with a bad conscience, Hawthorne gives scientific explanations for the supernatural phenomena of the moral cosmic order, always providing an alternative and leaving the decision up to the reader.

Chapter XII of *The Scarlet Letter,* "The Minister's Vigil," tells us how Dimmesdale is driven one night to the square where Hester had to atone for her infamy. Suddenly a light appears in the sky, making it as bright as noon, "but also with the awfulness that is always imparted to familiar objects by an unaccustomed light."

> It was doubtless caused by one of those meteors, which the night-watcher may so often observe, burning out to waste, in the vacant regions of the atmosphere. So powerful was its radiance, that it thoroughly illuminated the dense medium of cloud betwixt the sky and earth.[91]

The Puritans had always regarded the appearance of a meteor as the harbinger of some special event, since they regarded themselves as being under the special protection and supervision of the heavens: "It was, indeed, a majestic idea, that the destiny of nations should be revealed, in these awful hieroglyphics, on the cope of heaven." But at times someone would read a sign into an event afterwards and then embellish on it. This argument is now used to cast doubt on the phenomenon witnessed by Dimmesdale, who is nearly deranged by the torment of his conscience:

> We impute it, therefore, solely to the disease in his own eye and heart, that the minister, looking upward to the zenith, beheld there the appearance of an immense letter—the letter A,—marked out in lines of dull red light. Not but the meteor may have shown itself at that point, burning duskily through a veil of cloud; but with no such shape as his guilty imagination gave it; or, at least, with so little definiteness, that another's guilt might have seen another symbol in it.[92]

The sign of the heavens becomes a symbol that can mean something different to each individual. The direction of the development in American intellectual history could scarcely be displayed more clearly.

The contemporary reader who believed in science was thus assured that the miracle was partly a natural phenomenon and partly the delusion of a mind burdened with guilt. This substitutes a psychological explanation for a religious one. But two pages later we learn that this explanation cannot be correct. There were others who also saw the huge red "A," and on the next morning the sexton asks Dimmesdale:

> But did your reverence hear of the portent that was seen last night?—a great red letter in the sky,—the letter A, which we interpret to stand for Angel. For, as our good Governor Winthrop was made an angel this past night, it was doubtless held fit that there should be some notice thereof! [93]

Thus belief in the divine sign is admitted through the back door.

The basic question in Hawthorne's case seems to be the following: does he believe that his moral world principle is active in extra-human concrete phenomena, altering their laws of causality and probability, or is he satisfied with limiting its efficacy to the human mind, where he has it speak through symbols? The first alternative is near Calvinism and is carried on in the semi-miraculous world of the romance. The second has affinity with philosophical idealism and leads to poetic symbolism. Hawthorne seems to me to waver between the two, toying with both without making a decision. He offers both without taking either seriously. He could not bring himself to be satisfied with the second, and in view of his skeptical contemporaries he did not dare opt for the first, which probably did not fully correspond to his convictions.

His balancing act on this seesaw of his time is what modern critics call "the device of multiple choice" or "the formula of alternative possibilities." Did Young Goodman Brown really take part in a witches' meeting, or "Had Goodman Brown fallen asleep in the forest and only dreamed a wild dream of a witch meeting?" Was there a scarlet "A" on the breast of the dying Dimmesdale? Several theories (all supernatural) are offered for how it came to be there. He is said to have applied it himself by some horrible self-torture, or Chillingworth is said to have created it with magic and poisons. Some believe

> that the awful symbol was the effect of the ever-active tooth of remorse, gnawing from the inmost heart outwardly, and at last manifesting Heaven's dreadful judgment by the visible presence of the letter.[94]

But its existence is also denied flatly:

> It is singular, nevertheless, that certain persons, who were spectators of the whole scene, and professed never

once to have removed their eyes from the Reverend Mr. Dimmesdale, denied that there was any mark whatever on his breast, more than on a new-born infant's.[95]

"Out of such variety of symbolical reference, Hawthorne developed one of his most fertile resources, the device of multiple choice," F. O. Matthiessen said of this section of *The Scarlet Letter*, and since then it has been fashionable to praise this technique.[96] But Yvor Winters is skeptical and expresses himself more sharply when he calls it "the formula of alternative possibilities." [97] Richard H. Fogle sees it not only as a technique but as "a pervasive quality of mind." "It can be an evasion, and it is sometimes no more than a mannerism. But as a whole it embodies Hawthorne's deepest insights." [98]

I cannot follow Matthiessen's positive evaluation. Hawthorne's use of "multiple choice" reveals an inconsistency in style. It occurs wherever direct allegory breaks through a primarily symbolic-emblematic, *i.e.*, a natural, realistic context, at the expense of probability. Hawthorne asserts that the wild animals of the forest have manifested their kinship to Pearl, the wild, unruly child of sin. Then he takes back the assertion in the very same sentence: "A wolf, it is said,—but here the tale has surely lapsed into the improbable,—came up, and smelt of Pearl's robe, and offered his savage head to be patted by her hand." A deeper meaning is expressed by a miraculous event which is in turn immediately disavowed.

This "multiple choice" principle has some of the two-faced character of the Gothic romance, which also offers subsequent scientific explanations of its supernatural events. Critics do Hawthorne an injustice when they take such a superficial formula as evidence of his profundity. The embodiment of his insights into the ambiguities of life lies on a deeper, less readily accessible plane. "The formula of alternative possibilities" shows that Hawthorne never wholly succeeded in uniting the two main constituents of his mind, the Puritan and nineteenth-century ones. Despite his critical distance toward the New England past he had more affinity with the form of life and mentality of the Puritans than with those of his own era. Whereas Emerson and the Transcendentalists broke with Calvinism and made its forms of thought serve their new view of the world and nature, Hawthorne put these forms of thought to use in a more conservative manner. He too made "type," "emblem," and the concept of the divine "sign" suitable for literary use, but in his case they are put in service of a view of life still governed by the ancient drama of the Fall.

8 HERMAN MELVILLE

1. "THE LEXICON OF HOLY WRIT"

The heroes of Melville's novels—the sailor Tom in *Typee* and *Omoo*, Redburn, White Jacket, Ishmael, Pierre, Billy Budd, and even Israel Potter, who begins his wandering as a seaman on a whaler—are all created out of Melville's own experience, and are even more or less disguised projections of his own self. Yet rather than being individualities in the true sense of the word, they are something quite unusual: individual experience presented in the form of types. They are not developed as individual persons with specific pasts and differentiated talents and reactions. With the possible exception of Pierre, they are instead towering, solitary characters, drawn in simple contours, without pasts and without ties. Their character and their behavior can be deduced from a single foundation, albeit a complex one. The European novel of the era, *e.g.* that of

Balzac and Stendhal, had countless ways and varieties of presenting its characters in conjunction with their past, environment, and with fate. On the other hand, in Melville the character is identical with his fate. In some cases, such as Ishmael and White Jacket, the name even determines the fate. But in every case this fate rolls on inexorably and unchangeably according to true predestination. Melville's characters have no development, nor do they have any chance of altering the course of events to their advantage. They have been assigned a role, and this role they must play out. Even Ahab, who is on one side a modern, romantic character, knows that he must see his assigned role through to the end. His tragedy is that he knows this, and that his role is an evil, self-destructive one. If this is true of the principal characters, the minor ones are often purely "emblematic." This holds for Pip, Jackson (*Redburn*), Delly (*Pierre*), and for the various figures of the *Confidence Man*, each of whom expresses but a single quality or characteristic act in a scene that exhausts its significance.

American literary criticism has devoted much attention to the individualistic differentiation of character and situation in the European novel compared with the relative simplicity of the same in the American. From the time of Henry James's "negative catalogue," [1] the simplicity of social texture in America, the lack of cultural institutions, and the democratic equality of its citizens have been cited as responsible for this. Lionel Trilling's definition of "manners" as "a culture's hum and buzz of implication" is only a modernized version of the old argument, extended to human conduct as a whole.[2] But this certain simplicity of American literature encountered in Melville's characters or in the world depicted by Hawthorne does not in fact mirror a true meagerness of conditions. It results instead from the adoption of a special viewpoint toward life and people, and is thus more properly a phenomenon of intellectual history rather than of sociology. The American life of the time was filled with vitality, contrasts, and problems in its manifold aspects, but for the most part these were not regarded as worthy of literature. This is not only because they were thought to lack respectability and gentility, but because they were not considered "significant." Melville made new aspects of reality, such as the world of the whaler, worthy of literature by discovering and presenting their "significances," rather than by making them interesting in themselves as *tranche de vie* in the manner of later realists.

Melville like Hawthorne comes from the Calvinist tradition. Though he struggled passionately and bitterly all his life with the dogmas of the Calvinist faith, he was nonetheless decisively influenced by it. *Moby Dick* is an embittered debate over predestination and free will, conveyed in the rebellion of the "satanic" hero, Ahab.[3] Pierre too struggles with the unsolvable conflict of "Fixed Fate" and "Free Will." This is the debate of a man who is rebelling against Calvinism, yet who still sees the world through the eyes of a Calvinist. If this were not true the problem of predestination would not have been so significant for him.

Melville was raised in a religious home, educated in an especially pious school, and as a youth he listened to numerous sermons, mainly in the Calvinist Dutch Reformed Church. He read a great amount of religious literature: Bible commentaries, sermons, the great dogmaticians from Augustine to Calvin, and the great Christian poets from Dante to Milton.[4] All these poets and thinkers have left distinct traces in Melville's work. The Bible, above all the Old Testament, and especially Genesis, Kings, Job, Psalms, and Proverbs, pervades his entire creative work to the extent of giving it its structure. This makes it a unique example of a quasi-theological opus among nineteenth-century novels, which are generally of a secular nature. Biblical characters are not stylistic *décor*, but witnesses and participants in a dispute—so intense as only a Puritan could conduct—between a brooding, doubting Melville, and God: a dispute over the justification of human predetermination. As a man of his time and a rebellious prisoner of its taste, Melville carried out this dispute in the form of the "romance." [5] Melville's literary fate is expressed in this strange and forced connection of two so heterogenous elements. The radical change from religious to secular epochs, which in America took place at a pace so accelerated as to compress centuries of European development into the maturing process of a single individual, is evident in Melville's work. It is as if Milton had reached maturity in the nineteenth century and had chosen the "romance" vehicle of Walter Scott for the great theme of *Paradise Lost*.

Critics have recognized that Melville took his themes and subjects from the Bible and Christian literature generally.[6] Up to now, however, the extent to which his views of mankind, fate, and history embody theological traits and primarily typological ones has not been noticed. Not only does he seek "a certain significance" in everything; he also regards the world and even the present as recurrences of biblical models. He uses typological ideas in many ways, changes and develops them, and experiments with that dimension of the type-concept that refers to the future. For instance, he ascribes a "singularly indicatory" significance to the encounter of the American ship *Bon Homme Richard* with the English *Serapis* in the Revolutionary War, and he says, "it may involve at once a type, a parallel and a prophecy." It was the first naval battle between America and England, and Melville regarded the American victory as a prefiguration of things to come: "Sharing the same blood with England, and yet her proved foe in two wars—not wholly inclined at bottom to forget an old grudge—intrepid, unprincipled, reckless, predatory, with boundless ambition, civilised in externals but a savage at heart, America is, or may yet be, the Paul Jones of Nations." [7]

In one place the anonymous narrator of *Billy Budd*— without doubt Melville himself—steps out of the story and tells us something about himself. He is trying to fathom the mystery of Claggart's character, and he states that the normal standards do not apply.[8] He recalls an old scholar with whom he once discussed cases of mysterious people. His old friend told him that to know the world and to understand human nature were two different things, and that the ancient Hebrew prophets threw more light on the mysterious corners of the soul than did others whose knowledge covered only the world. "At the time my inexperience was such," the narrator continues, "that I did not quite see the drift of all this. It may be that I see it now. And, indeed, if that lexicon which is based on Holy Writ were any longer popular, one might with less difficulty define and denominate certain phenomenal men." [9] Unfortunately, other models had to be sought today, but in these too he discovered (not without irony) a Calvinist core: "In a list of definitions included in the authentic translation of Plato, a list attributed to him, occurs this: 'Natural Depravity: a depravity according to nature.'" A definition, which though savoring of Calvinism, by no means involves Calvin's dogma as to total mankind. Evidently its intent makes it applicable but to individuals." [10]

This *Lexicon of Holy Writ* is a literary paraphrase for typology, which is in turn the book of models used by God in forming his creatures.[11] As we will soon show, Melville leafed through this lexicon frequently. He characterized and explained his figures by assigning them models from it. The use of this lexicon of Calvinist interpretations of man signifies that men can be classified and grouped under different models. But the models themselves may well be enigmatical at their very core, and here Melville's insight is romantic and modern. This interpretation differs from the one prevalent in Europe at the same time, which in fact brought about the realistic European novel. That interpretation states that the individual is something unique and incomparable, something made inimitable by particular talents and the special constellation of his historical situation. Melville regards "phenomenal men"— exceptional men, in so far as they can be comprehended —as new fulfillments of prefigurations and types, not in mere imitation but in various transformations and combinations. The modern reader who regards this typological conception as hopelessly obsolete would do well to remember that a similar conception is gaining ground today, when people and literary characters are taken as repetitions of mythical originals, or archetypes. Here our own era has a hidden resemblance to Melville that may well have been a factor in his rediscovery.[12]

Like Cotton Mather, Melville draws his parallels not only from the Bible but from legend and history, and especially from the classical antiquity that has been canonized since the Renaissance. The process is not so simple that one type suffices to determine the essence of a character. For Billy Budd, Melville employs primarily three models as *leitmotifs* to depict his hero: "young Adam before the Fall," Christ, and the folk-lore character of the "Handsome Sailor." [13] He uses a remarkable, synthetic creative technique, wherein layers are projected one over the other to yield a three-dimensional effect. Billy Budd's appearance and manner are those of the "Handsome Sailor"; his natural innocence corresponds to Adam before the Fall; and his fate, being sacrificed, is related to Christ's death.

In addition to being a means of creating character, the

typological correspondence also enhances it. By means of it Melville's plain, democratic heroes become members in a brotherhood of the great figures of history. This involves more than only fixing the character type. Just as in Mather's sermons and in the Calvinist interpretation of reality, models are used to fix a person in a certain situation or frame of mind, in order to indicate that events and fateful coincidences are also related to eternal models. Thus for Captain Vere's tragic dilemma, being forced to sacrifice Billy Budd for sake of a higher principle, the parallel to Abraham is called up:

> He was old enough to have been Billy's father. The austere devotee of military duty letting himself melt back into what remains primeval in our formalized humanity may in the end have caught Billy to his heart even as Abraham may have caught young Isaac on the brink of resolutely offering him up in obedience to the exacting behest. But there is no telling the sacrament, seldom if in any case revealed to the gadding world wherever under circumstances at all akin to those here attempted to be set forth two of great Nature's nobler order embrace.[14]

The most difficult case is Claggart, who is—like Moby Dick—proof of the power of an incomprehensible evil in the world. The way Melville describes this pale intellectual with the curly black hair calls to mind Milton's Satan[15] and the ill-fated, nefarious heroes of Romanticism.[16] There is an intimation of a sort of love-hate relationship toward the innocent Billy Budd he so sorely provokes.[17] When Melville says that Claggart is best defined in the biblical lexicon, he must be thinking of Lucifer, because he counts him among the "mysteries of iniquity": ". . . Claggart, in whom was the mania of an evil nature, not engendered by vicious training or corrupting books or licentious living, but born with him and innate, in short 'a depravity according to nature'." [18] Thus his temptation of Billy is associated with Satan's temptation of Christ, and Billy's mortal blow symbolizes (as in the mystery plays) Christ's vanquishing of Satan. In its deepest abstract core, *Billy Budd* is a parable of the inexplicable enmity of evil toward good, embodied in Melville's favorite milieu, the world of the ship, and presented in a narrative the tragical culmination of which was based on famous incidents in the American Navy. The metaphysical and exemplary levels are connected by the types of Christ, Adam, and Satan, as well as by other models and parallels, with the level of fate and the figure of Billy Budd into a complex and richly significant whole.

Melville even views historical persons typologically. In *Israel Potter* he sketches a colorful and highly amusing portrait of Benjamin Franklin. Melville's pen has hardly given us its equal in extravagance and loving attention to individual characteristics. But Franklin too is assigned his place in the biblical book of models. He is said to have something of "primeval orientalness" in him:

> Neither is there wanting something like his scriptural parallel. The history of the patriarch Jacob is interesting not less from the unselfish devotion which we are bound to ascribe to him, than from the deep worldly wisdom and polished Italian tact, gleaming under an air of Arcadian unaffectedness. The diplomatist and the shepherd are blended; a union not without warrant; the apostolic serpent and dove.[19]

Finally, another historical type is added: "A tanned Machiavelli in tents," and a further parallel, to Hobbes, who is also compared to Jacob.

Israel Potter, also a historical figure, is much less complex. In his case it is his fate that constitutes his nature, and his name characterizes both the fate and the nature. Thus Melville can say: ". . . [he was] prophetically styled Israel by the good Puritans, his parents, since, for more than forty years, poor Potter wandered in the wild wilderness of the world's extremest hardships and ills." [20] Israel, the soldier of God, is moreover a type of which the Puritans liked to regard themselves as the fulfillment. In *White Jacket* Melville applies this conception to his ideal of a democratic America:

> Escaped from the house of bondage, Israel of old did not follow after the ways of the Egyptians. To her was given an express dispensation; to her were given new things under the sun. And we Americans are the peculiar, chosen pople—the Israel of our time; we bear the ark of the liberties of the world. [21]

Thus Israel Potter's struggles for his country's liberty represent the American struggle for liberty, and Potter has the dedication of a man called to do battle for the Lord. He is entirely beyond individual psychological traits. What characterizes him are such general qualities as courage, perseverence, love of liberty, and a fearlessness that lands him in captivity and exile again and again, just like the Israelites. The stages of his journey, as given in the chapter headings, carry forth this parallel: "Israel in the Lion's Den," "Samson among the Philistines" and "Israel in Egypt." His precarious existence in London up to his return to America is compared with the forty years spent by the children of Israel in the wilderness:

> For the most part, what befell Israel during his forty years' wanderings in the London deserts, surpassed the forty years in the natural wilderness of the outcast Hebrews under Moses. [22]

The type of forty years in the wilderness—it is well known
that the number forty has a special significance in the
Bible—turns up again in *Moby Dick*. Not long before his
downfall, Ahab laments that he has been at sea forty
years: "Forty years of continual whaling! forty years of
privation, and peril, and storm-time! forty years on the
pitiless sea! for forty years has Ahab forsaken the peaceful
land, for forty years to make war on the horrors of the
deep!" [23]

The hero of the Revolutionary War, Ethan Allen, is
characterized quite summarily, one might say in a typological telegraphic style. The fugitive Israel Potter encounters him as a picturesque prisoner in England. Instead of a lengthy description, Melville says simply:
"Allen seems to have been a curious combination of a Hercules, a Joe Miller, a Bayard, and a Tom Hyer; had a
person like the Belgian giants; mountain music in him
like a Swiss; a heart plump as Coeur de Lion's." [24] This
announces a technique that Melville makes considerable
use of, especially in *Moby Dick*: to link one analogy with
another in order to achieve, either partially concealed or
at times quite open and straightforward, an ironic or a
humorous effect. Thus he links Hercules with Joe Miller
and Tom Hyer, or again he forms a trio of Perseus, St.
George, and a man named Coffin from Nantucket. "Any
man may kill a snake, but only a Perseus, a St. George, a
Coffin, have the heart in them to march boldly up to a
whale." [25]

Melville biographers and scholars have established the
stylistic influences exhibited in *Moby Dick*. Shakespeare,
Sir Thomas Browne, Burton, Sterne, and Rabelais helped
shape certain parts of the novel. To this list we must add
Cotton Mather, who was read and studied by Melville.[26]
Mather's significance for American literature is greater

than has been suspected up to now. The salient stylistic feature of Melville's *Moby Dick* is the technique of finding an analogy for every character and situation. Though numerous examples and authorities are cited by Sir Thomas Browne, Robert Burton, and other seventeenth-century authors, Melville's technique is especially closely related to the one used by Mather in his *Magnalia Christi Americana*. In *Moby Dick*, just as in Mather, people, actions, situations, and things are linked up in an extensive network of parallels and connections, whereby they are simultaneously described and commented on. An example of such a series of parallels is found at the end of the introduction to the third book of Mather's *Magnalia*, which contains biographies of New England clergymen:

> Archilocus *being desirous to give prevailing and effectual advice unto* Lycambes, *by an elegant* Prosopopoeia, *brought in his* dead father, *as giving the advice he was now writing, and as it were put his pen into his* fathers hands. Cicero *being to read a lecture of temperance and modesty unto* Clodia, *raised up her father* Appius Caius *from the grave, and in his name delivered his directions. And now, by introducing the* fathers *of* New-England, *without the least fiction, or figure of* rhetorick, *I hope the plain* history *of their lives, will be a powerful way of propounding their* fatherly counsels *to their posterity.*[27]

Melville too uses exemplary analogies to connect strength and beauty more closely:

> Real strength never impairs beauty or harmony, but it often bestows it; and in everything imposingly beautiful, strength has much to do with the magic. Take away the tied tendons that all over seem bursting from the marble in the carved Hercules, and its charm would be gone. As devout Eckerman lifted the linen sheet from the naked

corpse of Goethe, he was overwhelmed with the massive chest of the man, that seemed as a Roman triumphal arch. When Angelo paints even God the Father in human form, mark what robustness is there.[28]

Melville's analogies attest to a Baroque delight in extravagance and often to hidden rebellion as well. At one place Ishmael says of Queequeg (who must bear other analogies in other situations): "Queequeg was George Washington cannibalistically developed." [29] Many capricious and unusual analogies are drawn to describe the *Pequod*: ". . . her masts stood stiffly up like the spines of the three old kings of Cologne", and "Her ancient decks were worn and wrinkled, like the pilgrim-worshipped flagstone in Canterbury Cathedral where Beckett bled." [30] These scenes from religious legends are linked up with Melville's reminiscences of his visit to Cologne Cathedral in 1849.[31] In contrast to them we have the characteristic name "Pequod," the predominantly heathen crew of the ship, and the total contrast of the mysterious, unchristian purpose of the voyage. Immediately thereafter Melville jumps to barbarian imagery:

> She was apparelled like any barbaric Ethiopian emperor, his neck heavy with pendants of polished ivory. She was a thing of trophies. A cannibal of a craft, tricking herself forth in the chased bones of her enemies. All round, her unpanelled, open bulwarks were garnished like one continuous jaw, with the long sharp teeth of the sperm whale, inserted there for pins, to fasten her old hempen thews and tendons to.[32]

Melville gives his imagination free rein in search of material for his linked analogies. At times he finds visual similarities, which may have either a deeper connection or a striking contrast. At times he finds similarities of content

—be they similarities by association or by memory, be they similarities hinted at or certain—but the similarity is usually only one aspect of the scene used. Melville's imagination works according to some one of these principles[33] and provides a rich selection of imagery, varied as to kind and meaning, an El Dorado for critics with evidence to support the most divergent and even contradictory interpretations. There is also evidence that some of Melville's linked analogies stem from a delight in wit and parody rather than from symbolical, speculative depths. For instance, the seamen on watch at the masthead in the chapter "The Mast-Head" are compared with the ancient Egyptians, who observed the stars from the tops of their pyramids, with the ascetic saints who lived on pillars in the desert, and finally even with the columns in memory of Napoleon and Washington, and of Nelson at Trafalgar Square.[34]

The chapter "The Prairie" gives us the physiognomy of the sperm whale. His brow is rendered—one cannot say described because the technique resembles more a montage or *collage* than description—by an abundance of bold analogy:

> In thought a fine human brow is like the East when troubled with the morning. In the repose of the pasture, the curled brow of the bull has a touch of the grand in it. Pushing heavy cannon up mountain defiles, the elephant's brow is majestic. Human or animal, the mystical brow is as that great golden seal affixed by the German emperors to their decrees. It signifies "God: done this day by my hand." But in most creatures, nay in man himself, very often the brow is but a mere strip of alpine land lying along the snow line. Few are the foreheads which like Shakespeare's or Melancthon's rise so high, and descend so low, that the eyes themselves seem clear, eternal, tideless mountain lakes; and all above them in

the forehead's wrinkles, you seem to track the antlered
thoughts descending there to drink, as the Highland
hunters track the snow prints of the deer. But in the
great Sperm Whale, this high and mighty god-like dignity inherent in the brow is so immensely amplified,
that gazing on it, in that full front view, you feel the
Deity and the dread powers more forcibly than in beholding any other object in living nature.[35]

The analogies almost always leap as boldly as these
with nations and ages. We seldom find them based on but
a single scene, as for example in the chapter "Schools and
Schoolmasters." Here a school of female whales is compared somewhat obviously to a harem ruled by its "Otto-
man" or "Grand Turk," who chases off intruding rivals,
"young Lotharios." Then a bold leap of imagination con-
verts such a Grand Turk to a "pious Salomon devoutly
worshipping among his thousand concubines."

The technique of illustrating every statement by analogies or contrasts becomes a structural feature of *Moby
Dick*, because characters and actions become embedded
in a network of such analogies with which contact is renewed again and again. Actual description, the backbone
of the realistic novel, recedes in importance. The examples cited above show that Melville's analogies go far
beyond even the extended, so-called epic simile. They no
longer have a primarily stylistic function like metaphor
and simile. They become instead part of the message of
the novel, witnesses to Melville's belief in "linked analogies" that pervade nature and the human soul, and bind
the universe together. One should note, however, that this
sort of analogy is not a symbolic relation wherein a
symbol stands for something invisible, incomprehensible,
and inexplicable. It relates two carefully delimited phenomena to each other with the intention of thereby illumi-
nating both. This illumination quite often occurs in an

ironic manner, so that the bold comparison of opposites sets them off in relief. Melville obviously enjoys juggling incongruent images, and he harnesses divergent things together, tongue in cheek, to produce a humorous or even grotesque effect. He is parodying Cotton Mather when he comments on the stiff shipboard dining ceremony presided over by Ahab by linking it to the dining customs of Belshazzar and Caesar, as well as to the coronation banquet of the German emperor in Frankfort.[36] Here the analogy is free to provide humour and an irony sovereignly balanced between earnestness and ridicule. The leap from Ahab to Belshazzar, who scornfully disregards God's handwriting on the wall, also involves prophetic seriousness, which is however immediately repressed:

> To have been Belshazzar, King of Babylon; and to have been Belshazzar, not haughtily but courteously, therein certainly must have been some touch of mundane grandeur. But he who in the rightly regal and intelligent spirit presides over his own private dinner-table of invited guests, that man's unchallenged power and dominion of individual influence for the time; that man's royalty of state transcends Belshazzar's, for Belshazzar was not the greatest.[37]

The analogy to Caesar and the coronation banquet derives mostly from Melville's delight in hyperbolic comparisons.

But when Melville relates something ordinary to something exalted, this is always accompanied by serious intent also. For instance, when he compares Queequeg with Washington, or when he makes the whalers of the Pequod members in an order with Perseus, St. George, and Hercules ("that antique Crockett and Kit Carson," [38]—the comparison can also be reversed): "Thus, then, . . . we harpooneers of Nantucket should be enrolled in the most noble order of St. George. And therefore, let not the knights of that honorable company (none of whom, I venture to say, have ever had to do with a whale like their great patron), let them never eye a Nantucketer with disdain, since even in our woollen frocks and tarred trowsers we are much better entitled to St. George's decoration than they." [39] This elevates the ordinary and brings the exalted closer to the level of a broader humanity. The typological analogy provides Melville the opportunity of giving literary expression to his democratic creed, and to do so with irony and humorous understatement rather than in bitter seriousness.[40] By putting the ordinary man, even the unfortunate wretch, on a plane with the momentous figures of the Bible and world history, he attests to the dignity and potential importance of every single person. In the chapter "Knights and Squires" Melville even goes so far as to make this the program of *Moby Dick*, thereby providing a foundation for the especially numerous and extravagant analogies in this book:

> Men may seem detestable as joint stock-companies and nations; knaves, fools, and murderers there may be; men may have mean and meagre faces; but man, in the ideal, is so noble and so sparkling, such a grand and glowing creature, that over any ignominious blemish in him all his fellows should run to throw their costliest robes. That immaculate manliness we feel within ourselves, so far within us, that it remains intact though all the outer character seem gone; bleeds with keenest anguish at the undraped spectacle of a valor-ruined man. Nor can piety itself, at such a shameful sight, completely stifle her upbraidings against the permitting stars. But this august dignity I treat of, is not the dignity of kings and robes, but that abounding dignity which has no robed investiture. Thou shalt see it shining in the arm that wields a pick or drives a spike; that democratic dignity which, on all hands, radiates without end

from God; Himself! The great God absolute! The centre and circumference of all democracy! His omnipresence, our divine equality!

If, then, to meanest mariners, and renegades and castaways, I shall hereafter ascribe high qualities, though dark; weave around them tragic graces; if even the most mournful, perchance the most abased, among them all, shall at times lift himself to the exalted mounts; if I shall touch that workman's arm with some ethereal light; if I shall spread a rainbow over his disastrous set of sun; then against all mortal critics bear me out in it, thou just Spirit of Equality, which hast spread one royal mantle of humanity over all my kind! Bear me out in it, thou great democratic God! . . . Thou who, in all Thy mighty, earthly marchings, ever cullest Thy selectest champions from the kingly commons; bear me out in it, O God.[41]

Here it is obvious that the idea of a typological linking up of people is one of the roots of democratic thought in America. The self-conscious Puritans cultivated typology among other reasons because they regarded their deeds and fate in a direct line of descent from the great biblical events and figures. Melville links up his characters in the same network of things ordinary and exalted. His political convictions stem from his belief in a democratic God.

Typological ideas also contributed toward the creation of the three main characters of *Moby Dick*. Moby Dick, Ahab, and Ishmael all have biblical models that determine certain aspects of their being. Moby Dick is not only a natural creature but also the whale of Jonas, which is treated, like a *leitmotif*, in Father Mapple's sermon at the beginning of the narrative. In the opinion of the superstitious seamen, he is "not only ubiquitous but immortal," the whale that swallowed God's disobedient prophet, Jonah. Father Mapple preaches on Jonah 2:1, "God had prepared a great Fish to swallow up Jonah." [42] But Moby Dick is also "a Job's whale," [43] the leviathan (the name constantly used for him) of which it is said in the Book of Job that man can make no covenant with him. This passage is quoted in the chapter "Cetology": "Will he (the leviathan) make a covenant with thee? Behold the hope of him is in vain!" [44] He is the element of danger that stands outside the covenant, against which man has no security.

When Melville relates of Captain Bildad, Captain Peleg, and the whaling Quakers of Nantucket in the chapter "The Ship," he remarks that many men receive biblical names there, and this seems to make the name "Ahab" plausible. But in fact no Puritan or Quaker ever named a son after an infamous biblical personage annihilated by God. This would be tantamount to a prophecy of damnation for the hapless child.[45] Melville also leaves it open whether "Ahab" is the given name or the surname. He is always "Ahab" or "Captain Ahab," and the first time he is mentioned in the narrative Captain Peleg declares: "He's a grand, ungodly, god-like man . . . *he's Ahab*, boy; and Ahab of old, thou knowest, was a crowned king!" And Ishmael replies: "And a very vile one. When that wicked king was slain, the dogs, did they not lick his blood?" [46] The man's predestined fate is to be Ahab.

Thus Ahab is named for the King of Israel who "wrought evil in the eyes of the Lord" (I Kings 16:25), who worshiped Baal and otherwise so enraged the Lord until he was destroyed by Him. Melville's Ahab is also another Job, a contentious man who wants to dispute with the Almighty (Job 40:1), and whom God confronts with the leviathan. In pursuing the leviathan-whale Ahab combats the divine world order, or to be more precise, the original evil power to which God allotted a place and function in the world. Ahab nourishes a wild vindictiveness against Moby Dick:

> . . . he at last came to identify with him, not only all
> his bodily woes and spiritual exasperations . . . He
> piled upon the whale's white hump the sum of all the
> general rage and hate felt by his whole race from Adam
> down; and then, as if his chest had been a mortar, he
> burst his hot heart's shell upon it.[47]

With a single stroke this motivation of his pursuit
makes Ahab into a modern hero. He is a man with a dam-
aged psyche. He has not only fallen out of the divine world
order, he also doubts, the passion of his accusations not-
withstanding, that its evils are capable of rational explanation. With monomaniac hatred he ascribes these evils
to a scapegoat, to Moby Dick as a symbol of all evil. He
regards this whale as the leviathan in the theological
sense of the "image of the primeval world powers created
and ruled by God" and of the "evil world powers." [48] Being
motivated by this abysmal despair of the divine world
order, which leads to a psychological compulsion with no
escape, makes Ahab more modern than the demonic heroes of Romanticism, who do evil because they are inex-
plicably fascinated by evil itself. Ahab yields a *post facto*
explanation and rationale of the demonic and satanic heroes of the Gothic novel, who resemble him in appearance
and behavior. He is the man enraged by the contradictions
in the divine world order, and who for this reason defies
that order.

The basic problem of the Calvinist world view, that of
predestination and free will, is also involved in this dispute with God. Melville struggled with this problem his
entire life.[49] The abstract core of this expansive novel
about whaling and human fate is a dialectical one. Melville wants an explanation for the triangular relation of
man, God, and evil (or that which man takes for evil be-

cause it is inimical to him and eludes his moral categories). Is the human will free or predetermined when it drives a man to destruction? Is it free will or divine predestination that drives a man to combat evil—when the combat ends in his own destruction? Is evil dependent on God, or is it independent? If it is dependent on God, why does God place it in man's path? The traditional reply is: so that man can resist it. But since Ahab even combats evil, why does God let him perish? Or could evil be an independent force, as the Manicheans believed?[50]

All these questions affected Melville deeply, and he found no final answers to them. This conflict too exhibits Melville at the turning point of a new epoch. He still thinks with the categories of Calvinism, the concepts of predestination and free will, but the orthodox solutions no longer satisfy him. Ishmael states the Calvinist version in the symbol of the "Mat-makers":

> The straight warp of necessity, not to be swerved from its ultimate course—its every alternating vibration, indeed, only tending to that; free will still free to ply her shuttle between given threads; and chance, though restrained in its play within the right lines of necessity, and sideways in its motions directed by free will, though thus prescribed to by both, chance by turns rules either, and has the last featuring blow at events.[51]

But Ahab cannot accept this account for his own case. He regards himself as part of an infernal fate that takes its unalterable course. Turning to Starbuck, he says:

> But in this matter of the whale, be the front of thy face to me as the palm of this hand—a lipless, unfeatured blank. Ahab is forever Ahab, man. This whole act's immutably decreed. 'Twas rehearsed by thee and me a bil-

lion years before this ocean rolled. Fool! I am the Fates'
lieutenant; I act under orders. Look thou, underling!
that thou obeyest mine.[52]

This conflict, with a seemingly free will leading him to
a predestined fate, is insoluble and inscrutable for Ahab
himself. This is another reason for his name. Melville did
not choose King Ahab as a type of his hero only because
he rebelled against God. He also chose him as the man
whom God deceives in order to destroy, as it is reported in
I Kings 22:20–23:[53]

Now therefore, behold, the Lord hath put a lying spirit in
the mouth of all these thy prophets, and the Lord hath
spoken evil concerning thee. (I Kings 22:23)

This makes Ahab into a truly tragic figure whose will and
insight are led astray by God. Ahab carries on his dispute
with a treacherous God. His monologue is:

What is it, what nameless, inscrutable, unearthly thing
is it; what cozzening, hidden lord and master, and cruel,
remorseless emperor commands me; that against all natural lovings and longings, I so keep pushing, and crowd-
ing, and jamming myself on all the time; recklessly
making me ready to do what in my own proper, natural
heart, I durst not so much as dare? Is Ahab, Ahab? Is it
I, God, or who, that lifts this arm? But if the great sun
move not of himself, but is an errand boy in heaven; nor
one single star can revolve, but by some invisible power;
how then can this one small heart beat; this one small
brain think thoughts; unless God does that beating, does
that thinking, does that living, and not I.[54]

The notion of typology itself contains an element of inevi-
tability and predestination that precludes a free will. With

his name, Ahab has set out on an Ahab fate, and he must see it through to the end after the example of his name-sake. According to Captain Peleg, Squaw Tistig prophe-sied "that his name would prove prophetic," and Ahab himself accepts the prophecy connected with his name:

> They think me mad—Starbuck does; but I'm demoniac, I am madness maddened! That wild madness that's only calm to comprehend itself! The prophecy was that I should be dismembered; and—Aye! I lost this leg.[55]

According to this, the loss of the leg, which Freudian interpreters of Melville have so dwelt upon,[56] is also an element in the fulfillment of a type.

In this conflict between a puzzled man and an omnipo-tent God, Melville was on man's side. Moreover, it is pre-cisely the notion of omnipotence, which the Calvinists emphasized, and Melville at first accepted, before calling it into question in *Moby Dick*, that provokes him against God. In *Pierre* he quotes a proverb that Ahab could call his own: *Nemo contra Deum, nisi Deus ipse.*[57] According to this, God is also responsible for the rebellion against God and for evil. A theological debate in literary form takes place in Melville's works, primarily in *Moby Dick*, with a God who claims the attribute of omnipotence yet dis-claims responsibility for evil and for destruction by evil. In this sense *Moby Dick* is "a wicked book," and when Melville nevertheless feels "spotless as a lamb," it is be-cause he sees himself, consciously or unconsciously, in imitation of Christ, who shouldered the world's burden of guilt and sorrow, and shielded mankind from a merciless God.

In a note to *Pierre*, Henry A. Murray has pointed out that the character Ishmael had a special appeal for the romantics because he combines two qualities they especially esteemed. Ishmael was "the innocent one" and at the same time "the indignant one"; in anger he rebelled against society, and in his suffering he pointed toward Christ.[58] According to one interpretation Ishmael is in fact a type of Christ, whereas according to another he is, as the son of the slave Hagar, excluded from the promise.[59] Those of the romantics who were still close to the religious tradition occasionally regarded their outcast heroes, or those that withdrew voluntarily, according to biblical types. The evil despisers of society were in the type of Lucifer, and the ones who bore their fate nobly were in that of Ishmael. For the Calvinists, Ishmael has a special fate: that of distinction with exclusion. He is indeed blessed by God, but he does not participate in the covenant God makes with Abraham.[60] Just like Bullinger and Zwingli, Calvin interprets Genesis 17:19–21 as meaning that the covenant of eternal life has no reference to Ishmael:[61]

> And God said, Sarah thy wife shall bear thee a son indeed; and thou shalt call his name Isaac, and I will establish my covenant with him for an everlasting covenant, *and* with his seed after him.
>
> And as for Ishmael, I have heard thee: Behold, I have blessed him, and will multiply him exceedingly; twelve princes shall he beget, and I will make him a great nation.
>
> But my covenant will I establish with Isaac, which Sarah shall bear unto thee at this set time in the next year.

Thus Ishmael lacks the assurance which the Calvinists derive from the contractual nature of the covenant. Anything can happen to him because God has not made a covenant with him.

Melville had a special affection for this outcast, for whose eternal fate God would not accept responsibility.

This is precisely what makes him a prototype of the modern man who is emancipated from all religious ties. Melville makes Ishmael the progenitor of several of his heroes, most obviously for the amiable and religiously tolerant Ishmael of *Moby Dick*. But the young Redburn too is "a sort of Ishmael on the ship, without a single friend or companion," [62] and Pierre recognizes that he is taking an Ishmael's fate upon himself when he stands by his sister.[63] Without doubt, James Baird goes too far when he proclaims an Ishmael figure the hero of every one of Melville's works.[64] But we can safely assume that Melville felt especially close to the literary characters he created in the image of Ishmael, because in relation to his environment he felt like an Ishmael himself.

Many interpreters of *Moby Dick* have recognized and explained how the Old Testament names of the ships *Rachel* and *Jerobeam* which the *Pequod* encounters indicate their fate and that of their crews. They belong among the numerous episodes and subordinate figures of the novel that attest to the influence of typology on Melville. These ships whose names designate their fates also indicate that ships occupied a special place in Melville's creative imagination.

During a life of seventy-two years Melville spent about three and a half years at sea as a sailor. In his writing the ratio of land to sea is reversed. By far the greater part of his fiction takes place at sea on board ship, and among his longer narratives only *Pierre* takes place wholly on the mainland. The reason for this is not only that Melville's relatively short tour at sea supplied the material for nearly all of his fiction. In addition, he regarded shipboard life as a compressed copy of life in society. In *Typee*, *Omoo*, and *Mardi*, the ship is the compulsory society from which the two heroes flee to the uncivilized paradise of the South Sea cannibals. In *Redburn*, the ship is the vehicle for the first trip out into life. *Mardi, Moby Dick, Israel Potter*, "Benito Cereno," and *Billy Budd* all have their action exclusively or mostly on board ship. And in *Confidence Man*, the appearances and transformations of the swindler take place between the stations of a Mississippi steamer.

There is a principle of delimitation at work in Melville's preference for the measurable planks of a deck as a stage for human life, similar to the principle of his art of characterization. It is a tendency to concentrate on the typical in the modern sense, at the expense of the individual and the nuance. Instead of a manifold of characters, customs, and events, we encounter on board only that which is in some way typical. Accordingly, the plot has only one strand even in the longer novels, and it is really only long enough for a short story. In *Mardi* the thread of action is taken up anew again and again, and the scheme of the plot in *Moby Dick* is only apparently enlarged by the whaling knowledge and philosophical discussions.

In *White Jacket* Melville gives us his idea of the ship as a symbol for the world, earth, community, and stage of human life: "We mortals are all on board a fast-sailing, never-sinking world-frigate, of which God was the shipwright; and she is but one craft in a Milky-Way fleet, of which God is the Lord High Admiral." [65] Here the earth is regarded as a ship, while the real ship becomes a replica of human society. "For a ship is a bit of terra-firma cut off from the main; it is a state in itself; and the captain is its king." [66] In an extended analogy the American warship *Neversink* becomes a swimming city with its hierarchical order corresponding to social classes:

> In truth, a man-of-war is a city afloat, with long avenues set out with guns instead of trees, and numerous shady lanes, courts, and byways. The quarter-deck is a grand

square, park, or parade-ground, with a great Pittsfield elm, in the shape of the mainmast, at one end, and fronted at the other by the palace of the commodore's cabin.

Or, rather, a man-of-war is a lofty, walled, and garrisoned town, like Quebec, where the thoroughfares are mostly ramparts, and peaceable citizens meet armed sentries at every corner.

Or it is like the lodging-houses in Paris, turned upside down; the first floor, or deck, being rented by a lord; the second, by a select club of gentlemen; the third, by crowds of artisans; and the fourth, by a whole rabble of common people.[67]

The ship as it is used in these three cases has at first a transcendent meaning and then a secular one: the world as a ship steered by God, and then the actual ship as a symbol for the city and society.[68] Both interpretations allude to the biblical Noah's ark, which was commanded by God, and which took on representatives of all species of living things. This manifold use of ship imagery, which contains symbolical, allegorical, and biblical elements, raises the question of the origin and type of the metaphors used by Melville.

2. THE TERMINOLOGY OF THE SYMBOLIC CONNECTIONS

One of Melville's peculiarities is that like Hawthorne he expressly states in an astounding number of cases that his images embody meanings. For this he uses above all the concepts "symbol," "emblem," and "sign," as well as "type" and "shadow," and the corresponding verbs. The frequent use of "type," "typify," and "shadow forth" (in the sense of "prefigure") shows that Melville's metaphorical language has been influenced and enriched by typological ideas. In Melville's long poem *Clarel*, the fruit of his pilgrimage to the Holy Land, "type" and "typic" occur several times, and in the original theological sense. For example:

> Lambs had he known by thunder killed,
> Innocents—and the type of Christ
> Betrayed . . .[69]

In other works we encounter "type" and "typify" where the meaning of these concepts is at a stage of transition from the specific meaning to the general one:

> It is deemed a fit type of all-forsaken overthrow, that the jackal should den in the wastes of weedy Babylon; but the Encantadas refuse to harbor even the outcasts of the beasts.[70]

> Now as the Memnon Statue survives down to this present day, so does that nobly-striving but ever shipwrecked character in some royal youths (for both Memnon and Hamlet were the sons of kings), of which that statue is the melancholy type.[71]

> Here reigned the dashing and all-fusing spirit of the West, whose type is the Mississippi itself, which, uniting the streams of the most distant and opposite zones, pours them along, helter-skelter, in one cosmopolitan and confident tide.[72]

In the *Confidence Man* it is said of bears that they are "true types of most destroyers of confidence." [73] Further examples could be cited where the verb form "typify" or the synonymous "to shadow forth" are used. Here we mention only one, from *Moby Dick*, in the much-quoted chapter "The Whiteness of the Whale":

. . . though in many climes, whiteness typifies the ma-
jesty of Justice in the ermine of the Judge, . . . though
even in the higher mysteries of the most august religions
it has been made the symbol of the divine spotlessness
and power; . . .[74]

Obviously these are not "types" in the original religious
sense. Rather, this connection has been transferred to the
most diverse secular phenomena. Only in the "Encantadas" quotation on the jackals of Babylon is a trace of the
biblical origin to be found. Today one could substitute
"symbol" for "type" in every case—with the possible exception of the bears who are called "true types of most
destroyers of confidence." Nonetheless a closer study reveals that Melville makes distinctions in the use of these
concepts. He regards them neither as wholly identical nor
as exchangeable in every case.

Let us first examine Melville's use of "symbol" in *Moby
Dick*. The albino whale is the symbol of all of the ambiva-
lent white horrors mentioned. "And of all these things the
Albino whale was the symbol," it is said at the end of "The
Whiteness of the Whale." [75] Queequeg, in "The First Low-
ering," with a lantern in his hand, is ". . . the sign and
symbol of a man without faith, hopelessly holding up
hope in the midst of despair." [76] Here "symbol" draws close
to "sign", of which the significance for Puritan thought
was discussed above (p. 15 ff.). At the beginning of the
chapter "Fast-Fish and Loose-Fish" we read: "The allusion
to the waifs and waif-poles . . . necessitates some account of the laws and regulations of the whale fishery, of
which the waif may be deemed the grand symbol and
badge." [77] In all of these cases the word "symbol" points to
an inherent meaning that is symbolically expressed in
outer phenomena. They are the sign and indicator of this

meaning, and this is why Melville speaks so readily of "symbol and sign" and "symbol and badge." For him the concept of the symbol always includes the idea that it is the visible and intentional embodiment of an invisible deeper meaning,[78] which has to be referred to expressly. The whiteness of the whale is a "most meaning symbol of spiritual things, nay, the very veil of the Christian's Deity";[79] the rope ladder to the pulpit of the Whaleman's Chapel, which causes Ishmael to ponder, "must symbolize something unseen";[80] and the wind that blew out their sails like great bellies "seemed the symbol of that unseen agency which so enslaved them to the race," [81] God or Leviathan. The symbol is the image through which God speaks.[82]

The passages where Melville uses "type" are something quite different. There is a complicated connection whereby two separate, autonomous phenomena are confronted with each other (*e.g.* Babylon—the Encantadas; the Memnon statue and Hamlet-Pierre). In some one respect they are comparable in regard to their deeper meaning. For this connection Melville employs and stretches the old biblical connection of the type, as it fits two things that are indeed independent, yet similar due to divine determination. The idea that God laid out the world according to great models with hidden connections and correspondences is still alive in Melville. It is quite obvious that the Memnon statue cannot be a symbol for Hamlet or Pierre. They have neither inner nor causal connection, and unless one allows for a divine providence, their only connection is the one recognized and put on them by the observer Pierre. The same occurs in the case of the Mississippi and "the dashing and all-fusing spirit of the West." This quotation is a specially good example of typological thought merging into an expanded symbolism:

> Here reigned the dashing and all-fusing spirit of the
> West, whose type is the Mississippi itself, which, uniting
> the streams of the most distant and opposite zones,
> pours them along, helter-skelter, in one cosmopolitan
> and confident tide.[83]

Here the Mississippi is made equivalent to the "spirit of
the West." Or to be more precise, it is made a type which
the spirit fulfills, because it too is "dashing and all-fusing"
as it unites streams of the most distant zones into a cosmopolitan and confident tide. The most important vehicle
of comparison at the foundation of this equivalence is the
"flowing together" of rivers or people of quite different
zones.[84] It is reinforced by the four attributes, "dashing,"
"all-fusing," "cosmopolitan," and "confident," which apply
to both river and people. Note however that the first two
originally apply to the river and the final two to the spirit.
The effect of this is to link up the two wholly disparate
phenomena, river and spirit, and to set them in a relation
that can be called symbolical in a broad sense, because the
river apparently represents the spirit of the West. With
the help of the type theory, this initiates the limitless practice of setting phenomena that are in any way comparable
into symbolic relationships. From the standpoint of logic
there is a fallacious syllogism at the bottom of this connection, which is a leap from religiously conditioned typology to symbolism: 1. The Mississippi unites streams
from the most different zones; 2. The spirit of the West
unites streams of people from the most different zones; 3.
The Mississippi is equivalent to the spirit of the West. The
typological parallels, and especially the extended typology
applied by the Puritans to all possible terrestrial things,
were based on a faith that sinks into oblivion at the transition to symbolism, at least on the rational plane, whereas

it still vibrates in resonance on the unconscious one. This foundation alone is what raises the symbolic connection above the arbitrary, noncommittal character of the mere comparison. Its recalling of mysterious connections in the structure of the universe is what gives this kind of symbolism its mysterious power to convince.

Melville's metaphorical language is of decisive importance for the understanding of his fiction, because in it he gives expression to his deepest artistic and religious convictions about the connection of the world with its creative principle, God. One might call the artistic style that grows from these convictions a "symbolic realism" in order to indicate the bipolarity of world and meaning so characteristic of Melville's most important works.

Thus *White Jacket*, from which we took the ship symbolism, is at first glance an almost nonfictional, realistic book. An actual experience, Melville's return voyage on an American warship, provides the material, which has scarcely been transformed at all for the purposes of fiction. The beginning and end of the voyage are the only formative element of the book. The contents comprise several portraits of crew members, descriptions of their activities, and of the darker sides of their lives, and reflections on inhuman punishment in the Navy. The symbolic illuminations of the described facts alone is what makes the book literary. In addition there is the motif of the white jacket, which quite obviously has a symbolic meaning. Not only does it mark its wearer as an unhappy lonewolf, it also provokes the other sailors to annoy him or avoid him. It seems a safe conjecture that at the core this symbol comes from Melville's own experience, because we encounter a similar motif as early as *Redburn*. Redburn begins his voyage in a gray hunting jacket that brings him ridicule and trouble.[85] This symbolic interpretation of actual experience proves Melville an heir to the Calvinist en-

deavor of finding "significances" in the world. Melville
continues this search, but his interpretations have grown
more secular and more sceptical. Often enough the meaning of his interpretation is so peculiar to him, and so bold
and independent, that his contemporaries did not understand it. But the origin of his thought is revealed on those
occasions when a traditional biblical interpretation ob-
trudes on him. White Jacket finds it strange that fallen
naval officers are honored with a gun salute:

> . . . I thought it a strange mode of honouring a man's
> memory who had himself been slaughtered by a cannon.
> Only the smoke, that, after rolling in at the port-holes,
> rapidly drifted away to leeward, and was lost to view,
> seemed truly emblematical touching the personage thus
> honoured, since that great non-combatant, the Bible,
> assures us that our life is but a vapour that quickly
> passeth away.[86]

Melville's much-quoted passage, "And some certain significance lurks in all things, else all things are little worth,
and the round world itself but an empty cipher, except to
sell by the cartload, as they do hills about Boston, to fill up
some morass in the Milky Way," [87] is the key to what we
have here called "symbolic realism." It is a position between faith and scepticism which yet makes faith the ultimate choice. If things had no "significance," Melville's
writing would lose its point. The belief that God uses real
phenomena and events as signs for human beings is the
presupposition of Melville's idea. Thus all of the world's
phenomena are potential bearers of significance; all of
them point to God's will, or more concretely, to biblical
models and types. For Puritans versed in the Scriptures,
these significances were wholly unequivocal. Without a
trace of doubt they could say, "This signifies . . .", and

then give the explanation. The heirs of the Puritans share their deeply-rooted disposition to see signs in real phenomena. The difference is that the interpretation is no longer an authoritative, definite matter. Rather, it is something to be sought and outlined by the liberated power of human knowledge and imagination, and at times it cannot even be determined unequivocally. A further characteristic of this Calvinistic tradition is the acceptance of the world and experience as divine creation, and thus as a source of insight into the meaning of the world and life. But the God of this creation grows ever more enigmatical and questionable until he finally becomes anonymous. The more the authority of dogmatically fixed religion fades, the more important reality itself becomes, for its testimony is the only accessible revelation of a hidden God. The realism that grew from this tradition is in fact a characteristically American form of literature. A modern realist like Hemingway, who wants to seize what happened in its pure form, undistorted by its being experienced, is a continuer of this tradition in his own way.[88]

By Melville's time Calvinism was no longer a living religious force, yet it still had a fundamental cultural significance. Its strict dogmas had lost their power, but certain basic ideas of the Calvinist world view continued to exert influence. Thus in Melville's conception of the symbol, faith is intermingled with usurpation: "We incline to think that God cannot explain His own secrets, and that He would like a little information upon certain points Himself." [89] Despite this facetious and self-ironic remark, the symbolic interpretation of reality is something extraordinarily serious for Melville rather than something arbitrary. It is a conversion of religious meanings to his own use, whereby a biblical style is often employed. What an extravagance of imagery we find in certain parts of the Bible! Above all in the Song of Solomon so loved by Melville. The late Puritan interpretations of reality which could have served as models, *e.g.* that of Cotton Mather, interlarded with quotations and parallels, Melville regards with a healthy dose of irony. His own linked analogies in *Moby Dick* are among other things also a parody of the learned Puritan style.

Melville was rediscovered around 1920, seventy years after his period of richest productivity, since which time he has been interpreted according to all the rules of art. Thus his rediscovery and interpretation fall in an era of conscious literary symbolism, whereas he produced his works in an era of transition from religious to symbolic thought. Since his rediscovery his metaphorical language has helped make the symbol an element of literature much discussed and admired in American criticism.

Some modern symbolists would like to give the symbol a sacramental character and regard the writer as a hero of redemption who creates symbols. Melville, a solitary figure tragically misunderstood by his own age, seems to fit the role well. Some years ago Alfred Kazin pointed out in an essay "On Melville as Scripture" [90] that some modern critics read and interpret Melville like a religious text. More recently James Baird has viewed the writer Melville as the "supreme example of the artistic creator engaged in the act of making new symbols to replace the "lost" symbols of Protestant Christianity." [91] Baird sets up a succinct equation: Christian sacrament = symbol. Thus the literary symbol becomes a sacrament. Symbolism is proclaimed the religion of modern man.[92]

In our connection it is important to note that this interpretation of Melville's symbolism is an example of the repudiation of historical thought described above in the Introduction. The sense of distinction, evolution, and transition in intellectual currents is abandoned for total generalization. Melville's place in history is that of a pioneer of literary symbolism, but he was not a symbolist in the modern sense of the term. At times, above all in *Mardi* and *Confidence Man*, he did base allegories on literary models. But in his most important works he is, as his native talent bids, a symbolic realist, *i.e.*, a writer for whom the actual world and experience are keys for a deeper, supernatural meaning. He had an innate conviction that everything contains a transcendental meaning. Even though he quarreled with the God of the Calvinists, he never doubted that the world with all its features was a divine creation. For Melville, writing did not mean to create a world but to interpret the world. In fact it is the impulse to interpret, to ferret out the hidden meaning, that made a writer of him.

"[To get] the meaning of this great allegory—the world" [93] was so much the mainspring of his creative work and an integral element of his viewing and experiencing that he even unconsciously seized upon the potentially symbolical in reality. This he describes in a letter to Mrs. Hawthorne in reply to the letter from her and Hawthorne:

> . . . your allusion for example to the "Spirit Spout" first showed to me that there was a subtile significance in that thing—but I did not, in that case, *mean* it. I had some vague idea while writing it, that the whole book was susceptible of an allegoric construction, also that *parts* of it were—but the speciality of many of the particular subordinate allegories, were first revealed to me, after reading Mr. Hawthorne's letter, which without citing any paticular examples, yet intimated the part-&-parcel allegoricalness of the whole. [94]

What Melville calls "allegoricalness" would be "symbolic meaning" in more precise terminology, because he means something that is part of reality. Wherever Melville actually does use an allegorical technique, *e.g.* in *Mardi*, where he constructs allegorical actions and figures in illustration of an abstract idea, he is outside his true *métier* and suffers reverses. And the novel *Pierre* too is a failure in the final instance because Melville cannot convert the ideas he wants to express into convincing actions. But wherever Melville goes to work on material from his own experience, or with his genial instinct for what is significant in reality, he produces literature of a high order.

9　CHRIST AND ADAM AS
"FIGURES" IN AMERICAN
LITERATURE

Among the important writers of the nineteenth century
only Melville and Hawthorne still regard the concepts
"type" and "emblem" in the light of their religious derivation and substance. In isolated cases later writers in the
New England tradition have used them in a way that recalls their religious meaning, without, so far as one can
see, a full and precise understanding of it. As early as the
time of Hawthorne and Melville the theory of the type
coalesced with literary symbolism, contributing to its
power to convince from its religious foundation. However,
the character components of the type concept exerted an
influence on American literature that persisted even
longer than this. It is a distinctive trait of American literature far beyond the characterization techniques of Hawthorne and Melville that its characters often are not cre-

ated as freshly conceived individuals but as based on fixed models, of which the most important are Adam and Christ.[1]

On Adam as the American hero *par excellence*, the ever newly modified archetypal hero of American literature, an important and interesting book has been written by R.W.B. Lewis: *The American Adam: Innocence, Tragedy and Tradition in the 19th Century*.[2] Lewis shows how the young American nation that had recently parted from Europe politically and from Calvinism spiritually chose Adam, the prototype of innocent man, as the symbol and ideal of its destiny. He also shows how the writers of the earlier nineteenth century, from approximately 1820 to 1860, take this ideal as the model for their heroes. In addition to Hawthorne and Melville, Oliver Wendell Holmes, Walt Whitman, and in another way, Charles Brockden Brown, Cooper, and Montgomery Bird all fashioned their heroes according to the type of Adam. As Lewis shows, even the historians Bancroft and Parkman are under the spell of the innocent Adam.

Thus we may refer to Lewis's account for evidence of Adam figures and symbolism in these authors, though his point of departure and in some ways his interpretation as well differ from those put forth here. As the guiding idea of his discussion Lewis chooses Emerson's comment on "The party of the Past and the party of the Future, of Memory and Hope," which he interprets as the party of "original sin" and that of "innocence." But this relativizes his argument in a way that is sometimes confusing. "Memory" and "Hope" cannot be exactly coordinated with past and future, and the latter pair of concepts can only be fixed relative to some given standpoint.

Lewis views the "American Adam" only as a myth and archetype, neither recognizing nor mentioning his being anchored in the Calvinist theory of types and antitypes.

But this involves a factor important for cultural history. This innocent Adam, who feels free of the burdens of history and faces the future—as anti-Calvinist as he appears in nineteenth-century literature—is as much a product of the Calvinist world drama as his counterpart, the Adam whose fall brought man to sin. With Adam God made the first covenant, the covenant of works; Adam is the "type" of Christ, the "second Adam." This link which comes originally from typology is the reason why the two figures so often appear together and even merge in their literary use, so that some literary Adam figures, for instance, Billy Budd, finally turn into Christ figures.[3] Whenever the hero meets a tragic fate, the model of the innocent Adam is linked to that of Christ suffering as, for example, Melville's Steelkilt from the "Town-Ho's Story" in *Moby Dick*,[4] Pierre, Billy Budd, or Israel Potter.

These works present a double Adam-Christ figure that originates in Calvinism, but is transformed by anti-Calvinist, secular tendencies. The fact is that the Christ of the New Testament was ever characterized by an antipredestination element, a gentleness and mercy that ill agree with the Old Testament sternness of Puritanism, and this is why Puritanism did not quite grant to Christ the predominant role given him by other Reformation sects. Those who began the rebellion against the severity of Puritanism in the later eighteenth century cast their lot with the merciful Christ.

Harriet Beecher Stowe has given us a fictional account of the beginning of this development in *The Minister's Wooing* (1859). Raised in a family of clergymen that cultivated an intellectual Calvinist tradition even in the middle of the nineteenth century, Harriet Beecher received a formidable education in theology.[5] Two events caused her great inner turmoil. When she was 11, her sister's fiancé was drowned in a shipwreck. She was plunged into a religious crisis over the question whether this dear friend, who according to the Calvinist view was unconfirmed in his faith and thus unregenerate, had been condemned by God to eternal damnation. She had a similar unfortunate experience in the period when *The Minister's Wooing* was being written. In 1857 Harriet Beecher Stowe's son Henry drowned in the Connecticut River. Here too, in addition to her grief, she was deeply troubled by the question about the eternal fate of the lad snatched away before his religious awakening.

The Minister's Wooing is a novel about Dr. Hopkins, a well known eighteenth-century New England clergyman. The problem about the early death of an unregenerate is inserted in the narrative.[6] This provides Harriet Beecher Stowe an opportunity to discuss the problems of predestination, divine grace, and election. She turns out to be mainly a follower of Calvinism on essential points, yet at the same time expresses unorthodox ideas. In the novel the heroine's fiancé is missed at sea, and his mother is driven to the verge of madness at the thought that her son, not at all a strict believer, might be condemned to eternal damnation. In her distress she is comforted by her Negro servant, Candace, a simple and uneducated woman (uneducated always means theologically uneducated for the Puritans) who is an ardent believer. This articulate lay priestess of religious feeling becomes the antagonist of Dr. Hopkins by invoking Christ's help against the sternly interpreted dogma of predestination. She comforts her desperate mistress with the following words:

> "I knows our Doctor's a mighty good man, an' larned,—
> an' in fair weather I hain't no 'bjection to yer hearin' all
> about dese yer great an' mighty tings he's got to say.

But, honey, dey won't do for you now; sick folks mus'n't
hab strong meat; an' times like dese, dar jest ain't but
one ting to cometo, an' dat ar's Jesus . . . Why, Jesus
did n't die for nothin',—all dat love ain't gwine to be
wasted. De'lect is more'n you or I knows, honey! Dar's
de Spirit,—He'll give it to 'em; and ef Mass'r James is
called an' took, depend upon it de Lord has got him
ready—course He has; so don't ye go to layin' on your
poor heart what no mortal creetur can live under, 'cause,
as we's got to live in dis yer world, it's quite clar de Lord
must ha' fixed it so we can, and ef tings was as some
folks suppose, why, we could n't live, and dar would n't
be no sense in anyting dat goes on." [7]

Although Christ's love is called upon here to mitigate
the harshness of the dogma of predestination, his role as
the divine redeemer is not generally affirmed in liberal
theology. On the contrary, Christ undergoes a transformation that brings him nearer to man. This is not only because religion grows more emotional, it also results from
debates on points of dogma.

When William Ellery Channing defined the position of
Unitarianism in 1819 in his ordination speech for Jared
Sparks, he staked out his position solidly on the ground of
the New Testament, in opposition to orthodox Calvinism:
"Jesus Christ is the only master of Christians." [8] But when
he proceeds to destroy the dogma of the Trinity, he has to
place Christ on a lower level than God if he is to avoid a
polytheistic conception: ". . . Jesus Christ is a being distinct from and inferior to God." [9] There is a new interpretation of Christ as mediator whereby rational explanation
is substituted for dogmatic conception. He did not sacrifice himself to redeem mankind from sin by his vicarious
suffering. Nor was he acting as God, who assumed human
shape because only God Himself could atone for the punishment exacted by divine justice for man's disobedience:

We regard him as a Saviour, chiefly as he is the light,
physician, and guide of the dark, diseased, and wandering mind. No influence in the universe seems to us so
glorious as that over the character; and no redemption
so worthy of thankfulness as the restoration of the soul
to purity . . . With these impressions, we are accustomed to value the gospel chiefly as it abounds in effec-
tual aids, motives, excitements to a generous and divine
virtue. In this virtue, as in a common centre, we see all
its doctrines, precepts, promises meet; and we believe
that faith in this religion is of no worth, and contributes
nothing to salvation, any farther than as it uses these
doctrines, precepts, promises, and the whole life, character, sufferings, and triumphs of Jesus, as the means of
purifying the mind, of changing it into the likeness of
his celestial excellence.[10]

Here Jesus is regarded primarily as the moral redeemer, by example and by doctrine. The Transcendentalist goes beyond the Unitarian theologian to make the Son
of God a figure of supreme humanity, whose brotherhood
with man attests to man's divine nature. Ralph Waldo
Emerson broke with the Unitarian Church in 1832. The
immediate cause was his scepticism about the rite of the
Lord's Supper, but his criticism of the church was much
more far-reaching. In his 1838 address to the young theologians of Harvard Divinity School, he accuses it of over-
emphasizing the personal, the positive, and the ritual, and
of worshipping Christ much as the Orientals and Greeks
worshipped their demigods: "The stationariness of religion; the assumption that the age of inspiration is past,
that the Bible is closed; the fear of degrading the character of Jesus by representing him as a man;—indicate with
sufficient clearness the falsehood of our theology." [11] And
he rises to almost hymnic rapture when he proclaims (p.
127 f.):

Jesus Christ belonged to the true race of prophets. He saw with open eye the mystery of the soul. Drawn by its severe harmony, ravished with its beauty, he lived in it, and had his being there. Alone in all history he estimated the greatness of man. One man was true to what is in you and me. He saw that God incarnates himself in man, and evermore goes forth anew to take possession of his World. He said, in this jubilee of sublime emotion, "I am divine. Through me, God acts; through me, speaks. Would you see God, see me; or see thee, when thou also thinkest as I now think."

The postulated divine nature of man logically requires the human nature of Christ. Three years after Emerson's "Address," Theodore Parker held his famous sermon on "The Transient and Permanent in Christianity," severing himself too from the Unitarian Church. Parker views the Bible and Christianity with a sense of history and the skepticism taught by history. What is variable and transient in Christianity are its dogmas: "Men are burned for professing, what men are burned for denying." He counts the typological interpretation of the Old Testament among the obsolete dogmas: "Every fact in the early Jewish history has been taken as a type of some analogous fact in Christian history. The most distant events, even such as are still in the arms of time, were supposed to be clearly foreseen and foretold by pious Hebrews several centuries before Christ." [12] Parker's conception of Jesus is as revolutionary as his Bible criticism. Jesus is said to combine divine and human features: "But still was he not our brother; the son of man, as we are; the son of God, like ourselves? His excellence—was it not human excellence? His wisdom, love, piety—sweet and celestial as they were —are they not what we also may attain?" [13] Then Parker completes the transformation of the Son of God into a divine human:

But if, as some early Christians began to do, you take a heathen view, and make him a God, the Son of God in a peculiar and exclusive sense, much of the significance of his character is gone. His virtue has no merit, his love no feeling, his cross no burthen, his agony no pain. His death is an illusion, his resurrection but a show. For if he were not a man, but a god, what are all these things? what his words, his life, his excellence of achievements? It is all nothing, weighed against the illimitable great-ness of Him who created the worlds and fills up all time and space! Then his resignation is no lesson, his life no model, his death no triumph to you or me, who are not gods, but mortal men, that know not what a day shall bring forth, and walk by faith "dim sounding on our perilous way." Alas! we have despaired of man, and so cut off his brightest hope.[14]

This is a logical development that had its parallels in Eu-rope in the eighteenth and nineteenth centuries. The secu-larization of early American culture, a pre-eminently theo-logical and rational culture, finds its expression in the humanization of Christ. Parker's words reveal a revolu-tionary transformation of values. Secular human life now has a significance all its own, and Christ is related to it in a naive and egoistical manner so that this alone lends his suffering significance. He must be human because, in Parker's opinion, this is the only way his suffering and his sacrifice can mean anything to us. Parker is the first to clearly state the necessity of making Christ the paragon of humanity. Christ is "our brother; the son of man as we are, the son of God, like ourselves."

"There was never an age, when men did not crucify the Son of God afresh," Parker says elsewhere in this ser-mon,[15] thereby making the tragic heroes of all ages Christ's brothers in suffering. We discern this same con-viction in literary disguise in the fates of Pierre and Billy

Budd, of Faulkner's Joe Christmas and his corporal. When Emerson and Parker linked the idealist conviction of man's divinity with Christ's humanity, they sensed that they were establishing a symbolic relation between the two. Christ must bear witness to man's divinity, and Christ's sacrifice is in vain unless man in his suffering regards it as a sign that consoles and exalts him. This means that Christ in his new role was suited for use in literature. Indeed, his metamorphosis even required this use as proof of his new, secularized service to mankind. In a secular age Christ becomes the literary symbol of the innocent man suffering for his brothers.

Even in a novel as deliberately realistic as William Dean Howells' *A Hazard of New Fortunes* (1889), there are unmistakable Christ features in the idealism and self-sacrifice of Conrad Dryfoos, who is shot during a strike. Allusions to Christ are also found in some twentieth-century writers: In Thomas Wolfe, the death of old Grant in *Of Time and the River*;[16] in Ralph Ellison, the shooting and burial of young Tod Clifton in *Invisible Man*;[17] and in Ernest Hemingway's *The Old Man and the Sea*,[18] the old man's endurance and suffering are crowned with the symbols of the Passion. As the luckless fisherman returns home from his battle with the sharks, he drags the mast of his boat to his hut as Christ did the cross, falling down several times with this burden on his shoulders. In his shack he lies face down on the bed with his arms extended out to the sides and the lacerated palms of his hands turned up. This is how he is found by his friend, the fisher boy, who then runs crying to the villagers to report what he has seen. Christ symbolism is used in another way by Nathanael West, namely, as social criticism: His novel *Miss Lonelyhearts* (1932) is the bitter portrait of a modern *ersatz* Christ. Miss Lonelyhearts, the "comforter of lonely hearts," is the fictitious person of a newspaper who dispenses smooth, tailored consolation in answer to letters from lovelorn readers. This is a cruel travesty of the role of Christ in our time. The hero of the book, the journalist who answers letters from distressed and lovelorn readers, breaks down under the burden of his imitation. He entangles himself in the affairs of those in need of consolation until one of his disappointed letter writers finally shoots him.

No author has invoked the shadow of Christ more often, covertly or openly, than William Faulkner. In *The Sound and the Fury* (1929) it is covertly. Only the Easter services of the Negroes, which Dilsey attends with the 33-year-old child Benjy, tell us that the three days revealing the decline of the Compsons, April 6, 7, and 8, 1928 (given in this order as chapter headings), are the Good Friday, Holy Saturday, and Easter Sunday of that year. *Light in August* (1932) is rife with signs that are more overt. No doubt Faulkner regards the unfortunate hero of this novel as Christ's brother. Joe Christmas, the man with the invisible "cross" of Negro blood in his veins, was born during the Christmas season and baptized Joseph. "It is so in the Book," his fanatical grandfather says, "Christmas, the son of Joe. Joe, the son of Joe. Joe Christmas." [19] His name is "an augur of what he will do," and his life follows the example of Christ's suffering in a cruelly twisted way. Every step of this way he is rebuffed, wounded, baited and beaten by fanatics of various sects. Finally, in a horrible reversal of Christ's deed, he is driven to murder the Calvinist Joanna Burden, who tries to hold him with a love distorted by nymphomania. Christmas' life ends in shocking analogy to that of the Redeemer, nor does Faulkner neglect to remind us that at his death he is the same age as Jesus on the cross. On a Friday he is seized, tormented, and murdered, and in death he achieves an entirely unearthly transfiguration and something like a spiritual resurrection:

> He just lay there, with his eyes open and empty of everything save consciousness, and with something, a shadow, about his mouth. For a long moment he looked up at them with peaceful and unfathomable and unbearable eyes. Then his face, body, all, seemed to collapse, to fall in upon itself, and from out the slashed garments about his hips and loins the pent black blood seemed to rush like a released breath. It seemed to rush out of his pale body like the rush of sparks from a rising rocket; upon that black blast the man seemed to rise soaring into their memories forever and ever. They are not to lose it, in whatever peaceful valleys, beside whatever placid and reassuring streams of old age, in the mirroring faces of whatever children they will contemplate old disasters and newer hopes. It will be there, musing, quiet, steadfast, not fading and not particularly threatful, but of itself alone serene, of itself alone triumphant. Again from the town, deadened a little by the walls, the scream of the siren mounted toward its unbelievable crescendo, passing out of the realm of hearing.[20]

The drama of the crucifixion is for Faulkner the archetypal human tragedy. Isaac McCaslin, one of his most likeable characters, decides to follow Christ's example. He gives up his life as a landowner and hunter, relinquishing the estate acquired by his ancestors with greed and guilt, and buys himself carpenter tools:

> . . . not in mere static and hopeful emulation of the Nazarene as the young gambler buys a spotted shirt because the old gambler won in one yesterday, but (without the arrogance of false humility and without the false humbleness of pride, who intended to earn his bread,

didn't especially want to earn it but had to earn it and for more than just bread) because if the Nazarene had found carpentering good for the life and ends He had assumed and elected to serve, it would be all right too for Isaac McCaslin. . . .[21]

In scene, plot, and style, *A Fable* (1954) falls so little within the compass of Faulkner's other work that it was an unpleasant surprise and disappointment for most American critics.[22] Yet the theme of the book is very much in the American tradition: the rebellion of an ordinary man against authority, the military, and the war. Some critics hold that in *A Fable* Faulkner's thought is naive and confused.[23]

> From a European writer of Faulkner's stature we would expect in the treatment of such a theme, even if no answer, at least a sharper and richer debate in contemporary theological and philosophical terms than Faulkner gives us: there is a considerable amount of debate in the book, but it tapers off into nebulous language . . . Faulkner's explicit handling of ideas, outside as well as within the domain of theology, is usually amateurish. When, for example, as happens repeatedly in the novel, a cause is assigned to the war, it is the familiar simplification current in the 1920's: that it was an international conspiracy of the munitions makers and the generals.

By stating this,[24] Philip Blair Rice shows only that he entirely fails to understand the monstrous, heretical conception that Faulkner presents us with here. It is absolutely false that by means of over-simplification "an international conspiracy of munitions makers and generals" is made responsible for the war. Faulkner's accusation is infinitely broader in its sweep: It is aimed at all civilization, at all who are ambitious, who thirst for fame, who perform great feats, cultural feats included, at all states, nations, armies, heroes, and at Christianity as well. His accusation is aimed at *rapacity* as the mother of all culture and civilization:

> Rapacity does not fail, else man must deny he breathes. Not rapacity: its whole vast glorious history repudiates that. It does not, cannot, must not fail. Not just one family in one nation privileged to soar cometlike into splendid zenith through and because of it, not just one nation among all the nations selected as heir to that vast splendid heritage; not just France, but all governments and nations which ever rose and endured long enough to leave their mark as such, had sprung from it and in and upon and by means of it became forever fixed in the amazement of man's present and the glory of his past; civilization itself is its password and Christianity its masterpiece, Chartres and the Sistine Chapel, the pyramids and the rock-wombed powder-magazines under the Gates of Hercules its altars and monuments, Michelangelo and Phidias and Newton and Ericsson and Archimedes and Krupp its priests and popes and bishops; the long deathless roster of its glory—Caesar and the Barcas and the two Macedonians, our own Bonaparte and the great Russian and the giants who strode nimbused in red hair like fire across the Aurora Borealis, and all the lesser nameless who were not heroes but, glorious in anonymity, at least served the destiny of heroes—the generals and admirals, the corporals and ratings of glory, the batmen and orderlies of reknown, and the chairmen of boards and the presidents of federations, the doctors and lawyers and educators and churchmen who after nineteen centuries have rescued the son of heaven from oblivion and translated him from mere meek heir to earth to chairman of its board of trade; . . .[25]

Christianity as "rapacity's masterpiece"—this is unmistakable evidence that Faulkner's interpretation of history

and Christianity is intended to jar its audience. As an institution that exercises power, Christianity belongs among
nations, generals, and heroes on the side of those who
crave fame, wealth, and glory—"glory" as a motive of historical deeds extends through the book like a *leitmotif*—
and whose actions begin wars. But Christ, the "Son of
Man," stands on the other side, the side of ordinary people
who want but to live in peace from the work of their own
hands. He is the noble hero of the unheroic, the unassum-
ing, the suffering. By setting the two parties in opposition,
one acting and one suffering from the action, Faulkner
provides his novel with a universal conception above and
beyond its treatment of the world war. The world war is
then only one of the historical catastrophes wherein the
ordinary man is "crucified."

"There was never an age, when man did not crucify the
Son of God afresh"—Faulkner has undertaken to prove
this statement by Theodore Parker several times. Joe
Christmas, the man between white and colored, is one
such crucified figure; the mutinous corporal of the *Fable*
is another. The "unknown soldier" of the world war is
Christ crucified: this comparison is the basic idea of *A
Fable*. This is not only expressed by the many analogies in
the life of the corporal. It also appears at the end of the
novel in a parable, a truely gruesome and grotesque
Faulknerian tale of a drunken detachment sent to Verdun
to get a corpse from the casemates for the monument to
the unknown soldier. Underway this corpse is exchanged
for that of the executed Christ-corporal, which in turn is
placed in the Paris monument.

The comparison of the hero with Christ is more direct
and detailed in *A Fable* than in *Light in August*. Faulkner
makes the analogy so exact in regard to Oriental descent,
birth, family, and disciples that one would call it an allegory if one forgot that a true allegory has an abstract, con-

ceptual core illustrated in personifications and figurative actions. Here we have a parallelism established between a contemporary character and a historico-religious one, Christ. This parallelism corresponds largely to the old typological comparison while it differs in decisive ways from modern techniques of symbolism and allegory.

Faulkner's reference to Christ does not fit in the category of symbolic structures that today's critics so readily investigate. It is related to the symbol but not identical with it. Where the usual symbol points from the limited to the boundless—it can be defined as a concrete, pictoral form with a nearly unlimited variety of interpretation— the Christ figure is summoned in literature to give a solid and consoling interpretation to the muddled abundance and ambiguity of life which might otherwise seem meaningless or miserable. This is a symbolism in the reverse direction, which points from the unsifted abundance of life to the *one* definite message. The use of exact historical facts represent another departure from usual symbolism and the mythical symbol. The date, day of the week, details of the Passion of Christ, his age, his disciples—all of these facts about unique events are employed symbolically to create the analogy of man with the son of God.[26] Unlike mythical symbols, Christ symbols cannot be freely manipulated and transformed. They stand immutable amidst the infinite variety of human suffering, from where they point toward the ideal, the redemption.

Faulkner's Christ parallelism is a modern continuation and modification of a typological thought that seeks reincarnations of eternal models in every age. But the age of Calvinism had to pass before Christ, to whom all types were originally connected, could himself become a type who is 'fulfilled' by a man who merges with him. The corporal with the twelve followers, who is betrayed by one of them, and who wants to end the slaughter in the trenches of World War I, fulfills Christ's role in our own time, and he is accordingly a character lacking individual traits and specific features.

Even though the basic idea of the Christ analogy was Calvinistic, its literary execution depended on the anti-Calvinist currents mentioned above. The corporal is a modern and even more radically humanized version of the Christ figure sketched by Emerson and Parker when they made the son of God into the divine brother of man. Faulkner's Christ is the man who suffers symbolically and actually for a mankind entangled in the tragic conditions of this world. The Christ of his conception is more tragic and earthly than Emerson's or Parker's. Both Christ and the corporal die without having provided more than a noble example for mankind. They are destroyed physically by the powers that have organized the world according to their own rules.

As we saw above, the transformation of the image of Christ by the Transcendentalists was the result of a rebellion against the absolute authority of a God conceived with Old Testament severity. Faulkner also continues this tendency in his own way, by putting the generalissimo in the place of God. The old general is the supreme military authority, to whom the three allied armies are subordinate —the threefold symbolism of three flags, three armies, is stressed—and in addition he is the natural father of the corporal. The military hierarchy he commands is described in religious terms:

> First and topmost were the three flags and the three supreme generals who served them: a triumvirate consecrated and anointed, a constellation remote as planets in their immutability, powerful as archbishops in their trinity, splendid as cardinals in their retinues and myriad as Brahmins in their blind followers; next were the three thousand lesser generals who were their dea-

cons and priests and the hierarchate of their households, their acolytes and bearers of monstrance and host and censer . . .[27]

Like Melville, Faulkner cannot see how an omnipotent God can avoid direct responsibility for the power exercised on earth. He makes the general represent this power, and this means above all the power that created and that perpetuates the conditions of this world. He is general, Caesar, God the father, and the devil, all in one person. He wants to induce the corporal to flight and to betrayal of himself, his rebellion and disciples, and his meeting and conversation with the corporal correspond to the temptation of Jesus by the devil. Just as the devil takes Jesus to a mountain and then to the pinnacle of the temple overlooking Jerusalem, so the old general takes his son to the Roman citadel overlooking the city and offers him the world:

"Then take the world," the old general said. "I will acknowledge you as my son; together we will close the window on this aberration and lock it forever. Then I will open another for you on a world such as caesar nor sultan nor khan ever saw, Tiberius nor Kubla nor all the emperors of the East ever dreamed of. . . ." [28]

But the corporal—and herein lies Faulkner's heretical interpretation of Christ—rebels against this father and refuses to submit to him, for which he is executed. Dostoyevsky's *The Great Inquisitor* was mentioned in the discussion of *A Fable*, and Faulkner also coincides with Dostoyevsky in his argument that rather than Christ it was the opposite party of bloody force that converted the world to Christianity:

It wasn't He with his humility and pity and sacrifice that converted the world; it was pagan and bloody Rome which did it with His martyrdom; furious and intractable dreamers had been bringing that same dream out of Asia Minor for three hundred years until at last one found a caesar foolish enough to crucify him. . . . Because only Rome could have done it, accomplished it, and even He . . . knew it, felt and sensed this, furious and intractable dreamer though He was.[29]

But Faulkner goes much further than Dostoyevsky. His Christ-corporal opposes not only the church and its rulers but also the ultimate basis of power, God Himself, by Whom he must necessarily be defeated. He is therefore a tragic character, much as Christ himself is a tragic figure in Faulkner's view. Both go down to defeat because they defend the cause of peace against force. But in each case defeat brings a moral victory. As Christ refuses to win followers by deception, changing stone into bread, so the corporal resists the coaxing of the priest whom the general charged with persuading him to save himself and his followers:

"Remember—" the priest said. "No, you cant remember, you dont know it, you cant read. So I'll have to be both again: defender and advocate. *Change these stones to bread, and all men will follow Thee.* And He answered, *Man cannot live by bread alone.* Because He knew that too, intractable and furious dreamer though He was: that He was tempted to tempt and lead man not with the *bread,* but with the *miracle* of that bread, the deception, the illusion, the delusion of that bread; tempted to believe that man was not only capable and willing but even eager for that deception, that even when the illusion of that miracle had led him to the point where the bread would revert once more to stone in his very belly and destroy him, his own children would be panting for the opportunity to grasp into their hands in their turn the delusion of that miracle which would destroy them. . . ."

. . . "Tell him that," the corporal said.

"Power," the priest said. "Not just power over the mere earth offered by that temptation of simple miracle, but that more terrible power over the universe itself—that terrible power over the whole universe which that mastery over man's mortal fate and destiny would have given Him had He not cast back into the Tempter's very teeth that third and most terrible temptation of immortality: which if He had faltered or succumbed would have destroyed His Father's kingdom not only on the earth but in heaven too because that would have destroyed heaven, since what value in the scale of man's hope and aspiration or what tensile hold or claim on man himself could that heaven own which could be gained by that base means—blackmail: man in his turn by no more warrant than one single precedent casting himself from the nearest precipice the moment he wearied of the burden of his free will and decision, the right to the one and the duty of the other, saying to, challenging his Creator: *Let me fall—if You dare?*"

"Tell him that," the corporal said.[30]

This rejection of power involves both an external defeat and an inner victory. The priest who wanted to change the corporal's mind bows to him and asks to be saved. Then he goes out and falls on a bayonet.

A Fable is the fable about the tragic fate of the ordinary, peace-loving man in this world. According to the other possibility of interpreting the title, it is the legend of Christ suffering symbolically in the name of the ordinary man. By making Christ into a "type" of the nonviolent rebel against power, Faulkner colors the latter and his cause with a saintly glow. The corporal is the common man ennobled by brotherhood with Christ, an ordinary man who, as the ideal of the unheroic hero, is the true prototype of American literature.

Hemingway, Wolfe, and Ellison had similar aims of elevation and glorification when they lent their modern heroes in suffering features of Christ. Their works share with Faulkner's a world view that is tragic in a certain way, something seldom encountered otherwise in American literature. In American fiction Christ becomes the "type" of the hero who suffers despite his innocence, or perhaps precisely because of it. He thereby fulfills a special function resulting from the peculiar dilemma of the tragic hero in America.

Actually it seems to be a paradox to speak of a "tragic American hero." Can there be such a thing as an openly confessed tragic world view in American literature? Does the American regard tragic experience as the unavoidable and necessary lot of man? In both cases the answer is no, and this is a basic difference between American literature and European. A literature that is acknowledged to be democratic, of a nation with an optimistic belief in life, cannot openly affirm the tragic experience of life. If tragic problems are encountered nonetheless, a situation arises where a redeemer is needed and Christ is summoned in aid. The ideal of the American is basically the innocent man, the new Adam of the new world, who lives in the best of all nations, a nation and a society he has shaped according to his own ideals. In this society he devotes himself to peaceful endeavors and the pursuit of happiness, firmly convinced that he is fairly entitled to a happy life.

Of course defects may appear in the social order; at times it may fall short of its ideal and then expose its heroes to distress. This is what happened for instance toward the end of the nineteenth century, and the conflicts that arose were vigorously exploited by naturalistic and sociocritical writers. Their goal, however, was the removal of defects and the restoration of an originally just order rather than revolutionary transformation. This is one possibility of discovering conflicts for literary use in an ideal society without calling the society itself into question and without becoming aware of an inescapable tragedy in life. Henry James explored another possibility by sending his "innocent" heroes and heroines to old and sinful Europe to become involved in tragic or near-tragic experiences, as innocent victims if not as collaborators.[31]

But the writers now being considered are concerned with a deeper level of experience. Melville, Hemingway, and Faulkner depict innocent people, ordinary Americans, who encounter inexplicable and invincible adversities given along with life itself. Their optimistic view of life yields no explanation for evils that are of an entirely different nature from social abuses. In this sense Billy Budd is the prototype of the tragic American hero. He is absolved of the Calvinist dogma of original sin, but he encounters an evil that persists and "for which God alone is made responsible," because in this respect He is still the "omnipotent God" of Calvinism. As in *Moby Dick* Melville here too places evil in close proximity to God. Faulkner's corporal is a more radical successor to Melville's Billy Budd. He rebels against the omnipotent lord of all powers and wars, God-Satan, for which intentional rebellion he meets the same fate encountered by Billy Budd for his unintentional one: a death compared to the Crucifixion by the author to tell us that we view an innocent man suffering vicariously.

For Melville, Billy Budd is wholly innocent. He has not the least share in any human failing which for the Greek hero is a precondition of his tragic consummation. Basically the same can be said of Melville's Pierre, and of

Faulkner's corporal as well, a character without human weaknesses and faults. At bottom even the cruel Joe Christmas is a basically innocent person who is prevented from being innocent all his life. His constant violence is really nothing other than his reaction to the inexplicable and incessant adversities in life, the helpless rage of innocence defiled that culminates in the murder of his unwelcome benefactress. The enemies of the innocent include not only evil people but good and well-meaning ones in addition. One gets a glimpse of this insight in *Billy Budd*. But the innocent can neither endure nor vanquish evil; instead, they are crushed by it.

The rage, the white-hot indignation and abysmal despair at the world one so often encounters in American literature is frequently the result of this perplexed, helpless innocence of an optimistic faith in life. When the hero who cherishes his own innocence encounters life's adversities, he cannot avoid the conflict. The dilemma of such heroes is that their very innocence prevents them from accepting life's adversities and thereby transcending their fates. The innocent man is at the same time an incomplete man: he must shun experience, for experience brings guilt. His only escape from such a conflict is madness or death. The bitter outbursts of innocent heroes, who often leave an entire world in ruins behind them, would be meaningless if Christ did not lend them the significance of innocence suffering magnificently. Even evil and embittered "innocents" are apparently unable to do without Christ. Thus we encounter in American literature the strange phenomenon of negative Christ figures, in whom an outraged and unbending "innocence" is converted to cruelty. This is the case with Joe Christmas, as with the Quaker "Nick of the Woods" in the novel of the same name by Montgomery Bird. His family having been murdered by Indians, he conceals beneath the mask of a peace-loving Quaker the murderous avenger who slaughters his Indian victims with an ax and marks them with a chilling bloody cross. It is also the case with Ahab, wounded by the incarnation of a neutral evil, Moby Dick, an Ahab who baptizes his helpers in the pursuit of this evil *"in nomine diaboli"* and who hunts Moby Dick with a suicidal, holy madness.

Tragic consummation, the supreme nonreligious blessing attainable by man in his earthly struggles, demands of its conferee, paradoxically enough, that he be initiated into guilt. Only the man who can acknowledge that neither he nor life is blameless can transcend his fall. He must accept responsibility and punishment as the price for his inner victory in defeat. But for the innocent hero there is no escape. He cannot be reconciled with his situation as a tragedy because he is convinced that he does not deserve his misfortune. The American hero freed of the conviction of total depravity is unable to deal with the problem of evil in the world. The radical suppression of the dogma of original sin created a dilemma to escape from which American authors called on Christ, not so much the son of God as the innocent one made to suffer persecution and crucifixion. He suffers for mankind and this sanctifies his suffering: it needs no explanation. The innocent hero is consoled at the thought of a brotherhood of all who suffer represented by Christ. The symbol of the crucified one, impressed on the unfortunate American Adam like a stamp, lends him a consecration and transfiguration he could not have attained alone, and it may also satisfy a secret ambition for distinction from and elevation above an egalitarian society.

Christ, the "hero of the lowest station," is invoked when the ordinary, innocent, suffering democratic hero is defeated by life. His presence lends the defeat the splendor of victorious transcendence that is the mark of tragedy.

Santayana once called it "glorification of life," the glorification of life in the face of death. In American literature it is not the mortal hero that glorifies life in defeat, it is instead the Christ invoked who brings transfiguration and explanation.

CHAPTER I

[1] (New York, 1931), p. 12.

[2] F. O. Matthiessen, *American Renaissance. Art and Expression in the Age of Emerson and Whitman* (London, Toronto, New York, 1941).

[3] Perry Miller has rendered us the service of documenting this in his anthology, *The Transcendentalists* (Cambridge, Mass., 1950). Miller affirms in his "Introduction" (p. 8) ". . . that the Transcendental movement is most accurately to be defined as a religious demonstration."

CHAPTER II

[1] *E.g.* take the symbol of the cross: it was originally part of an event, then it came to symbolize Christ sacrificing his life, and ultimately it came to be a symbol for the Christian religion.

[2] C. S. Lewis, in *The Allegory of Love* (London, 1936), p. 57 ff., describes the first century AD as an era sympathetic to allegory, and he explains this sympathy as due to the victory of monotheism over polytheism.

[3] One exception is Edwin Honig, who investigates poetical allegory and its relation to biblical allegory in his work, *Dark Conceit: The Making of Allegory* (London, 1959).

[4] In English and American literary criticism this divergent evaluation is largely derived from Coleridge's distinction of "Imagination" and "fancy," and the classification of allegory as "fancy."

[5] We occasionally encounter comparable convictions of an undoubted and missionary nature, together with a group of disciples, in the sphere of politics and ideology today. In this respect George Orwell's *Animal Farm* is a distant relative of *Pilgrim's Progress*.

[6] In his *Anatomy of Criticism* (Princeton, 1957), Northrop Frye argues that the modern critic is averse to allegory because it prescribes one exclusive mode of interpretation for him. This is a psychological explanation of the same state of affairs.

[7] Three vols. (Berlin, 1923/29).

[8] *Essay on Man* (New Haven, 1944), p. 25.

[9] Susanne K. Langer, *Philosophy in a New Key. A Study in the Symbolism of Reason, Rite, and Art* (Cambridge, Mass., 1942), p. 32.

[10] (Chicago, 1953), p. 56.

[11] (New York, 1955), p. 68.

[12] When we speak of "modern" symbolism we refer to the ideas and theories of the modern symbolist critics, which are mainly derived from the symbolism of modern poetry from the time of the French Symbolists.

[13] *Cf.* Max Schlesinger, *Geschichte des Symbols* (Berlin, 1912), p. 162 ff.

[14] Maxim No. 752, *Goethes Werke*, Vol. XII (Hamburg, 1953), p. 471.

[15] See Ursula Brumm, "Symbolism and the Novel," *Partisan*

Review (Summer, 1958), where an attempt is made to indicate the nature and function of this sort of symbol.

[16] The genesis of the elderly Goethe's use of symbolism in *Faust II* has been investigated by Wilhelm Emrich in *Die Symbolik von Faust II* (Berlin, 1943). It arises from Goethe's ideas on art, biology, geology, the theory of art, and history. Emrich examines the symbols and symbolic figures from their first appearance in Goethe's work up to their final form in Part Two of *Faust*.

[17] In a discussion that is far more subtle than anything we could attempt here Emrich refers to a typical symbol of Goethe's as a "condensed image," in which the relation between the sign and the thing signified is always paradoxical. He points out an example in the "Novelle" where Goethe "attempts to represent the sum total of the national budget without referring to currency" (p. 57) in the barter of the market place. "The exchange of goods reveals to everyone the essence of the economy, yet conceals it at the same time, because the economy cannot be wholly identified with the visible goods of the market place. If for the purpose of theory, however, one seeks to express this in abstract terms (*e.g.* to transfer barter into financial units) this destroys the economy at its very core. You cannot transfer "activity" and "exchange" into abstract terms without nullifying and destroying them.

[18] In the first chapter of *Maule's Curse: Seven Studies in the History of American Obscurantism*, to be found in *In Defense of Reason* (Denver, 1947), Yvor Winters speaks of an "allegorical disposition," without, however, defining allegory and distinguishing it from symbolism.

[19] *American Renaissance*, p. 243.

[20] *Symbolism and American Literature*, p. 81 f.

[21] Hans Leisegang, in his *Denkformen*, 2nd ed. (Berlin, 1951), distinguishes large families of thought forms according to the type of logic applied in them. *E.g.* he classifies St. Paul and his typological ideas (p. 88 ff., especially p. 93) in the group of thinkers whose inferences are circu-

lar. I here apply the concept "form of thought" in a more restricted sense to those views based on belief or conviction which (like "providences" or types), due to their dogmatic and clearly defined basis, have a certain formal structure.

22 *The Letters of Herman Melville*, ed. M. R. Davis and William H. Gilman (New Haven, 1960), p. 141 f.

23 But in his essay, "Hawthorne and His Mosses" (most readily accessible in Edmund Wilson, *The Shock of Recognition*, 2nd ed. [New York, 1955], p. 192), Melville did admit to "that Calvinistic sense of Innate Depravity and Original Sin, from whose visitations, in some shape or other, no deeply thinking mind is always and wholly free."

24 Poe, the real transmitter of the ideas of symbolism to Europe, is a special case among these writers, and he is not treated in Matthiessen's *American Renaissance* either. His imagination—so fertile in creating symbols—was nourished in part by the Gothic novel of Europe and in part by his own peculiar mental constitution. Even though one cannot agree with all of Marie Bonaparte's analyses (*The Life and Works of Edgar Allan Poe* [London, 1949], of which the criticism by Mario Praz in "Poe and Psychoanalysis," *Sewanee Review* [Summer, 1960] should be taken into account), it seems highly probable that many aspects of Poe's symbolism are psychologically conditioned. Thus Poe cannot be treated in our present essay on intellectual history.

Chapter III

1 Second ed. (Springfield, Mass., 1955).

2 See Johannes Erich Heyde, "Typus," *Wege zur Klarheit* (Berlin, 1960), pp. 66–79. In his derivation of the modern meanings of *Typ* and *Typus*, Heyde does not consider their use in medieval theology. For the modern use in English the *Oxford English Dictionary* cites examples for meanings 5, 6, and 7 from about 1840 on.

3 Ed. by James A. H. Murray *et al.* (Oxford, 1933).

4 A thorough treatment of the early history of the word *Typos*

and its use in the Bible will be found in Heinz G. Jantsch, *Studien zum Symbolischen in der frühmittelhochdeutschen Literatur* (Tübingen, 1959), p. 19 ff. Jantsch investigates the typological notions in early Middle High German literature in particular.

[5] On typology cf. *The Encyclopedia of Religion and Ethics*, Vol. XII (Edinburgh, 1921); *Lexikon für Theologie und Kirche*, founded by Michael Buchberger, Vol. X (Freiburg, 1931); *Dictionnaire de Théologie Catholique*, Vol. XV (Paris, 1946); and Wetzer-Welte, *Kirchenlexikon*, Vol. V, 2nd ed. (Freiburg, 1888). Leonhard Goppelt's *Typos. Die typologische Deutung des Alten Testaments im Neuen* (Gütersloh, 1939) is a recent discussion.

[6] Goppelt, *Typos*, p. 5 f.

[7] *Lexikon f. Theol. u. Kirche*, Vol. X, p. 345 f.

[8] Because it used the word "shadow," typology came to be confused with related theories of Plato's. See William G. Madsen, "Earth the Shadow of Heaven: Typological Symbolism in *Paradise Lost*," *PMLA*, LXXV (1960). This biblical use of "shadow" is the source for the phrase *to shadow forth*, meaning to prefigure, which is quite frequently encountered in typology.

[9] Although it is not limited to the Middle Ages, the doctrine of the fourfold meaning of the Bible was most widespread at that time.

[10] The source for what follows is Ernst von Dobschütz, "Vom vierfachen Schriftsinn," in *Harnack-Ehrung* (Leipzig, 1921), pp. 1–13, and Wetzer and Welte, *Kirchenlexikon*, *s.v.* "Hermeneutik, biblische."

[11] There are (less precise) alternatives with the same meaning: *effigies, imago, exemplum, similitudo,* and *umbra*.

[12] Originally in *Archivum Romanicum*, XXII (1938), pp. 436–489; reference is made hereafter to the English trans. by Ralph Manheim in Auerbach, *Scenes from the Drama of European Literature* (New York, 1959), pp. 11–76.

[13] Among the other literary historians who touch upon typology is Perry Miller, in the foreword to his edition of *Images or Shadows of Divine Things by Jonathan Edwards* (New

Haven, 1948) [*cf.* below, p. 37]; in the foreword of *Anatomy of Criticism* (Princeton, 1957), p. 14, Northrop Frye points out the significance of typology for literature; and Rosamund Tuve, in *A Reading of George Herbert* (London, 1951), describes the influence of typological thought on Herbert.

[14] This early type already exhibits the manifold parallelism later to become so popular with the Puritans. They too often refer to the antitype as the "second Moses," "the second children of Israel," etc.

[15] *Cf.* Harry A. Wolfson, *Philo, Foundations of Religious Philosophy in Judaism, Christianity, and Islam,* 2 vols. (Cambridge, Mass., 1948), esp. Vol. I, p. 115 ff.

[16] Auerbach, "Figura," *Scenes from the Drama of European Literature,* p. 53 f.

[17] Auerbach, *op. cit.,* p. 58 f.

[18] See below, p. 88 ff.

[19] Auerbach, *op. cit.,* p. 50 f.

[20] Another study by Auerbach which also treats Dante is the lecture, *Typologische Motive in der mittelalterlichen Literatur,* Schriften und Vorträge des Petrarca-Instituts, II (Cologne, 1953).

[21] Goppelt, *Typos,* p. 7.

[22] See Albrecht Ritschl, *Geschichte des Pietismus in der reformierten Kirche* (Bonn, 1880), esp. p. 130 ff. and p. 505 f., and Gottlob Schrenk, *Gottesreich und Bund im älteren Protestantismus, vornehmlich bei Johannes Coccejus* (Gütersloh, 1923).

[23] Schrenk, *Gottesreich,* p. 28 ff.

[24] On Ames see Karl Reuter, *Wilhelm Amesius, der führende Theologe des erwachenden reformierten Pietismus* (Moers, 1940).

[25] *Cf.* Perry Miller on Ames' significance as a teacher of the Puritans, *The New England Mind: The Seventeenth Century* (Cambridge, Mass., 1954), pp. 51, 165 ff., and 432 f. In his biographical sketch of Thomas Hooker (*Magnalia,* Book III, First Part, Appendix, ¶ 13), Cotton Mather renders Hooker's estimate of Ames with the following words: "And

such was the regard which . . . he had for Dr. Ames, that he would say, if a scholar was but well studied in Dr. Ames his *Medulla Theologiae,* and *Casus Conscientiae* . . . would make him (supposing him versed in the scriptures) *a good divine."*

26 With reference to an Amsterdam, 1628 edition of the *Medulla,* Liber Primus, Cap. XXXVIII, "De administratione foederis gratuiti ante Christum adventum," p. 173 ff.

27 See Schrenk, *Gottesreich,* p. 40 ff.

28 Albrecht Ritschl, *Geschichte des Pietismus in der reformierten Kirche,* and *Geschichte des Pietismus in der lutherischen Kirche,* Part I (Bonn, 1884), pp. 346, 393.

29 Karl Christian Bähr, *Symbolik des Mosaischen Cultus,* Vol. I (Heidelberg, 1837), pp. v and 17.

30 *Op. cit.,* p. 15.

31 Perry Miller (*Images or Shadows,* p. 142 n. 30) says of Witsius and Cocceius that ". . . since these men were leaders of the 'federal' or 'covenant' school of Calvinism, to which the New Englanders belonged, they were much respected and read in America."

32 *Journal of Jasper Danckaerts, 1679–1680,* ed. by Bartlett Burleigh James and J. Franklin Jameson, Original Narratives of Early American History, Vol. XV (New York, 1946), p. 45.

33 One can see this clearly in Ch. VII, "Of God's Covenant with Man," of Book Five, "The Faith and the Order in the Churches of New England," of Cotton Mather's *Magnalia Christi Americana.* The close connection between the Adam-Christ parallel and the two covenants is also affirmed by Samuel Mather, in *The Figures or Types of the Old Testament* (London, 1705), p. 63. See also below, p. 41 f.

34 The American Puritans constructed an independent theological system on a Calvinist foundation. On this see John T. McNiell, *The History and Character of Calvinism* (New York, 1954), p. 339 ff., and Perry Miller, *The New England Mind, passim.* Among the notions they stressed particularly was that of the covenant, which was also elaborated in Scotland and by the Cocceians.

[35] *Magnalia*, Fifth Book, Ch. VIII, vi.

[36] See William Haller, *The Rise of Puritanism* (New York, 1938), p. 151.

[37] On the connection between covenant theology and political thought *cf.* Gerhard Oestreich, "Die Idee des religiösen Bundes und die Lehre vom Staatsvertrags," *Festchrift für Hans Herzfeld* (Berlin, 1959), pp. 11–32.

CHAPTER IV

[1] *Images or Shadows*, p. 24: "For, in the literature of New England, during the years in which the moralists were perfecting the art of spiritualizing the commonplace, a resurgence of typology can be traced, as it can in the literature of all Protestant communities. It ran parallel to the spiritualizing, and separate, but was often allied." Miller accounts for it in the following manner: "Probably the increasing demand for sensational preaching explains both tendencies." I am not wholly satisfied by this explanation. As Samuel Mather's *Figures or Types of the Old Testament* (London, 1673) and Edward Taylor's "Meditations, Second Series" (see below pp. 43 ff. and 56 ff.) show, the Puritans were led to typology for reasons immanent in the logic of their theology.

[2] *The Dictionary of American Biography* has nothing on this Samuel Mather; he is treated in Vol. XIII (London, 1909) of the *Dictionary of National Biography*, ed. by Sidney Lee.

[3] *Magnalia Christi Americana, or, the Ecclesiastical History of New England* (London, 1702), Book IV, Ch. II. Subsequent quotations are from the first American ed., 2 vols. (Hartford, Conn., 1820).

[4] *Magnalia*, Vol. II, p. 39.

[5] This typological argument against church music did cause the Puritans some difficulty, because they had trouble indicating what instrumental music was typical of. The prohibition of church music occurred again in the explanatory appendix of the Cambridge Synod of 1680, which confirmed the Faith of the Churches of 1648. Thus we read in Book

5 of the *Magnalia* ("Historical Remarks upon the Discipline practised in the Churches of New-England," Vol. II, p. 228): "In our asserting, a matter of the *Old Testament*, to have been *typical*, 'tis not needful, that we be always able to particularize any *future mysteries* of the *New Testament* therein referred unto . . ."

6 *Magnalia*, Vol. II, p. 45.

7 Subsequent quotations are from the 2nd ed. (London, 1705).

8 Samuel Mather, *The Gospel of the Old Testament, Rewritten from the Original Work of S.M. by the author of "The Listener," "Christ Our Example,"* etc. (London, 1834). The author was Mrs. Catherine Fry Wilson.

9 *Figures or Types*, p. 52.

10 *Loc. cit.*

11 *Ibid.*, p. 118. See below, p. 170, for Herman Melville's use of this type.

12 *Ibid.*, p. 126.

13 *Ibid.*, p. 129 f.

14 *Ibid.*, p. 128.

15 *Magnalia*, Vol. I, p. 23.

16 See above, p. 25 f.

17 *Magnalia*, Vol. I, p. 32.

18 *Loc. cit.*

19 *Magnalia*, Vol. I, p. 48.

20 *Magnalia*, Vol. II, p. 426.

21 *Cf.* Donald A. Stauffer, *English Biography Before 1700* (Cambridge, Mass., 1930), pp. 287–372; and in addition, R. E. Watters, "Biographical Technique in Cotton Mather's *Magnalia,*" *William and Mary Quarterly*, II (1945), pp. 154–63.

22 Kenneth B. Murdock, "Clio in the Wilderness. History and Biography in Puritan New England," *Church History*, XXIV (1955), pp. 221–38.

23 William R. Maniere II emphasizes these negative features of Mather's method in "Cotton Mather and the Biographical Parallel," *American Quarterly*, XIII (1961), pp. 153–60.

24 *Magnalia*, Vol. I, p. 104.

[25] *Ibid.*, p. 109.

[26] *Ibid.*, p. 251.

[27] Some of Cotton Mather's other fulfillments of Moses are Francis Higginson, Theophilus Eaton, and John Davenport.

[28] *Magnalia*, Vol. I, p. 259.

[29] *Ibid.*, p. 254.

[30] *Magnalia*, Vol. I, p. 167 f.

[31] *Ibid.*, p. 152.

[32] *Ibid.*, p. 251. The deeper reason for the choice of terms in the present case is probably that John Cotton could not fulfill the Moses type in its full sense. He was more a theologian than a man of action and could thus fulfill only the spiritual aspect of the Moses type. The parallel to Melanchthon emphasizes the primarily spiritual and intellectual nature of his achievement.

[33] Jonathan Edwards made the attempt one generation later to write contemporary history from the standpoint of theology and typology; see below, p. 87 ff.

[34] Mather gathered cases of "providences" in the Sixth Book of his *Magnalia*. He urged his colleagues to gather cases of miraculous rescue at sea or from Indian captivity, and other "providences," and report them to a department of Harvard College, created especially for that purpose.

[35] See Friedrich Meinecke, *Die Entstehung des Historismus*, 2 vols. (Berlin, 1936).

CHAPTER V

[1] *The Poems of Edward Taylor*, ed. by Donald E. Stanford, with a Foreword by Louis L. Martz (New Haven, 1960).

[2] This is also the opinion of Louis L. Martz, *ibid.*, p. xiii.

[3] *E.g.*, Austin Warren, "Edward Taylor," in *Rage for Order* (Chicago, 1948); Herbert Blau, "Heaven's Sugar Cake: Theology and Imagery in the Poetry of Edward Taylor," *NEQ*, XXVI (1953); and Mindele Black, "Edward Taylor: Heaven's Sugar Cake," *NEQ* XXIX (1956).

[4] Mindele Black (see above, note 3) speaks of "aesthetic schizophrenia"—"Doctrinal liberalism and Hebraic rigor do

not blend happily" (p. 179), because he fails to understand how the images are connected by types. The same may be said of Blau (see note 3): he is unaware of the typological use of 'circumcise' (p. 353 f.), which occurs again and again in the theological literature of the era. Meditation 70, Second Series, presents a typological interpretation of circumcision.

5 On this see Willie T. Weathers, "Edward Taylor and the Cambridge Platonists," *American Literature*, XXVI (1954), pp. 1–31.

6 *Literature & Theology in Colonial New England*, pp. 168–169.

7 "Edward Taylor: A Revaluation," *NEQ*, XXI (1948), pp. 518–30.

8 *The Poetical Works of Edward Taylor* (Princeton, 1939), p. 24. But it seems to me misleading to postulate a marked gap between these two tendencies. Covenant theology was derived from an important conception of Calvinism and it was developed within the framework of Calvinism.

9 This is also the vantage point from which to regard the discussion about whether the New England Puritans were Calvinists. On the role of covenant theology in New England Calvinism *cf.* Perry Miller, "The Marrow of Puritan Divinity" in *Errand into the Wilderness* (Cambridge, Mass., 1956), p. 48–98.

10 Meditation 22, First Series.

11 *E.g.*, Samuel Mather's *Old Testament Types Explained and Improved* (London, 1673), see above, p. 40 ff.; or Benjamin Keach's *Tropologia: A Key to Open Scripture Metaphors . . . Together with Types of the Old Testament* (London, 1681). See also notes 30 and 31 in *Images or Shadows of Divine Things by Jonathan Edwards*, ed. by Perry Miller (New Haven, 1948), p. 141 f.

12 There is a theoretical discussion of typology in Sermon IX (to Meditation 50) of the *Christographia*, ed. by Norman Grabo (New Haven, Conn., and London, 1962).

13 Meditation 12 of the First Series already makes use of a typical idea, but it is not characterized as such. See there

the note to line 3. There are also other Meditations before and after the specifically typological period which deal with types: for instance, Meditations 29, 37 (First Series) and 113 (Second Series) on the Tree of Life.

[14] *The Poems of Edward Taylor*, p. 83.

[15] In his *Tropologia* Benjamin Keach also provides a thorough definition of the distinction, which is quoted in *Images or Shadows*, p. 142.

[16] When he developed this style Taylor was not unaware of the English religious poets; George Herbert's influence on his work is too pronounced to be overlooked. On this point *cf.* the Foreword by Louis L. Martz in *The Poems of Edward Taylor*, p. xiii ff.

[17] Meditation 20.

[18] On the emblem see below, p. 125 f.

[19] The italics are mine in both cases.

[20] As the opening stanzas show, the oxymoron "fiery flood" is derived from the typical connection of flood with hellish deluge of sinfulness.

[21] Meditation 80 says: "Except you eate the flesh of the Son of Man, etc. ye have no Life in you."

[22] This is discussed by Rudolf Bultmann in "Ursprung und Sinn der Typologie als hermeneutischer Methode," *Theologische Literaturzeitung*, LXXXV (1950), col. 210.

[23] This also marks the distinction between type and antitype.

[24] *Magnalia Christi Americana*, Fifth Book, "The Faith and the Order in the Churches of New England," Chapter XXX, vi., Vol. II, p. 178.

[25] *Ibid.*, Fifth Book, Chap. XXX, vii.

[26] This also accords with the Profession of Faith. The chapter "Of the Sacraments," *ibid.*, Ch. XXVIII, p. 176, states: "Sacraments are holy signs and seals of the covenant of grace, immediately instituted by Christ."

[27] Meditation 102.

[28] Meditation 103.

[29] From Meditation 106, *ibid.*, p. 273.

[30] Meditation 22, First Series; Meditation 13 is similar.

[31] Meditation 36 of the Second Series states the same: "My Metaphors are but dull Tacklings tag'd / With ragged Non-Sense . . ."

[32] Meditation 152, Second Series. Meditation 153 states:

> You Holy Angells lend yee mee your Skill.
>   Your Organs set and fill them up well stuft
> With Christs rich praises whose lips do distill
>   Upon his Spouse such ravishing dews to gust
> With Silver Metaphors and Tropes bedight.
> How fair, how pleasant art, Love, for delight?

[33] This is from Meditation 151, Second Series. In Meditations 100 and 101, even "glory" occurs as a metaphor: "Then Glory as a Metaphor, Il'tende / And lay it all on thee, my Lord! to bring My Heart in Flames of love . . .": God's "glory" has a spiritual significance and is thus a metaphor.

[34] On the question whether sensual imagery is useful and permissible, *cf.* Kenneth Murdock's comments on Richard Baxter's approval of such imagery, in *Literature & Theology in Colonial New England* (Cambridge, Mass., 1949), p. 54.

[35] Meditation 148, Second Series.

[36] We find emblems in *e.g.* Meditations 122, 140, 149, and 160.

[37] See below, p. 95 ff.

[38] Ralph Waldo Emerson, "Nature"; both quotations are from Ch. IV, "Language," *Emerson's Complete Works*, ed. by Edward W. Emerson (Cambridge, Mass., 1883), Vol. I, p. 31 f.

Chapter VI

[1] "The Perpetuity and Change of the Sabbath," *The Works of President Edwards* (New York and London, 1849), Vol. IV, p. 628.

[2] Perry Miller, *Jonathan Edwards* (New York, 1949). The modernity of Edwards alleged there is criticized by Vincent Thomas in "The Modernity of Jonathan Edwards," NEQ, XXV (1952).

[3] *Jonathan Edwards, Representative Selections*, with Introduction, Bibliography and Notes, by Clarence H. Faust and Thomas H. Johnson (American Book Company, 1935).

[4] I cannot share Perry Miller's opinion (*Jonathan Edwards*, p. 311) that this is "a pioneer work in American historiography."

[5] The original letter is dated May 30, 1735; an expanded version dated November 6, 1736, was published in London in 1737 under the title "A Faithful Narrative of the Surprising Work of God. . . ."

[6] *The Works of President Edwards*, Vol. III, p. 274 ff.

[7] The rationalist faction in the New England clergy rejected this belief. Edwards' opponent, Charles Chauncey, who objected to Edwards' "preaching of terror," advanced some criticisms of Edwards' *Revival of Religion* in his *Seasonable Thoughts on the State of Religion in New England* (Boston, 1743). Cf. *Jonathan Edwards, Representative Selections*, p. xxi.

[8] *The Works of President Edwards*, Vol. III, p. 314. "The other continent" refers as the context shows to "the old world," Asia and Europe together.

[9] *Ibid.*, p. 319.

[10] *Ibid.*, p. 315.

[11] *Ibid.*, p. 316.

[12] *Ibid.*, p. 323.

[13] See above, p. 27.

[14] "Type" occurs in Dwight in Bk. I, 1. 756 and Bk. V, 1. 195 ff.

[15] Timothy Dwight, *The Conquest of Canaan* (Hartford, 1785), Bk. X, 1 479 ff.

[16] *The Works of President Edwards*, Vol. IV, p. 403.

[17] *Ibid.*, p. 403 f.

[18] Vol. III, p. 593.

[19] The Passover is also termed symbolical rather than typical.

[20] *Images or Shadows of Divine Things*, ed. by Perry Miller (New Haven, 1948), p. 44.

[21] *Ibid.*, p. 65. Quite similar ideas will be found in Image 19, p. 46 f.

[22] Perry Miller treats this in his Introduction, mainly on p. 7 ff: "By an unavoidable compulsion, typology was forced to seek for a unity greater than that of the Bible, a unity of history, nature, and theology."

[23] *Ibid.*, p. 63 f.

[24] Image 156, *ibid.*, p. 109.

[25] *Cf.* Miller on this point, *Images*, p. 18.

[26] Image 79, *ibid.*, p. 79.

[27] Image 146, *ibid.*, p. 102.

[28] Image 25, *ibid.*, p. 48.

[29] Image 12, *ibid.*, p. 45.

[30] Differences in handwriting, pens, and inks prove that the entries were made at different times; the editor Perry Miller states "throughout his life," *Images*, p. 1.

[31] Erich Auerbach, *Typologische Motive in der mittelalterlichen Literatur*, p. 15.

[32] In *Errand Into the Wilderness* (Cambridge, Mass., 1956), p. 185.

[33] *Ibid.*, p. 192.

[34] Swedenborg, the son of a Swedish Lutheran bishop, whose bold visions Emerson accepted with but few reservations (as his essay "Swedenborg: or, The Mystic" shows), based his work upon a similar theological foundation. From the first volume of Swedenborg's *Animal Kingdom* Emerson quotes the following: "In our doctrine of Representations and Correspondences we shall treat of both these symbolical and typical resemblances, and of the astonishing things which occur, I will not say in the living body only, but throughout nature, and which correspond so entirely to supreme and spiritual things that one would swear that the physical world was purely symbolical of the spiritual world." Here we also encounter "typical resemblances." *Emerson's Complete Works*, ed. by Edward W. Emerson (Cambridge, Mass., 1883) Vol. IV, p. 112.

[35] *Cf.* Robert E. Spiller, "Ralph Waldo Emerson," in *Literary History of the United States* (New York, 1949), p. 365, who perhaps overstates the case: "Many volumes have been written to prove that Emerson's final position was based on

Neo-Platonism, German idealism, or Oriental mysticism; but a study of his sermons and of his early reading indicates that he never departed from his loyalty to the faith of his fathers, the Christian tradition as developed by Christ, Paul, Thomas Aquinas, and Calvin."

36 Perry Miller has gathered the most important contributions to this dispute in *The Transcendentalists. An Anthology* (Cambridge, Mass., 1950).

37 *Emerson's Complete Works*, Vol. XI, p. 9 ff.

38 This is Emerson's free rendition, *ibid.*, p. 16.

39 *Emerson's Complete Works*, Vol. XI, p. 18.

40 See above, p. 98.

41 *Emerson's Complete Works*, Vol. VIII, p. 14.
Edwards says in Image 19: "So it is God's way in the natural world to make inferiour things in conformity and analogy to the superiour, so as to be the images of them . . . And from the lowest animal to the highest, you will find an analogy, though the nearer you come to the highest, the more you may observe of analogy."

42 *Ibid.*, p. 23 f.

43 This is where Emerson derives his definition of the distinction between "imagination" and "fancy" which he adopted from Coleridge: as opposed to "imagination" (see the quotation in the text), "fancy" is that which "at leisure plays with the resemblances and types, for amusement, and not for its moral end . . ." (*ibid.*, p. 32).

44 *Emerson's Complete Works*, Vol. III, pp. 33, 38.

45 *Ibid.*, p. 18.

46 *Ibid.*, p. 21 f.

47 *Ibid.*, p. 22.

48 The "sign" is employed for a certain purpose: "The poet alone knows astronomy, chemistry, vegetation and animation, for he does not stop at these facts, but employs them as signs." *Emerson's Complete Works*, Vol. III, p. 25.

49 In the above examples Emerson speaks several times of things of visible nature being *used* as types.

50 *Emerson's Complete Works*, Vol. I, p. 32 f.

51 *Ibid.*, p. 32.

CHAPTER VII

1 *The Works of Nathaniel Hawthorne*, with introductory notes by George Parsons Lathrop (Cambridge, Mass., 1882), Vol. IX: American Notebooks, pp. 24 and 26.

2 The literary concept of the motif as defined in detail by Wolfgang Kayser (*Das Sprachliche Kunstwerk*, 5th ed., [Bern and Munich, 1959], pp. 59–71) is used here with certain reservations. The motif in Hawthorne is the pattern of a humanly significant situation that gives rise to action. But rather than echo a motif that occurs elsewhere in literature, Hawthorne usually discovers or invents his own motifs.

3 "The only way of expressing emotion in the form of art is by finding an 'objective correlative'; in other words, a set of objects, a situation, a chain of events which shall be the formular of that particular emotion; such that when the external facts, which must terminate in sensory experience, are given, the emotion is immediately evoked," in T. S. Eliot, *Selected Essays* (New York, 1950), p. 124 f.

4 *American Renaissance*, p. 243 f.

5 From *In Defense of Reason*, p. 157; *cf.* p. 164.

6 (Norman, Okla., 1952), p. 7.

7 (Cambridge, Mass., 1955), p. 58.

8 J. W. Shroeder, "Hawthorne's 'Egotism, or, The Bosom Serpent' and its Source," *American Literature*, XXXI (1960) and H. A. Leibowitz, "Hawthorne and Spenser: Two Sources," *American Literature*, XXX (1959).

9 *Hawthorne's Works*, Vol. IX, p. 34.

10 *Hawthorne's Works*, Vol. II, p. 308.

11 *Ibid.*, p. 309.

12 *Ibid.*, p. 314.

13 *Ibid.*, p. 315.

14 *Ibid.*, p. 320.

15 *Hawthorne's Works*, Vol. I, p. 26.

16 *Ibid.*, p. 29.

17 *Ibid.*, p. 31.

18 *Ibid.*, p. 31.

[19] On the other hand, Mary Goffe, in "The Man of Adamant," "typifying pure Religion," is closer to pure allegory. In fact, she is allegory embellished only by her individual name.

[20] With "type" and "typify" we may count "shadow" and "shadow forth," which Hawthorne occasionally uses in this specific sense.

[21] *Hawthorne's Works*, Vol. I, p. 54.

[22] *Ibid.*, p. 63.

[23] *Ibid.*, p. 62.

[24] *Ibid.*, p. 62.

[25] Elizabeth is said to be "of a firmer character than his own." *Ibid.*, p. 63.

[26] *Ibid.*, p. 69.

[27] It is possible that traits of Christ can be identified in the character of Colcord in *Doctor Grimshaw's Secret.*

[28] See above, p. 22.

[29] *Hawthorne's Works*, Vol. XI, p. 41.

[30] *Cf.* Samuel Mather, *The Figures or Types of the Old Testament*, 2nd edition (London, 1705), p. 55: "Men must not *indulge their own fancies*, as the Popish Writers use to do, with their Allegorical Senses, as they call them; except we have some Scripture ground for it. It is not safe to make any thing a Type meerly upon our own fansies and imaginations; it is *Gods* Prerogative to make *Types.*"

[31] *Hawthorne's Works*, Vol. I, p. 247.

[32] *Ibid.*, p. 506.

[33] Jonathan Edwards, *Images or Shadows*, p. 130.

[34] *Hawthorne's Works*, Vol. II, p. 502.

[35] *Images or Shadows*, p. 108.

[36] *Hawthorne's Works*, Vol. II, p. 180 f.

[37] *Ibid.*, p. 455.

[38] *Hawthorne's Works*, Vol. V, p. 160.

[39] *Ibid.*, p. 161.

[40] The *Oxford English Dictionary* has four basic meanings, the first two of which are obsolete: "1. An ornament of inlaid work" (examples from 1656–1775) and "2. A drawing or picture expressing a moral fable or allegory; a fable or allegory such as might be expressed pictorially" (examples

from 1430–1730). In addition: "3. A picture of an object (or the object itself) serving as a symbolical representation of an abstract quality, an action, state of things, class of persons, etc.," plus "b. In wider sense: A symbol, typical representation, sometimes applied to a person: The 'type' personification (of some virtue or quality)." And "4. A figured object used with symbolic meaning, as the distinctive badge of a person, family, nation, etc. Chiefly of heraldic devices, and of the symbolic objects accompanying the images of saints."

41 W. Kayser, *Das Sprachliche Kunstwerk*, p. 75 f.

42 *Hawthorne's Works*, Vol. I, p. 138.

43 *Ibid.*, p. 312.

44 Yvor Winters, *In Defense of Reason*, p. 158.

45 "Allegory" and "allegorical" occur very seldom in Hawthorne's tales. In "Howe's Masqeurade" Hawthorne speaks of the "allegorical figures" of the masks. But allegory is usually only referred to in forewords and introductory remarks, because as a literary *terminus technicus* it does not belong in the narrative.

In the introductory remarks to "Rappaccini's Daughter" Hawthorne speaks with irony towards himself of M. de l'Aubépine's "inveterate love of allegory."

46 Henry James, *Hawthorne* (London, 1879), most readily accessible in Edmund Wilson, *The Shock of Recognition* (New York, 1955), p. 521.

47 In a certain sense, with respect to Priscilla, this also holds for *The Blithedale Romance*.

48 The Puritan category that applies to these cases is not retribution, which would be redemption by works, but regeneration.

49 *Hawthorne's Works*, Vol. III, p. 375.

50 "Type," "typify," and related concepts occur in *HoSG* in the following connections: Of Clifford Pyncheon's old, faded dressing-gown it is said (Vol. III, p. 132): "It was the better to be discerned, by this exterior type, how worn and old were the soul's more immediate garments"; the phantasmagoria that Clifford sees in Maule's well (p. 186) is "a

stern dreadful shape that typified his fate," and "A cab; an omnibus, with its populous interior, dropping here and there a passenger, and picking up another, and thus typifying that vast rolling vehicle, the world. . . ." (p. 193).

[51] *Hawthorne's Works*, Vol. III, p. 34.

[52] *Ibid.*, p. 36.

[53] *Ibid.*, Vol. III, p. 13.

[54] *Ibid.*, p. 14.

[55] *Ibid.*, p. 14.

[56] Essays and Studies on American Language and Literature, IV (Uppsala-Cambridge, Mass., 1946), a part of her larger work, *Nathaniel Hawthorne and European Literary Tradition* (*loc. cit.*, 1947).

[57] Jane Lundblad, *Nathaniel Hawthorne and the Tradition of Gothic Romance*, p. 29.

[58] *Hawthorne's Works*, Vol. III, p. 358.

[59] *Ibid.*, Vol. III, p. 147 f.

[60] *Ibid.*, p. 277.

[61] *Ibid.*, p. 374 f.

[62] Hawthorne even states this two times: *Works*, Vol. III, pp. 112 f. and 182.

[63] *Ibid.*, p. 113.

[64] *Ibid.*, p. 186.

[65] *Ibid.*, p. 377.

[66] *Hawthorne's Works*, Vol. VI, p. 15.

[67] *Hawthorne's Works*, Vol. VI, p. 522 f.

[68] Hawthorne's contemporaries were not the only ones to encounter difficulty with Donatello. We find modern interpreters trying to explain his faun-like nature symbolically without recognizing its typological derivation. See H. H. Waggoner, *Hawthorne*, p. 207.

[69] *Hawthorne's Works*, Vol. VI, p. 491.

[70] *Hawthorne's Works*, Vol. VI, p. 37.

[71] "Did Adam fall, that we might ultimately rise to a far loftier paradise than his?" asks Kenyon at the end by way of summing up the events (*Hawthorne's Works*, Vol. VI, p. 519). Whether or not Hawthorne here embraces the *felix culpa* doctrine is a question thoroughly discussed by

scholars, many of whom take the affirmative view. Richard Fogle seems to me to be right when he says (*Hawthorne's Fiction*, p. 163) that Hawthorne makes no ultimate decision but offers the thesis for serious consideration.

[72] *Hawthorne's Works*, Vol. VI, p. 21.

[73] Richard Fogle has pointed out (*Hawthorne's Fiction*, p. 166 ff.) how often in *The Marble Faun* the Golden Age and Arcadia are described, and that they are somehow connected with the Garden of Eden of Christianity's earliest era: "Eden is the Christian counterpart of the pagan Golden Age. Hawthorne does not venture to identify the two, Eden having always a special sanctity, but in *The Marble Faun* they are clearly copresent, simplicities of similar import" (p. 168).

[74] *Hawthorne's Works*, Vol. VI, p. 268 f.

[75] *Ibid.*, p. 272.

[76] *Ibid.*, p. 273.

[77] *Ibid.*, p. 57.

[78] As Maturin's *Melmoth, the Wanderer* and other novels of terror show, this is a popular theme in the genre.

[79] *Hawthorne's Works*, Vol. III, p. 236 f.

[80] *Hawthorne's Works*, Vol. I, p. 303: "It seemed as if the picture, while hidden behind the cloud of immemorial years, had been all the time acquiring an intenser depth and darkness of expression, till now it gloomed forth again, and threw its evil omen over the present hour." Later on there was a rumour "that the dark mysterious picture had started from the wall, and spoken face to face with Lieutenant-Governor Hutchinson."

[81] *Hawthorne's Works*, Vol. VI, p. 488.

[82] *Ibid.*, p. 48.

[83] *Ibid.* p. 491.

[84] Hyatt H. Waggoner (*Hawthorne*, p. 60) also calls Hilda an emblematic character, but he offers no explanation why.

[85] *Hawthorne's Works*, Vol. VI, p. 471.

[86] H. H. Waggoner, *Hawthorne*, p. 256.

[87] *The English Notebooks*, ed. by Randall Stewart (New York, 1962), p. 106.

88 Edward H. Davidson, *Hawthorne's Last Phase* (New Haven, 1949), p. 16 f. and p. 22 ff.

89 *Ibid.*, p. 45 f. and p. 70 f.

90 I presume that it was just the romance character of this image that made Hawthorne stick to it, even though he could not find suitable material to fill it out.

91 *Hawthorne's Works*, Vol. V, p. 187.

92 *Ibid.*, p. 189.

93 *Ibid.*, p. 192.

94 *Ibid.*, p. 305.

95 *Ibid.*, p. 306.

96 F. O. Matthiessen, *American Renaissance*, p. 276.

97 Yvor Winters, *In Defense of Reason*, p. 170.

98 Richard H. Fogle, *Hawthorne's Fiction*, p. 11.

Chapter VIII

1 See above, p. 27 f.

2 Lionel Trilling, *The Liberal Imagination* (New York, 1950), p. 205 f.

3 On Ahab as a satanic figure *cf.* Henry A. Murray, "In Nomine Diaboli," NEQ, XXIV (1951), pp. 435–52.

4 Nathalia Wright, *Melville's Use of the Bible* (Durham, N.C., 1949), p. 5 ff. The authoress, who has very creditably traced the Bible passages used by Melville, pays no heed to typology. Also, she has little understanding of Melville's religious problems: "For all this interest in it, however, Melville's thought upon the subject of religion remained relatively immature. Though he speculated endlessly on the natture of God and on man's relationship to him, his implications were always ethical, his favorite presentation allegorical" (p. 6).

5 Not until relatively late does Melville read novels in the true sense. *The Melville Log, A Documentary Life of Herman Melville, 1819–1891*, ed. by Jay Leyda (New York, 1951), records that Thackeray's *Vanity Fair* was ordered in 1848, but Melville obviously did not read other realistic novels until much later. Not until 1870 do we hear of him reading

and commenting on Balzac. Interestingly enough, it is a bitter comment on a passage where Balzac describes how his hero has been negatively influenced by society. Melville's comment: "This describes man in his consummate flower of civilization" (*The Melville Log*, p. 715).

6 On Melville's religious thought see William Braswell, *Melville's Religious Thought. An Essay in Interpretation* (New York, 1943).

7 *The Works of Herman Melville*, Standard Edition (London, 1922), Vol. XI, Israel Potter, p. 158.

8 *Melville's Billy Budd*, ed. by F. Barron Freeman (Cambridge, Mass., 1948), p. 184: "But for the adequate comprehending of Claggart by a normal nature these hints are insufficient."

9 *Ibid.*, p. 185.

10 *Loc. cit.*

11 Howard P. Vincent, *The Trying-Out of Moby Dick* (Boston, 1949), p. 271 ff., shows that Melville probably used John Kitto, *A Cyclopedia of Biblical Literature*, for *Moby Dick*. "Lexicon of Holy Writ" could be (at least in connotation) an allusion to this book. But in the final instance this is not important, because Melville is clearly referring to its substance, *viz.*, the order of biblical characters in the Bible itself which Kitto rearranges.

12 Thus modern interpreters, as *e.g.* Richard Chase, *Herman Melville: A Critical Study* (New York, 1949), are misled into analyzing Melville in the light of a modern mythologism.

13 The first two are the original type designations that have become so important for American literature. See above p. 23 and below p. 209.

14 *Billy Budd*, p. 252.

15 It is quite clear that Melville did think of Milton in this connection: to the motto-like heading of the description of Claggart, "Pale ire, envy and despair," he remarks in a note in the manuscript, "Pale ire, envy and despair is Miltonic" (*Billy Budd*, p. 190).

16 See *ibid.*, pp. 168 and 190 f. Claggart's "silken jet curls" (p.

168) even recall the dark heroine as she is commonly described in the romances.

[17] *Ibid.*, p. 207: "Then would Claggart look like the man of sorrows. Yes, and sometimes the melancholy expression would have in it a touch of soft yearning, as if Claggart could even have loved Billy but for fate and ban."

[18] *Billy Budd*, p. 187.

[19] *Israel Potter*, p. 59.

[20] *Ibid.*, p. 5.

[21] *White Jacket*, p. 189, a literal echo of I Pet. 2.9. Melville states further: "God has predestinated, mankind expects, great things from our race; and great things we feel in our souls . . . Long enough have we been sceptics with regard to ourselves, and doubted whether, indeed, the *political Messiah* had come." (my italics). We meet here a combination of typological and nationalist though similar to that of Jonathan Edwards. See above, p. 9.

[22] *Israel Potter*, p. 214.

[23] *Moby Dick, or, The Whale*, ed. by Luther S. Mansfield and Howard P. Vincent (New York, 1952), p. 534.

[24] *Israel Potter*, p. 198.

[25] *Moby Dick*, p. 360.

[26] See the *Melville Log*, pp. 477 and 515.

[27] *Magnalia*, Vol. I, p. 212.

[28] *Moby Dick*, p. 373.

[29] *Ibid.*, p. 49.

[30] *Ibid.*, p. 68.

[31] Cf. *Journal of a Visit to London and the Continent by Herman Melville, 1849–1850*, ed. by Eleanor Melville Metcalf (Cambridge, Mass., 1948), p. 62.

[32] *Moby Dick*, p. 68 f.

[33] In the above example Melville's imagination leaps from the image chosen by visual criteria, "her masts stood stiffly up like the spires of the three old kings of Cologne," to another image also from the realm of religious devotion where something worn and wrinkled is compared with "the pilgrim-worshipped flag-stone in Canterbury Cathedral where Beckett bled"—an early indication of Ahab's martyrdom,

which, however, occurs under an entirely different sort of omen.

[34] *Ibid.*, p. 151 f.

[35] *Ibid.*, p. 344.

[36] *Ibid.*, p. 146 f.

[37] *Ibid.*, p. 146.

[38] *Ibid.*, p. 361.

[39] *Loc. cit.*

[40] Wright states similar ideas in *Melville's Use of the Bible*, p. 175 f., but without the reference to typology.

[41] *Moby Dick*, p. 113 f.

[42] *Ibid.*, p. 40.

[43] *Ibid.*, p. 184.

[44] Job 41:4–9; *Moby Dick*, p. 131. Job 41:7 is quoted in the Chapter "The Pequod Meets the Virgin": "Canst thou fill his skin with barbed irons? or his head with fish-spears? The sword of him that layeth at him cannot hold, the spear, the dart, nor the habergeon: he esteemeth iron as straw; the arrow cannot make him flee; darts are counted as stubble; he laugheth at the shaking of a spear!" (p. 354).

[45] The editors of the critical edition discuss in all earnestness whether the New Englanders ever used the name "Ahab" (p. 637).

[46] *Moby Dick*, p. 79.

[47] *Ibid.*, p. 181.

[48] Thus the definition of "Leviathan" in the *Lexikon für Theologie und Kirche*, Vol. IV (Freiburg, 1961).

[49] "Melville, as he always does, began to reason of Providence and futurity, and of everything that lies beyond human ken," reports Hawthorne in 1856 of his re-encounter with Melville; *cf. English Notebooks*, p. 432.

[50] Ahab considers this: ". . . be the white whale agent, or be the white whale principal . . ." *Moby Dick*, p. 162.

[51] *Ibid.*, p. 213.

[52] *Ibid.*, p. 554.

[53] *Cf.* Lawrence Thomson, *Melville's Quarrel with God* (Princeton, 1952), p. 153. Marius Bewley calls this interpretation into question with a very thorough interpreta-

tion of the entire chapter in his "A Truce of God for Melville," *Sewanee Review*, LXI (1953), pp. 682–700. What is important for the interpretation of *Moby Dick*, however, is the manner in which Melville understood these difficult verses rather than a theologically correct interpretation. That he actually did understand them in the above sense seems to me to be confirmed by Milton's *Paradise Regained*, which is regarded as a source for *Moby Dick* (see Henry F. Pommer, *Milton and Melville*, Pittsburgh, Pa., 1950). There Satan says to Jesus (I, 368 ff.):

> I came, among the Sons of God, when he
> Gave up unto my hands Uzzean Job,
> To prove him, and illustrate his high worth;
> And, when to all his Angels he proposed
> To draw the proud king Ahab into fraud,
> That he might fall in Ramoth, they demurring
> I undertook that office, and the tongues
> Of all his flattering prophets glibbed with lies
> To his destruction, as I had in charge.

Thus Milton also regarded Ahab as the man deceived by God.

[54] *Moby Dick*, p. 536.

[55] Ibid., p. 166.

[56] *E.g.* Newton Arvin, *Melville* (n.p., 1950), p. 171 ff.

[57] *Pierre, or the Ambiguities,* ed. by Henry A. Murray (New York, 1949), p. 14; Henry A. Murray points out that Melville took this quotation from Goethe's *Dichtung und Wahrheit*.

[58] *Pierre, or the Ambiguities*, p. 456.

[59] Gal. 4:22–31; *Encyclopedia of Religion and Ethics*, Vol. XII (Edinburgh, 1921), p. 502.

[60] The editors of the critical edition of *Moby Dick* have collected all the possible literary Ishmael characters and fates that could have influenced Melville. They advance the opinion in all earnestness that "James Fenimore Cooper's *The Prairie* (1827) probably introduced Melville to the actual use of the name for the Character Ishmael Bush" (p. 587). They do identify Ishmael as a biblical figure. But they do

not take into consideration that, for a culture based on the Bible, Ishmael was a characteristic figure referred to in countless sermons, and that he could have become important for Melville in this way, as a type in the biblical as well as in the modern sense. They have also overlooked the fact that for the covenant theologians among Calvinists, Ishmael had a special role because he was excluded from the covenant.

[61] Gottlob Schrenk, *Gottesreich und Bund im älteren Protestantismus, vornehmlich bei Johannes Coccejus* (Gütersloh, 1923), p. 46. This interpretation is also in Edward Taylor: see above, p. 63.

[62] *Redburn*, Standard Edition, Vol. V, p. 79.

[63] *Pierre*, p. 105.

[64] James Baird, *Ishmael* (Baltimore, 1956), p. 93.

[65] *White Jacket*, Standard Edition, Vol. VI, p. 502.

[66] *White Jacket*, p. 27.

[67] *Ibid.*, p. 94 f.

[68] Ships can also stand for nations and the ideas they represent, like the American merchant ship *Rights-of-Man*, and the English warship *Indomitable* in *Billy Budd*.

[69] *Clarel, A Poem and Pilgrimmage in the Holy Land*, ed. by Walter Bezanson (New York, 1960), p. 59.

[70] "The Encantadas," Sketch First, Standard Edition, Vol. X, p. 182 f.

[71] *Pierre*, p. 159.

[72] *The Confidence Man*, ed. by Elizabeth S. Foster (New York, 1954), p. 8.

[73] *Ibid.*, p. 53. In addition p. 283: "True, this aptly typifies that internal freshness. . . ."

[74] *Moby Dick*, p. 186.

[75] *Ibid.*, p. 194.

[76] *Ibid.*, p. 224.

[77] *Ibid.*, p. 393.

[78] In *Melville's Quarrel with God*, p. 133 f., Lawrence Thompson points out that Melville had to criticize Carlyle's definition of "symbol": "In a Symbol there is concealment and yet revelation. . . ."

[79] *Moby Dick*, p. 193.

[80] *Ibid.*, p. 38.

[81] *Ibid.*, p. 548.

[82] Since Melville sees the symbol primarily as a sign, it differs almost not at all from the emblem, which he uses the same way as "symbol."

[83] *Confidence Man*, p. 8.

[84] In German one can apply *Zusammenströmen* to people in a metaphorical sense, but Melville cannot use the English "flowing together" in the same way.

[85] *Redburn*, Standard Edition, Vol. V, p. 11.

[86] *White Jacket*, p. 162.

[87] *Moby Dick*, p. 427.

[88] Malcolm Cowley has established a connection of Hemingway to Hawthorne, Poe, and Melville on the basis of other but related characteristics in his Introduction to *The Viking Portable Library Hemingway* (New York, 1944), p. xxiii.

[89] Quoted in Eleanor Melville Metcalf, *Herman Melville, Cycle and Epicycle* (Cambridge, Mass., 1953), p. 105.

[90] *Partisan Review*, XVII (1950), pp. 67–79.

[91] James Baird, *Ishmael* (Baltimore, 1956), p. xv.

[92] In his essay "Psychoanalysis and Literary Culture Today," *Partisan Review*, XXVI (1959), p. 50, Alfred Kazin remarks, "For just as art is really a religious ritual, so religion is really art; sacrament, says Mr. Baird, is symbol 'representing corporateness in which the individual is subsumed, and ultimately these new compensatory symbols transcend the artist in the collective of the archetype.' " Kazin classes this sort of "pseudo-metaphysics" as the wishful thinking of contemporaries who are alienated from faith.

[93] *The Letters of Herman Melville*, p. 142.

[94] *Ibid.*, p. 146.

Chapter IX

[1] Ursula Brumm, "The Figure of Christ in American Literature," *Partisan Review*, XXIV (1957). Parts of this article are used in the present chapter.

2 (Chicago, 1955).

3 Lewis notes this too and comments on it thus (p. 130): "When this conviction [the saving strength of the Adamic personality] became articulate in *Billy Budd*, the American hero as Adam became the hero as Christ and entered, once and for all, into the dimension of myth."

4 *Cf.* Don Geiger, "Melville's Black God. Contrary Evidence in the 'Town-Ho's Story,'" *American Literature*, XXV (1954), pp. 464–71.

5 This has been shown by Charles H. Foster, *The Rungless Ladder. Harriet Beecher Stowe and New England Puritanism* (Durham, N.C., 1954).

6 *Cf.* what Edmund Wilson has recently said of this novel in *Patriotic Gore* (London, 1962), p. 38 ff.

7 *The Writings of Harriet Beecher Stowe*, Vol. V (Boston, 1896), *The Minister's Wooing*, p. 253 f.

8 *The Works of William E. Channing* (Boston, 1878), p. 367.

9 *Ibid.*, p. 376.

10 *Ibid.*, p. 380.

11 *Emerson's Works*, Vol. I, p. 142.

12 Theodore Parker, "A Discourse of the Transient and Permanent in Christianity," in Perry Miller, *The Transcendentalists*, p. 267 f.

13 *Ibid.*, p. 275.

14 *Loc. cit.*

15 *Ibid.*, p. 274.

16 Thomas Wolfe, *Of Time and the River* (New York, 1935).

17 Ralph Ellison, *Invisible Man* (New York, 1952).

18 Ernest Hemingway, *The Old Man and the Sea* (New York, 1952).

19 *Light in August*, The Modern Library (New York, 1950), p. 337.

20 *Ibid.*, p. 407.

21 "The Bear," *Go Down, Moses* (New York, 1942), p. 309.

22 It is indeed a matter for debate whether this book is successful in conception, form, and style. There are stretches where Faulkner's narration is mushy and lacking in contour, bogged down with unproductive detail, and the tone

and technique of Saturday evening village small talk is sometimes out of place.

[23] The German reviews were mostly favorable. The one by Wolfgang von Einsiedel in *Merkur*, X (1956), p. 282 ff., is worthy of special note.

[24] *Kenyon Review*, XVI (1954), p. 668 f.

[25] *A Fable* (New York, 1954), p. 259 f. "Rapacity does not fail" is a parody on I. Cor. 13.8, "charity never faileth," and the entire section on rapacity is the ironic counterpart of Chapter 13 of I Corinthians, the theme of which is 'charity.'

[26] In addition there is a mythical sort of Christ symbolism: *cf.* Eliot's "Christ the tiger," *The Complete Poems and Plays* (New York, 1952), p. 21. The animal parallels for Christ are reminiscent of Physiologus.

[27] *A Fable*, p. 239 f.

[28] *Ibid.*, p. 348.

[29] *Ibid.*, p. 363 f.

[30] *Ibid.*, p. 365 f.

[31] James occasionaly uses Christ symbolism with these heroes, for instance Milly Theale, the heroine of *The Wings of the Dove*, but it is not pronounced enough to be studied from our standpoint.

BIBLIOGRAPHY

Ames, William, *Medulla Theologiae*, Amsterdam, 1628; *The Marrow of Sacred Divinity*, London, 1638.

Arvin, Newton, *Melville*, n.p., 1950.

Auden, Wystan Hugh, *The Enchafèd Flood, or, The Romantic Iconography of the Sea*, New York, 1950.

Auerbach, Erich, *Scenes from the Drama of European Literature*, New York, 1959.

———, *Typologische Motive in der mittelalterlichen Literatur*, Schriften und Vorträge des Petrarca-Instituts Köln, II, Krefeld, 1953.

Bähr, Karl Christ., *Symbolik des Mosaischen Cultus*, Vol. I, Heidelberg, 1837.

Baird, James, *Ishmael*, Baltimore, 1956.

Bell, Millicent, "Pierre Bayle and *Moby Dick*," *PMLA*, XLVI (1951), pp. 626–648.

Bewley, Marius, *The Eccentric Design*, London, 1959.

————, "A Truce of God for Melville," *Sewanee Review*, LXI (1953), pp. 682–700.

Black, Mindele, "Edward Taylor: Heaven's Sugar Cake," *New England Quarterly*, XXIX (1956), pp. 159–181.

Blackmur, Richard P., "The Craft of Herman Melville," in *The Lion and the Honeycomb*, New York, 1955, pp. 124–144.

Blau, Herbert, "Heaven's Sugar Cake: Theology and Imagery in the Poetry of Edward Taylor," *New England Quarterly*, XXVI (1953), pp. 337–360.

Blau, Joseph L., *Men and Movements in American Philosophy*, 4th ed., New York, 1955.

Braswell, William, *Melville's Religious Thought. An Essay in Interpretation*, New York, 1943.

Brumm, Ursula, "The Figure of Christ in American Literature," *Partisan Review*, XXIV (1957), pp. 403–413.

————, "Symbolism and the Novel," Partisan Review, XXV (1958), pp. 329–342.

Bultmann, Rudolf, "Ursprung und Sinn der Typologie als hermeneutischer Methode." *Theologische Literaturzeitung*, LXXV (1950), col. 205–212.

Cassirer, Ernst, *An Essay on Man, An Introduction to a Philosophy of Human Culture*, New Haven, Conn., 1944.

————, *Philosophie der symbolischen Formen*, 3 vols., Berlin, 1923–1929.

Channing, William Ellery, *The Works of William E. Channing*, Boston, 1878.

Chase, Richard, *The American Novel and its Tradition*, New York, 1957.

————, *The Democratic Vista. A Dialogue on Life and Letters in Contemporary America*, New York, 1958.

————, *Herman Melville. A Critical Study*, New York, 1949.

Chauncey, Charles, *Seasonable Thoughts on the State of Religion in New England*, Boston, 1743.

Curtius, Ernst Robert, *Europäische Literatur und lateinisches Mittelalter*, 2nd ed., Bern, 1954.

Danckaerts, Jasper, *The Journal of Jasper Danckaerts, 1679–*

1680 (Original Narratives of Early American History, Vol. XV), New York, 1952.

Davidson, Edward H., *Hawthorne's Last Phase*, New Haven, 1949.

Dictionnaire de Théologie Catholique, Vol. XV, Paris, 1946.

Dobschütz, Ernst von, "Vom vierfachen Schriftsinn," *Harnack-Ehrung*, Leipzig, 1921, pp. 1–13.

Dwight, Timothy, *The Conquest of Canaan*, Hartford, Conn., 1785.

Edwards, Jonathan, *The Works of President Jonathan Edwards*, 4 vols., New York, 1849.

——, *Images or Shadows of Divine Things by Jonathan Edwards*, ed. by Perry Miller, New Haven, Conn., 1948.

——, *Representative Selections*, with Introduction, Bibliography and Notes by Clarence H. Faust and Thomas H. Johnson, New York, 1935.

Eliot, Thomas Stearns, *Selected Essays*, New Edition, New York, 1950.

Emerson, Ralph Waldo, *Journals*, 10 vols., Cambridge, Mass., 1909–1914.

——, *Complete Works of Ralph Waldo Emerson*, 11 vols., Cambridge, Mass., 1883.

Emrich, Wilhelm, *Die Symbolik von Faust II*, Berlin, 1943.

Encyclopedia of Religion and Ethics, ed. by James Hastings, Vol. XII, Edinburgh, 1921.

Feidelson, Charles, Jr., *Symbolism and American Literature*, Chicago, 1953.

Fogle, Richard H., *Hawthorne's Fiction: The Light and the Dark*, Norman, Okla., 1952.

Foster, Charles H., *The Rungless Ladder. Harriet Beecher Stowe and New England Puritanism*, Durham, N.C., 1954.

Frothingham, Octavius B., *Transcendentalism in New England: A History*, New York, 1876.

Frye, Northrop, *Anatomy of Criticism*, Princeton, 1957.

Gabriel, Ralph Henry, *The Course of American Democratic Thought. An Intellectual History Since 1815*, New York, 1940.

Geiger, Don, "Melville's Black God. Contrary Evidence in the 'Town-Ho's Story,'" *American Literature*, XXV (1954), pp. 464–471.

Gilman, William, *Melville's Early Life and Redburn*, New York, 1957.

Goppelt, Leonhard, *Typos. Die typologische Deutung des Alten Testaments im Neuen*, Gütersloh, 1939.

Haller, William, *The Rise of Puritanism*, New York, 1938.

Hawthorne, Nathaniel, *The Works of Nathaniel Hawthorne*, 15 vols., Boston, 1882–1888.

————, *The English Notebooks*, ed. by Randall Stewart, New York, 1962.

Heyde, Johannes Erich, "Typus. Ein Beitrag zur Bedeutungsgeschichte des Wortes Typus," *Wege zur Klarheit*, Berlin, 1960, pp. 66–72.

Hinrichs, Carl, *Friedrich Wilhelm I. König von Preussen. Eine Biographie*, Hamburg, 1944.

Honig, Edwin, *Dark Conceit: The Making of Allegory*, London, 1959.

James, Henry, "Hawthorne," London, 1879, in Edmund Wilson, *The Shock of Recognition*, New York, 1955.

Jantsch, Heinz G., *Studien zum Symbolischen in der frühmittelhochdeutschen Literatur*, Tübingen, 1959.

Johnson, Thomas H., *The Poetical Works of Edward Taylor*, Princeton, 1939.

Kayser, Wolfgang, *Das Sprachliche Kunstwerk. Eine Einführung in die Literaturwissenschaft*, 5th ed., Bern, 1959.

Kazin, Alfred, "On Melville as Scripture," *Partisan Review*, XVII (1950), pp. 67–79.

————, "Psychoanalysis and Literary Culture Today," *Partisan Review*, XXVI (1959), pp. 45–55.

Keach, Benjamin, *Tropologia: A Key to Open Scripture Metaphors . . . together with Types of the Old Testament*, London, 1681.

Künstle, Karl, *Die Ikonographie der christlichen Kunst*, 2 vols., Freiburg, 1926 and 1929.

Langer, Susanne K., *Philosophy in a New Key. A Study in the*

Symbolism of Reason, Rite, and Art. Cambridge, Mass., 1942.

Leibowitz, Herbert A., "Hawthorne and Spenser: Two Sources," *American Literature*, XXX (1959), pp. 459–466.

Leisegang, Hans, *Denkformen*, Berlin, 1951.

Levin, Harry, *The Power of Blackness. Hawthorne, Poe, Melville*, New York, 1958.

————, *Symbolism and Fiction*, Charlottesville, Va., 1956.

Lewis, Clives St., *The Allegory of Love*, London, 1936.

Lewis, R. W. B., *The American Adam. Innocence, Tragedy and Tradition in the Nineteenth Century*, Chicago, 1955.

Lexikon für Theologie und Kirche, founded by Dr. Michael Buchberger, 2nd ed., Vol. II, Freiburg, 1958, Vol. IV, Freiburg, 1961; 1st ed., Vol. X, Freiburg, 1931.

Leyda, Jay, *The Melville Log. A Documentary Life of Herman Melville, 1819–1891*, 2 vols., New York, 1951.

Lind, S. E., "Edward Taylor: A Revaluation," *New England Quarterly*, XXI (1948), pp. 518–530.

Lundblad, Jane, *Nathaniel Hawthorne and European Literary Tradition*, Essays and Studies on American Language and Literature, No. 6, Uppsala, 1947.

Madsen, William G., "Earth the Shadow of Heaven: Typological Symbolism in *Paradise Lost*," *PMLA*, LXXV (1960), pp. 519–526.

Male, Roy, R., *Hawthorne's Tragic Vision*, Austin, Texas, 1957.

Maniere II, William R., "Cotton Mather and the Biographical Parallel," *American Quarterly*, XIII (1961), pp. 153–160.

Mather, Cotton, *Magnalia Christi Americana, or, The Ecclesiastical History of New England*, 2 vols., Hartford, Conn., 1820.

Mather, Samuel, *The Figures or Types of the Old Testament*, 2nd ed., London, 1705.

Matthiessen, F. O., *American Renaissance. Art and Expression in the Age of Emerson and Whitman*, New York, 1941.

McNeill, John T., *The History and Character of Calvinism*, New York, 1954.

Meinecke, Friedrich, *Die Entstehung des Historismus*, 2 vols., Berlin, 1936.

Melville, Herman, *The Works of Herman Melville*, Standard Edition, 16 vols., London, 1922–1924.

——, *Clarel, A Poem and Pilgrimage in the Holy Land*, ed. by Walter Bezanson, New York, 1960.

——, *The Confidence Man*, ed. by Elizabeth S. Foster, New York, 1954.

——, *Journal of a Visit to London and the Continent by Herman Melville, 1849–1850*, ed. by Eleanor Melville Metcalf, Cambridge, Mass., 1948.

Melville, Herman, *Moby-Dick, or The Whale*, ed. by Luther S. Mansfield and Howard P. Vincent, New York, 1952.

——, *Pierre, or The Ambiguities*, ed. by Henry A. Murray, New York, 1949.

Melville's Billy Budd, ed. by Barron Freeman, Cambridge, Mass., 1948.

Melville, Herman, *The Letters of Herman Melville*, ed. by Merrell R. Davis and William H. Gilman, New Haven, 1960.

Metcalf, Eleanor Melville, *Herman Melville, Cycle and Epicycle*, Cambridge, Mass., 1953.

Miller, Perry, *Errand into the Wilderness*, Cambridge, Mass., 1956.

——, "From Edwards to Emerson," in *Errand into the Wilderness*, Cambridge, Mass., 1956, pp. 184–203.

——, *Jonathan Edwards*, New York, 1949.

——, "Melville and Transcendentalism," in *Moby Dick Centennial Essays*, ed. for the Melville Society, Dallas, Texas, 1953.

——, *The New England Mind: The Seventeenth Century*, Cambridge, Mass., 1939, reiss. 1954. *The New England Mind: From Colony to Province*, Cambridge, Mass., 1953.

——, *The Raven and the Whale*, New York, 1956.

———— and Thomas H. Johnson, *The Puritans*, New York, 1938.

————, *The Transcendentalists. An Anthology*, Cambridge, Mass., 1950.

Mills, Barris, "Hawthorne and Puritanism," *New England Quarterly*, XXI, (1948), pp. 78–102.

Morison, Samuel Eliot, *The Founding of Harvard College*, Cambridge, Mass., 1935.

Müller, Curt, *Die geschichtlichen Voraussetzungen des Symbolbegriffes in Goethes Kunstanschauung*, Leipzig, 1937.

Murdock, Kenneth B., *Literature & Theology in Colonial New England*, Cambridge, Mass., 1949.

————, "Clio in the Wilderness. History and Biography in Puritan New England," *Church History*, XXIV (1955), pp. 221–238.

Murray, Henry A., "In Nomine Diaboli," in *Moby Dick Centennial Essays*, Dallas, Texas, 1953, pp. 3–21.

The New England Primer, ed. by Paul Leicester Ford, New York, 1899.

Oestreich, Gerhard, "Die Idee des religiösen Bundes und die Lehre vom Staatsvertrag," *Festschrift für Hans Herzfeld*, Berlin, 1959, pp. 11–32.

Orians, G. H., "The Angel of Hadley in Fiction. A Study of the Sources of Hawthorne's 'The Grey Champion,'" *American Literature*, IV (1932/33), pp. 257–269.

The Oxford English Dictionary, ed. by James A. H. Murray *et al.*, 12 vols., Oxford, 1933.

Parker, Theodore, "A Discourse of the Transient and Permanent in Christianity," in Perry Miller, *The Transcendentalists*.

Parrington, Vernon L., *Main Currents in American Thought*, Vol. I: *The Colonial Mind*, Vol. II: *The Romantic Revolution*, New York, 1927.

Pearce, Roy H., "Edward Taylor: The Poet as Puritan," *New England Quarterly*, XXIII (1950), pp. 31–46.

Pommer, H. F., *Milton and Melville*, Pittsburgh, Pa., 1950.

Reuter, Karl, *Wilhelm Amesius, der führende Theologe des erwachenden reformierten Pietismus*, Moers, 1940.

Ritschl, Albrecht, *Geschichte des Pietismus in der luther-ischen Kirche des 17. und 18. Jahrhunderts*, Div. 1, Bonn, 1884.

———, *Geschichte des Pietismus in der reformierten Kirche*, Bonn, 1880.

Rusk, Ralph L., *The Life of Ralph Waldo Emerson*, New York, 1949.

Sann, Auguste, *Bunyan in Deutschland. Studien zur literar-ischen Wechselbeziehung zwischen England und dem deutschen Pietismus*. Giessener Beiträge zur deutschen Philologie, Giessen, 1957.

Schirmer, Walter F., *Antike, Renaissance und Puritanismus*, München, 1924.

Schlesinger, Max, *Geschichte des Symbols*, Berlin, 1912.

Schneider, Herbert W., *The Puritan Mind*, London, 1931.

Schrenk, Gottlob, *Gottesreich und Bund im älteren Protestan-tismus, vornehmlich bei Johannes Coccejus*, Gütersloh, 1923.

Schwietering, Julius, *Die deutsche Dichtung des Mittelalters*, Walzels Handbuch der Literaturwissenschaft, Potsdam, 1941.

Schroeder, John W., "Hawthorne's 'Egotism, or, The Bosom Serpent' and its Source," *American Literature*, XXXI (1959).

Spiller, Robert E., *et al.*, *Literary History of the United States*, 3 vols., New York, 1949.

Stanford, Donald E., "Edward Taylor and the Lord's Supper," *American Literature*, XXVII (1955), pp. 172–178.

———, *An Edition of the Complete Poetical Works of Edward Taylor*, Thesis, Stanford, 1953.

Stauffer, Donald A., *English Biography Before 1700*, Cambridge, Mass., 1930.

Stein, W. B., "The Parable of the Antichrist in 'The Minister's Black Veil,'" *American Literature*, XXVII (1955/56), pp. 386–392.

Stewart, Randall, *Nathaniel Hawthorne. A Biography*, New Haven, Conn., 1948.

Stowe, Harriet Beecher, *The Minister's Wooing*, The Writings of Harriet Beecher Stowe, Vol. V, Cambridge, Mass., 1896.

Sundermann, K. H., *Herman Melvilles Gedankengut. Eine kritische Untersuchung seiner weltanschaulichen Grundideen*, Berlin, 1937.

Sweet, William Warren, *Religion in Colonial America*, New York, 1951.

Taylor, Edward, *Christographia*, ed. by Norman Grabo, New Haven, 1962.

———, *The Poems of Edward Taylor*, ed. by Donald E. Stanford with a Foreword by Louis L. Martz, New Haven, Conn., 1960.

Thomas, Vincent, "The Modernity of Jonathan Edwards," *New England Quarterly*, XXV (1952), pp. 60–84.

Thompson, Lawrence, *Melville's Quarrel with God*, Princeton, 1952.

Tindall, William York, *The Literary Symbol*, New York, 1955.

Trilling, Lionel, *The Liberal Imagination*, New York, 1950.

Tuve, Rosemond, *Elizabethan and Methaphysical Imagery. Renaissance Poetic and Twentieth-Century Critics*, Chicago, 1947.

———, *A Reading of George Herbert*, London, 1951.

Tyler, Moses Coit, *A History of American Literature during the Colonial Period, 1607–1765*, Ithaca, N.Y., 1949.

Vincent, Howard P., *The Trying-Out of Moby Dick*, Boston, 1949.

Waggoner, Hyatt H., *Hawthorne. A Critical Study*, Cambridge, Mass., 1955.

Warren, Austin, "Edward Taylor," in *Rage for Order*, Chicago, 1948, pp. 1–18.

Watters, R. E., "Biographical Technique in Cotton Mather's *Magnalia*," *William & Mary Quarterly*, II (1945), pp. 154–163.

Weathers, Willie T., "Edward Taylor and the Cambridge Platonists," *American Literature*, XXVI (1954), pp. 1–31.

Weaver, Raymond, *Herman Melville. Mariner and Mystic*, New York, 1921.

Webster's New International Dictionary of the English Language, 2nd ed., 2 vols., Springfield, 1955.

Wellek, René, "Emerson and German Philosophy," *New England Quarterly*, XVI (1943), pp. 41–62.

———— and Austin Warren, *Theory of Literature*, New York, 1949.

Wetzer-Welte's *Kirchenlexikon*, Vol. V, Freiburg, 1888.

Wilson, Edmund, *Axle's Castle. A Study in the Imaginative Literature of 1870–1930*, New York, 1931.

————, *The Shock of Recognition. The Development of Literature in the United States Recorded by the Men who Made it*, 2nd ed., New York, 1955.

Winters, Yvor, "Maule's Curse. Seven Studies in the History of American Obscurantism," in *In Defense of Reason*, Denver, 1947.

Wolfson, Harry A., *Philo. Foundations of Religious Philosophy in Judaism, Christianity and Islam*, 2 vols., Cambridge, Mass., 1948.

Wright, Nathalia, *Melville's Use of the Bible*, Durham, N.C., 1949.

INDEX

This book was set in Primer Linotype and printed by letterpress on P & S F/W Book manufactured by P. H. Glatfelter Co., Spring Grove, Pa. Composed, printed and bound by H. Wolff Book Manufacturing Company Inc., New York, N. Y.